AHHHH!

A
Tribute to
Brother Blue

(Dr. Hugh Morgan Hill)

&

Ruth Edmonds Hill

Ruth

Brother Blue

"LOVE" Forever

ISBN: 0-938756-67-2

Copyright © 2003 Yellow Moon Press

All rights revert to the individual authors upon publication.

No part of this book may be reproduced or transmitted in any form or by any electronic or mechanical means including photocopying or information storage and retrieval systems without the permission in writing from the publisher/copyright owner except by a reviewer, who may quote brief passages in a review.

Front Cover & Bottom Back Cover photo:Susan Wilson

A Joint Project of:

Yellow Moon Press

P.O. Box 381316

Cambridge, MA 02238

(617) 776 - 2230 • www.yellowmoon.com

&

League for the Advancement of New England Storytelling (LANES)

411A Highland Avenue, #351

Somerville, MA 02144

www.lanes.org • lanes@lanes.org

The Brother Blue Tribute Committee:

Ann Hoban • Glenn Morrow

Robert B. Smyth • Magdalen Cantwell

Barbara Lipke

With help from

Laura Packer • Pam Kristan

Mary Skousgaard • Ruth Edmonds Hill

Editorial Interns: Kathyrn Berg, Carrie Breman, Laura Chandler, Mackenzie Kohrn, Katie White, Katy McNally

CONTENTS

Ahhhh!

iv

AHHHH !

Ahhhh!

Ahhhh!

viii

Ahhhh!

Ahhhh!

Ahhhh!

Ahhhh!

Ahhhh!

Ahhhh!

Ahhhh!

Preface
by Glenn Morrow

This book is a celebration of an extraordinary storyteller, and like all books it needed a title. Brother Blue is a master of the spoken word, shaping it improvisationally into rhymes and rhythms as a jazz musician bends notes. Blue has birthed a thousand phrases, each uniquely his own. Yet when we sought a title for this book, there was only one real possibility. Ahhhh, a wordless exhalation of awe and wonder, an assertion of the ineffable.

Is it odd that a book about a storyteller, a limber magician of language, should take a title of dumbstruck speechlessness? Not for those who know Brother Blue. The word is his (if word it is). It is perhaps his favorite word. It is, perhaps, the title of his favorite story, the tale of a crawling caterpillar awestruck by the sight of a butterfly and a vision of his own transformation. Ahhhh is the statement, endlessly repeated, that what is most essential and beautiful and holy can no more be captured in words than a butterfly.

Brother Blue's other name is Dr. Hugh Morgan Hill, holder of multiple graduate degrees from prestigious universities. But Brother Blue is not a stage name, a persona to be put on and taken off. Blue is always Blue. Whether bedecked in balloons and ribbons, with blue beret and butterflies pinned to clothes and painted on palms, or dressed in simple blue from head to shoes, Brother Blue is always himself. His passionate commitment to telling the stories that will transform the planet, and an equal or greater commitment to listen, really listen, to every single person's story is continual. It is who he is. Brother Blue knows that stories are bread for the soul, and must be taken where they are most needed. He, famously, can be found storytelling to passersby on the streets of Harvard Square. But he is equally likely to be spinning his tales on festival stages, in pulpits and academic lecture halls, on radio and

Ahhhh!

television, and in hospitals, shelters, nursing homes, prisons, and pre-
schools.

Wherever Brother Blue is found, Ruth will not be far away. His constant companion, helpmate, and muse, Ruth is as pragmatic as Blue is
extravagant, as quietly calm as Blue is verbosely enraptured. Brief acquaintance makes it clear that Ruth grounds Blue, keeps him tethered to
this world of time and schedules, of eating and sleeping. The longer you
know them, the more Ruth grows in your estimation. Ruth Edmonds
Hill is far more than Blue's beloved wife and indispensable support; she
is a fully equal co-creator of the spiritual and artistic endeavor that is
their lifework. In addition, Ruth Edmonds Hill is a noted scholar, a
respected authority in the field of oral history. She is dedicated to the
work of collecting and preserving the stories of women's lives, stories
that far too often have fallen through the cracks of established history.

The love that Blue and Ruth share is profound and palpable. It is an
exemplar of the love that they seek to embody, a love that heals this
broken world. Brother Blue can't say enough words about Ruth, his
muse, his Beatrice, his soulmate. Ruth smiles and replies with looks and
small gestures that speak volumes.

There are a lot of words in this book. There would be even more
words, but to publish the flood of loving material that was sent in response to our simple (so we thought then) request for words about, or
for, or inspired by Brother Blue and Ruth Edmonds Hill would have
been more than impractical, it would have been technically impossible.
For you see, responses to Brother Blue are as idiosyncratic as Blue
himself. In addition to memoirs, poems, letters, and stories, we received
sheet music, audio recordings, photographs and series of photos that
approximate a movie of Blue in motion, contributions from around the
world in several different languages, and a few in languages created
expressly for the occasion, artworks from portraits to symbolic abstrac-
tion in media ranging from drawing, watercolor, and pastel, through oil
painting, postcard art and collage, to metal sculpture and a hand-pieced
crazy quilt. We even received a message in a bottle.

So what you hold in your hands is just a selection which the committee
has cobbled together from this great outpouring of praise for the Praise-
singer, of love for the Lovers. We revel in awe and amazement, wonder
and disbelief , we are (as Blue is fond of saying) non-plussed. And having
reached the point where words of praise and words of thanks don't reach
high enough or deep enough, we raise our hands and say Ahhhh.

Ahhhh!

"Always, always call the Muse. It's a sacred thing."

Brother Blue

Invocation *(Latinate: "to put into voice")*

Brother Michael Wing

SOROR CAELESTIS
MUSA CAERULIS.
FLAGRANS FLAGITAMUS
UT FACULAS FIAMUR
ET FABULAS AFFLES.
PERVOCES FLAMMEAS
GERMANITAS VOCES.

Celestial sister,
Muse to heaven-blue souls!
We crave your ardent fire
to be torches inspired
by your breath upon our stories.
Through our blazing voices,
may you forge siblinghood.

Ahhhh!

Ahhhh!

3

Brother Blue's Application Statement: Jacques Lecoq Workshop August 1972

Began serious study of acting and playwriting while a student at the Yale Drama School. Wrote book and libretto of opera, <u>The Journey</u>, produced at Yale, also in Naples, Italy, and Rockford College in Illinois. Since graduating from Yale I have been studying theatre constantly, writing for theatre, and performing my own work. I have continuity credit for a national television show "Omnibus," have staged drama for WNAC-TV in Boston. My work is a mixture of dance, mime, story-telling, drama, tableaux, finger popping, shouts, and stomps. I have performed in mime and dance presentations from my own works in religiously oriented programs on television. I have taken my work to homes, nursery schools, colleges, lecture halls, graduate seminars, the fields, the street, prisons, theaters, coffee houses, to many churches for worship services, to the psychiatric ward of a hospital, to geriatric patients, to camps, to all kinds of children and adults, together and separately. I am trying to develop the language of motion, which is of the utmost importance in my work. My Ph.D project is a total effort to fuse the arts of theatre into new forms of worship, to body forth reality in us which is beyond verbalization, music, all sound. In the language of motion I long and pray to reveal something of the invisible, the inaudible in man, woman, child. I believe that physical gesture can and does express the God within us. I have seen Jacques Lecoq perform at Harvard, and I have attended one of his Master classes here at Harvard two years ago. Up until now, I have been rather alone, for the most part, in my groping and struggling with the language of motion. I would count it a most wonderful blessing to study further, to learn more about body movement and mime from this superb artist and mime, Jacques Lecoq.

AHHHH!

Tribute from Africa In April

David & Yvonne Acey

Africa in April Committee

P. O. Box 111261 ~ Memphis, Tennessee 38111
(901)947-2133 p ~ (901)947-2414 f ~ (901)785-2542 h
www.africainapril.org ~ aiafest@bellsouth.net

OFFICERS

David L. Acey, Sr.
Executive Director

Yvonne B. Acey
Associate Director

Willie H. Gregory
Board Chairman

Senator John Ford
Rep. Barbara Cooper
Honorary Chairs

Cynthia Green
Secretary

Joe C. Harmon
Treasurer

COMMUNITY ADVISORY BOARD

David L. Acey, II
Craten Armmer
D' Army Bailey
Julian Bolton
Noah Bond
Judy Card
Kenneth O. Cole, Sr.
Clifford Dates
John Elkington
Congressman Harold Ford, Jr.
Senator John Ford
Art Gilliam
Edna House
Minerva Johnican
John Jordan
Reverend Samuel B. Kyles
Arvis Latting
Reverend James Netters
Donald Smart
Maxine Smith
Todd Strickland
Shepperson Wilbun
Reverend Delnoah Williams

Portrait Of An International Professional Africa In April Humanitarian Storyteller... Brother Blue

The Africa In April Cultural Awareness Festival, Incorporated
is pleased to pay tribute to our Brother Blue.
The Butterfly Man brought joy and happiness to thousands
in Memphis, Tennessee for four years at our Festival.

Brother Blue 's Portrait showed us love, compassion,
and affection, coupled with diversity, talent, and
"Spiritual Intelligence."

Professor, Brother Doctor Blue thrilled the hearts of children,
family, adults, seniors, the nation, and the African Diaspora.
He called up the Butterfly in everyone and at the same time,
touched the Butterfly in us.
For he would say soulfully, eloquently and sincerely...
"Hello to the Butterfly in you from the Butterfly in me."

~ ~ ~ ~ ~ ~ ~

Brotherly,

David L. Acey, Sr.
Executive Director

Yvonne B. Acey
Associate Director

David L. Acey   April 30, 2000   *Yvonne B. Acey*

1234 Mississippi Boulevard ~ Memphis, Tennessee 38106

AHHHH!

Brother Blue

Samuel Allen

In these harried, post-modern times, it is Brother Blue who sustains the spirit of the wandering troubadours of the Middle Ages. Characteristically on the commandeered stage of the city streets, with improvisational flair in speech and pantomime, he spins his tales of fantasy, often imbuing them with sub-texts of serious moral intent. He is a cheering sight to come upon with his colorful multi-hued garb, his acrobatic gestures, as he transforms the mundane street or the bleak meeting hall into a place of magic and enchantment.

In this beguiling enterprise, Brother Blue would be the first to affirm he is not alone. It is a partnership fashioned over the years with his devoted wife, Ruth Hill. She has been his loyal follower, his whither-thou-goest Ruth, his not-without-whom Ruth, an inseparable part of the team. Ruth is his indispensible chief of staff whose efficient and unfailing support has made the story possible.

Brother Blue is now legend, as he adds so richly to the cultural life of Cambridge, the Boston area, and to venues in other regions as well. It was inevitable that his talents would come to be recognized in other countries. It is in impressive tribute that he is frequently invited abroad where he is warmly received and highly appreciated.

Let it not be forgotten that we, too, though a brash and younger nation, are enthusiastic about and warmly grateful to Dr. and Mrs. Brother Blue.

Samuel Allen is the author of four collections of poetry, including *Every Round*, published by Lotus Press. A recipient of an NEA Creative Writing Award in Poetry, and former professor at Tuskegee, Wesleyan, and Boston University, Samuel Allen lives in retirement in the Boston area.

Ahhhh!

Improvising with Blue

David Amram

I first met Brother Blue in 1971 when Boston University presented the Boston premier of my opera "Twelfth Night," which I conducted with a cast of student singers and the BU Orchestra. After the opening night performance, I went to Passim to see my old friend Bob Donlin. We were both friends of Jack Kerouac, and wanted to talk for the first time since his untimely demise in 1969. While we were talking, Dave Bromberg, who was performing there, invited me to sit in and play penny whistles, French horn and piano with him, even though I was still dressed in my white tie and tails. After the set was over, a distinguished looking man came up to me and said, "Brother David, I'm Brother Blue!" As soon as he spoke, and as I looked into his eyes and shook his hand, I felt an immediate warmth as if I had known him all my life. Over the past 31 years, I have always noticed Brother Blue's ability to make everyone in his presence feel that way not only about him, but before the day or night is over, about one another. Like Dizzy Gillespie, Willy Nelson, Odetta, Jack Kerouac, Mahatma Gandhi, and Pablo Casals, Brother Blue is a lifelong master of spreading joy.

In his programs for children, he is a one-man taskforce in promoting the principles of self-respect, love of family, sharing, and caring.

Over the years, from coffeehouses and the Cambridge Festival (1979), to symphony stages and Lowell Celebrates Kerouac (1994), and also, when I was with the share-a-composer program through the auspices of Harvard University, we have often performed together. Never having had a rehearsal, yet having it always come out miraculously. He sits in, and we trade off on-the-spot topical improvised rhymed lyrics and scat singing. Often I accompany his dancing and storytelling and whatever occurs spontaneously at the moment. I accompany him playing flute, penny whistle, french horn, piano, and percussion. Blue joined in when I played with my jazz group, or world music group, or when I worked with

Ahhhh!

folkloric musicians from around the world, and even one time when I was conducting a symphonic wind ensemble.

He and his wife, Ruth, make everyone who knows them want to come to Cambridge or wherever they are on the planet to be in their presence and share their light.

David Amram has composed over 100 orchestral and chamber works, written two operas, and early in his career, wrote many scores for theater and films. Long acknowledged as a pioneer of World Music and a performer, conductor and composer of uncompromising originality, he has conducted and performed as a soloist with symphony orchestras around the world and participated in major music festivals.

May 24, 1948 - Christian Science Monitor - Clay models portraying the parable of the Good Samaritan, made by children of the Lower School at the First Congregational Church in Cambridge, under the direction of Hugh Hill, a Pre-Theological student, in connection with a project for sending used clothing and money to a camp for displaced children near Rome, Italy.

Ahhhh!

Eight Comments on Brother Blue

Michael Anderson

When you walk down the streets of Cambridge, Massachusetts, you'll occasionally see a man walking toward you, a tall, handsome, 80-year old black man dressed in fifteen shades of electric blue, festooned in butterflies and ribbons, sometimes with bells and rattles on his trousers, like an English Morris dancer or a Sioux holy man. And your first instinct will be: Get the children out of the way! There's a crazy man coming!

Because you can't see someone that vivid, that far over the top, without thinking he's a lunatic or an acid casualty. And it never occurs to you, until later, that he may really be a prophet.

1. Playing Defense

People assume that Blue uses his vividness as a weapon. They assume wrong. Blue's radiance is primarily *defensive*.

If you can discover the Technicolor in your soul, if you can close your eyes and see the lilies of the field (*behold they toil not, neither do they spin, yet I say to you even Solomon in all his glory did not clothe himself like one of these*) and then open your eyes and see a world in gray on gray, drowning in fear and silence, wouldn't you want to turn the volume all the way up? Not because you expect to change the world, but to keep the world from changing you.

2. Singing

The greatest victories of the civil rights movement were all about singing. In free-speech cases like *Cox v. Louisiana*, the issue was what to do when Southern sheriffs threw a couple of dozen NAACP marchers in jail, and then several hundred would march outside the jailhouse. "*We shall overcome . . .*" And when they heard their friends inside the jail singing along, they cheered, and the sheriffs went berserk, arresting everyone in sight. Because this was the worst kind of jailbreak, some-

Ahhhh!

---

thing that made the bars of the jailhouse completely irrelevant.

Blue is a member of the only truly chosen generation still living—middle-class, African-American intellectuals born between 1910-1930. This is the generation of Martin Luther King, Medgar Evers, Malcolm X. No one was going to make him Governor of Mississippi, but the liberal Northern Harvard elites would have loved to make Blue a respectable Sidney Poitier figure, an engineer, or a doctor. But sometimes people like Blue just got away.

There's an old union poster with a striking worker in jail, pointing out at the viewer like Uncle Sam: "We're in here for you. You're out there for us." And whether Blue feels he is in prison or out of it, he has always been in or out *for* someone, for everyone else.

3. Johnny Carson

To call Brother Blue a storyteller is like calling Johnny Carson a comedian. Sure, that's what he does, but it misses the bigger picture.

Every week, same time, same channel, Blue comes out, gives the opening monologue (with Ruth as Ed McMahon), while his audience knows all the rituals. We shout and cheer and wave our arms as he has taught us, without even needing a studio prompter. And then Blue tells us we've got a really good show coming up, and every one, every comedian, or starlet, or musician, gets to sit on the couch afterward, as Blue puts his arm around us and says: "That was God talking to you, folks. And we'll be back after these messages."

4. Evil Twin

Blue should pick one day a year to offset his relentless positive energy, to put it into context. Every Halloween or April Fool's, he should become his evil twin, say, Agent Orange, some super-negative, condescending, genre priest who follows tellers with "That just *sucked*! You call yourself a *storyteller*?!"

5. Blue vs. Hitler

Blue was a US Army officer during World War II. This means he was, quite literally, someone who stopped the Third Reich directly across the line of scrimmage from Adolf Hitler. And if you were to go back to 1944 and show Hitler his worst nightmare, it would be hard to do better than a handsome young black American officer destined to become a psychedelic Harvard-educated Pied Piper whose mind would blow into the

AHHHH!

wind like a dandelion, like the 101st Airborne, to plant thousands of seeds.

Some strange similarities between these two opposites: 1) They both like public speaking; 2) they both dress in unusual costume; 3) they both have a certain charisma. The most obvious difference, though, is that Hitler didn't share his stage, while for Blue, that's the whole point. What's the point of being a fanatic, if it makes you sour and dull?

6. Shadrach

There is a certain safety in Blue's Tuesday room. No nasty slam poetry attitude, no snobby Olympic-skating-judge aesthetics. There's no poisonous sense of authority, because the king is also the fool.

When Stalin's army would come upon a minefield, they would force a prisoner from the penal battalion across. If he blew up, he was just a dead prisoner, but if he miraculously made it, like Shadrach, Meshach, and Abednego walking through the fire, he was an avatar, a hero: follow that man!

Why aren't people always the way we are in Blue's room? Because of shame, because we're afraid of looking ridiculous. Blue makes things safe—no one could be as ridiculous as this prophet. And if he stays alive, why do the rest of us have to be afraid?

7. Changing History

When people talk about changing history (usually late at night or during sci-fi conventions), they usually think about being some kind of time-travelling James Bond. "I'd go back and stop the plague! I'd go back and kill [name of bad person]!"

Blue intends to change history, but in a different way. They say that World War I (and all the wars that followed it) would have been stopped if only the troops had more soccer balls in the trenches when the Christmas truce broke out in 1914. In a few places, the singing and handshakes gave way to all-out schoolyard football, and in those sections of the line, both the British and the Germans had to pull the tainted regiments out and bring mass court-martials to restore a proper sense of hatred. If there had been 10,000 more soccer balls in no man's land, history might have skipped forward a century. Which is something like what Blue does. He's not a poetry commando, not a storytelling secret agent. He's just lobbing 10,000 soccer balls into no man's land, inviting everyone else to climb out and change.

AHHHH !

8. Immortality

Blue defies fear the way life defies death. You can't look that way, you can't act that way, you can't talk that way, if you're afraid of anything.

Blue is really a kind of architect. OK, it's art, what he does, but it's also a kind of *building*. Christopher Wren built the most beautiful buildings in London. On his memorial, it says: "If you seek his monument, look around."

By day, Michael Anderson is a mild-mannered First Amendment lawyer. Once he takes off his tie, he does the kind of frenzied political monologues that are not allowed in federal court. He thinks there's no such thing as free speech if you don't use it.

Performing in a play at The Loeb Drama Center
in the 1960's

Ahhhh!

A Letter to Blue Light

Eva Apfelbaum

Dear Brother Blue,

As I prepared myself to write about you, many thoughts crossed my mind until I finally decided to address you more directly via a personal letter.

While attending the School of Education at Harvard University in the early seventies, I often crossed the path of a man dressed all in blue with a slightly tilted blue beret. I was told that it was you, Brother Blue, but at that time I had never heard you speak, and we never really met. This spotting of a slim, blue-attired man continued for years. By then, butterflies had also alighted upon your hat and jacket.

Years later, my good friends, Jane and David, participated in your weekly story hours. I came to hear their presentations and was finally on your turf. I could feel and see the delicate iridescent brilliance of creative bubbles given life by the breath of the storytellers and listeners. The Bookcellar Cafe was festive with dancing and bursting words.

Finally, I too joined. There is something irresistible and magical about the inflow of old timers and newcomers, butterflies alighting ever so lightly, butterflies laying eggs to continue life, crawling caterpillars, cocoons, motionless silence, followed by the breaking out and birth of another modestly clad or brilliantly dappled butterfly. And then their flights. That is when you and your magic appear.

Rain or shine, almost always twenty to thirty people come—old, young, students, professionals, laborers, rich, poor, a diverse group. Your dear wife, Ruth, a co-magician, waits quietly for your butterfly wings to open up in greeting. Then the call comes for the willing storyflyers who have previously rolled up their names inside small pieces of paper to be picked out of a box.

Ahhhh!

Stories vary so, fantasy, folklore, biographical, traditional, poetic, song, and dance. Each story unique to its creator, spills, stumbles, and breaks through the air.

I watch you, totally entranced. When the story ends, you join the teller, put your hand in his or hers, look into their eyes, smile. You always find encouraging words. You always make each person feel special. By your deep, sincere belief in the holiness of sharing stories, the essence of people, you help to create a sacred space.

You studied to be a minister, and without a building, your being and your strong beliefs create temples on street corners, in prisons, here, wherever you are.

You light up the commonplace without denying the darkness in existence. You love, love, love kittens, dogs, children, youth, everyone. You thank us for being present, you thank us for the opportunity to love, which, to a person like you, is life itself.

I, in turn, thank you for your rare gifts, for your multi-colored flights of fancy and of courage, for your dreams, for your beautiful madness to see gods within each being and, through stories, to have these gods reborn over and over again.

May you and your gentle assistant be blessed.

Eva Apfelbaum has lived a life filled with stories, starting with her family's escape from Nazi Germany, to years spent in France, through wartime and another move to the USA. She eventually became an elementary and arts and crafts teacher with a strong interest in our precious and fragile environment and in the well-being of peoples with different backgrounds.

Blue Performing in Harvard Square in the 1960's

AHHHH!

Brother Blue,
Way Down in the Magic

David A. Anderson/Sankofa

Now and then—now and then, a being comes stomping down the street, strapped into a formula on how to make a living, when rib-bib-dee-drip-drop, precipitation, the sidewalk-pounding brother gets rained on. Not with the polluted stuff that causes so much concern, but an especially potent essence fit for absolving the anointee of major sin. But anointed ones have a lot to deal with. It's a risky business, this being absolved of major sins. Anointed ones can injure themselves and be seriously misunderstood. They can fly over the horizon and to infinity, and Nowhere don't do nobody no good.

So what's Blue to do? How then, does Brother Blue get over? The question kept me awake all night, and then some. I mean how does one ask a man to explain where/how he got his blessing? It is not a commodity; can't find it on the web, in the catalog, the mall or on the NASDAQ. It soars, cloud-like across the New England sky, awaiting the right combination of cosmic, human conditions.

So Dr. Hugh Morgan Hill—Brother Blue is in the hands of a lady of fine mind; a woman called Ruth. She tacks through the straits and shoals, navigates the updrafts, and the windshears of the Butterfly Cosmos. We don't know where-why-how cometh Ruth Hill. But we thank Heaven for that mellow-dispositioned pilot-navigator keeping our magic man on this side of infinity.

Blue tells of an encounter with a little boy who lived in a home for mentally handicapped people: the "greatest storyteller I ever met—a little boy who couldn't talk." The little boy smiled at the attention Blue gave him, and Blue was reminded of his brother Tommy who had smiled that way, long ago. But the smile gave way to tears of frustration because the little boy couldn't understand the words Blue spoke.

Ahhhh!

Blue stopped "trying to make sense with words," and, with his harp and hands "made up words out of my heart," and in a while, the child who couldn't talk, danced for Blue; gave Blue his heart.

Brother Blue was right to call that little boy the greatest storyteller he ever met. The boy gave his heart, and that, says Brother Blue, is all that storytellers do.

David A. Anderson/Sankofa, Ph.D., is Chair of the Rochester-Monroe County Freedom Trail Commission, created to research and make more accessible the sites, personalities and events that characterized the Underground Railroad. He also serves as program director of Akwaaba, The Heritage Associates, a non-profit education and tourism organization. He is a highly regarded storyteller, and served as Director of the 18th Annual National Black Storytelling Festival and Conference. He is the author of several books, including the storybook, *The Origin of Life on Earth: an African Creation Myth* which was named Outstanding Children's Book on Africa by the African Studies Association in 1992. With Ruth Brown Anderson, he is parent of three adult children.

Ruth - 1980's

AHHHH!

Night, Near Accra

Anthony Appiah

Stars blossom—and the moon how bright!
All human life a secret in this park.
Cicadas break the silence, stir in strum,
Frogs overstate their stature, I succumb
To all that is mysterious, to the spark
That is the coming day, seeded in present night.

Agnostic paradox: this emptiness demands
Tomorrow's plentitude, the sun must rise
Or everything is false, signs insignificant.
Cicada song promises as if I can't
Be wrong. Frog filibuster swears: no lies.
Stars blossom—as the night commands

Anthony Appiah served as the Charles H. Carswell Professor of Afro-American Studies and of Philosophy at Harvard University, after holding faculty positions at Duke, Cornell and Yale universities. His writings include books, essays and articles along with reviews, short fiction, three novels and a volume of poetry.

Ahhhh!

Brother Blue / The Storyteller

C. C. Arshagra

(In the Key of Listen)

First
…the sky shakes
…and then it fills with fine fools

wearing light hearts
and spirited wings

Then the good mother mud-of-Earth
rises through his soul being
…and here come all of the children

—on this world of ears and eyes
as they witness life
lifting from his butterfly palms
Then still as a universe moving
he soul-showers you
from the spirit of his ageless heart
onto all your happiness, so hungry
Here, listening souls vibrate
and the sky-wings come round
and on-down to give him
his barefoot Earth voice
A story
                improvised
begins to dance
God arrives dressed
as nobody and wants no thing;
accepting the skin of everyone
and all the hope of every child

Ahhhh!

18

Here, he speaks
the first word…haaaaaaa…
and you hear
the breath of sound

A storyteller's epic,
inside
quiet
spoken motions

The first word
He understands
He lives sharing
the earned respect of this

And he loves
word expressions

Loving the utter eloquence
of all rainbows and all people
Loving all the lost hopes
of each one who surrendered to the impossible dream

Loving
the finest gift
of every sense
of human nature

Loving
the simple strength of being

while living
gratitude

and giving

wonder

For you, my human brother

Veteran public poet, C.C. Arshagra is an events producer/host, publisher, lyricist, movement and visual artist, recipient of "Marcel Kopp Award" Boston Poetry Awards 2000, and nominee for the "Poet of the Year," Cambridge Poetry Awards 2001. His published works include *Poems*, and *Emotional Geography*.

Ahhhh!

The Butterfly Man

W. Kirk Avery

It was one of those steaming, oppressive, dead summer afternoons. Ruth and Blue had been invited to attend a wedding celebration and I had volunteered to drive them there and back. Whenever I think about Blue, the memory of that particular afternoon comes to mind. The reception after the wedding was louder than I had anticipated it might be. As so often it happens to me when crowds of people seem suddenly to be pressing too tightly all around and against me, the white noise crushing me under, the space enclosing me begins to shrink. I could feel myself panicking, suffocating as though drowning far from shore, frantic, unable to breathe.

For me, the Korean War, my experiences while there, what I was a part of, what I had witnessed, has a hold deep inside me. It is my own private haunting.

Flailing about—at least in my mind as it was shutting down—quite literally at the very edge of whatever keeps us from falling off, I lost track of who I was, or where. All that mattered was to shove the bodies aside. I felt only that I was in extreme danger, that *they* were surrounding me once again, *closer, closer;* that I had to escape, flee for my life. And right then, right at the deepest heart-of-darkness, the blackness and despair, as though in slow motion from all that frightful rush of sound and fury, something magical happened.

I could see him, *Blue*, his faithful *Ruth* by his side. Where there had been storming, now there was calming; where there had been stress and terror, there was now stillness, a clearing. In the very center of that clearing were Blue and Ruth.

I was seeing him, *truly seeing the person he was, not just the legend, for the very first time.* He was telling someone a story, or so it seemed. Or perhaps someone had stopped simply to say hello. The person soon left,

Ahhhh!

20

and, for just that frozen second of suspended time, there they were, the two of them, so very real, vulnerable, alive.

"Believe in yourself," he had challenged us the previous Tuesday. "Tell from your heart. Reach out and change the world," his special music we've all heard him sing ten thousand times, and yet, each time never quite the same. For me, lost as I had been, it was as though the words had a meaning and wonder to them I had never envisioned before. It was very clear and simple. If I could but make my way over to them, I *could* trust that he *would* be there. I *would* be safe—from myself most of all.

He smiled his special smile when he saw me coming. I touched his shoulder. "My man," he said, his eyes embracing my very soul. And I began to cry. Then, so gently spoken, "Ready to leave?" I put my arms around Ruth, wise woman of all the world. "Yes," I managed, when I could. "Are you?" He nodded; Ruth as well.

Thus, we were on our way together, weaving through the thinning clutches of people and back outside again into the white heat, the blinding glare of the cloudless tall sky, Blue emerging *after* us, of course. As always, there had been a story or two or three left to tell. Ruth and I were waiting in the shade cast by a high wall, with a woman, her baby carriage and two or three others, chatting quietly. Oblivious to all, Blue saw only the carriage. Leaning into it like the holy man he is, he began to tell a story to the tiny infant sleeping innocently inside.

Witnessing the butterfly man kneeling there, sharing his story with the infant child, heart and soul, the world seemed somehow gentler, somehow a place of wonder and caring and love.

And somehow a place with room enough for someone like me.

W. Kirk Avery is a Korean War survivor (USMC, 1952). His background includes 5 academic degrees; 30 years college teaching; citations for "extraordinary service to students"; honors for support provided domestic violence/sexual assault survivors. He is a licensed mental health counselor; SAG member; hospice volunteer; and committed to storytelling as a healing art.

Blue Performing *Little Blue Riding Hood* in 1978.

Photo: Lisa Hirsch

Ahhhh!

The Bird: A Story for Blue

Joan Bailey

When I first "discovered" storytelling, a friend told me about the Bookcellar and Storytelling with Brother Blue and Friends saying, "You have to come with me, you'll love it!" And I did. I found an open friendly place where new tellers were warmly welcomed and encouraged to try their voices, and experienced tellers could have fun with familiar material or experiment with new ideas. There was always an experienced featured teller to listen to and learn from. And there were Blue and Ruth.

I always think of them as kindly gardeners gently tending their plants, lovingly feeding the birds and, of course, encouraging caterpillars to transform into butterflies. Over the years I went often, though not as often as I would have liked, and learned a great deal. I offer Blue and Ruth this story as a thank you for all the tender care they have given the storytelling community.

The Bird

On the peak of a mountain at the top of the world a wise woman sat, waiting. She was waiting for the dawn. And it came slowly. At first, there was a pale light spreading across the eastern sky. And then it glowed soft rose and touched all the surrounding peaks, turning the snow on their summits pink. And the color grew and spread and deepened until the great red disk of the sun was visible on the eastern horizon. And all this happened to a chorus of bird song which grew with the dawning light, until there was a swelling of music which filled the valleys and climbed the peaks.

But the woman was waiting for something else. Because of her powers she knew that someone was journeying to see her. And so she sat and waited. Then, in the distance, she saw what she was expecting. At first a small speck, it came swiftly closer until she could discern a small bird. It

Ahhhh!

flew right to her and settled on the arm of her seat.

The bird opened her beak but no sound came; she ruffled her feathers in despair and her bright eyes looked pleadingly into the wise woman's. The woman smiled and said, "Do not worry. I know why you have come and what you seek. But you have two tasks to complete before you will find your heart's desire. And they will not be easy. Listen carefully. This is what you must do.

"First you must travel west, to the edge of the world, and there, deep in the bowels of the earth, you will find the castle of doom. Its gate is guarded by three huge and savage dogs. You must pass by them unseen, for they are fierce guardians and will devour you if they can. Go to the center of the castle and from the fire, which burns there, you must take a glowing coal.

"You must then take this coal to the far north to the land of ice where you will find a crystal castle made from towers of ice. There, in the heart of the castle, you will find a frozen queen sitting on her frozen throne. Before her there is a frozen fountain, and your second task is to put the coal in the fountain. The journey will be hard, and these tasks will not be easy to fulfill. But I tell you to summon your courage and do your best."

And so the little bird began her journey. And the wise woman was right. It was not easy. The little bird flew a vast distance into the wild, west wind. Tossed and buffeted by fierce storms, she searched for the edge of the world. She crossed the icy oceans where the salt spray stung her like darts of steel. She crossed deserts where the scorching air seared her lungs with every breath, and every beat of her wings took the greatest effort of will. Many times the little bird thought she would never be able to complete her task. But something kept her going, from somewhere she found the strength to continue.

And finally, exhausted to the limits of her strength, she came to the edge of the world. Then she gripped her courage and dove into the bowels of the earth. And there she found the castle of doom, its dark towers threatening and black in the distance. From the narrow slits of its windows there came a dull red glow. Guarding the gate were three huge, black dogs. Their slavering jaws gaped wide, showing huge red tongues and rows of razor-sharp white teeth. Even the forest seemed to fear the castle and its fierce guardians, for the trees thinned and shrank so that only straggly scrub survived closer to the castle walls.

The little bird flew down to a tree at a distance from the castle, and, her heart beating rapidly, she considered what she should do. There seemed to be no way out, for the three dogs watched in every direction.

AHHHH!

They looked out over the barren waste surrounding the castle, unsleeping, unblinking, allowing no creature to pass—only the Queen of the castle could come and go as she desired. From time to time she came out and strode along the road, glaring about as if she did not trust her savage pets to keep the castle safe. The dark Queen was a terrible figure; tall, thin and angular, with a wild mass of wiry hair that stood out from her head. She wore her anger like a badge on her scowling face. She trod the earth with utter contempt for any living thing around her; with each step her feet stamped the ground like a punishment. And the little bird's heart quailed at the thought of entering her domain. But, as the dark Queen came through the gate and strode out along the open road, the little bird made her way carefully toward her. Flying from branch to branch, flitting from tree to bush, she made her way unseen until she was hidden on a branch right beside the Queen. Then she took her chance and flew up into the wild black mass of the queen's wiry hair and lightly settled there hidden, unnoticed.

So it was that the proud Queen herself carried the little bird into the castle of doom. The bird wasted no time in finding the source of the dull red glow that filled the castle. It was a huge fire of glowing coals, roaring with power, in the deepest part of the castle. The little bird did not know how she was going to complete the next part of her task. How could she even touch one of the embers? She did not think she could bear to come close to the fire, so fierce was its heat. But the wise woman had said she must do this thing, and so she tried. She flew to the fire as fast as she could and gripped a tiny coal in her little claws. She expected to be seared by a savage heat, but to her surprise, she felt no pain. She flew up and above the fire.

Suddenly, the dark Queen noticed the little bird and her anger knew no bounds. She lashed the guardian dogs and screamed, "You worthless creatures! Why did you not stop her? Seize her! Stop her now! Do not let her go!"

But it was already too late. The little bird was beyond the gate and beyond the reach of the dogs. And with every beat of her fragile wings her strength seemed to grow, taking power from the burning coal she carried.

And so she began the second task she had been set. She flew fast and well toward the frozen north, growing in strength as she traveled. And swiftly she came to the land of ice. There she found the crystal castle, and within it, seated on a throne of ice, was the frozen Queen, beautiful, pale and still, frozen in time and place. She sat in her exquisite palace,

Ahhhh!

her gaze locked upon the fountain of ice before her.

The little bird did not hesitate, but flew at once to the frozen fountain and dropped the glowing coal as she had been instructed. Suddenly, there was music in the air, as though thousands of tiny crystals vibrated and chimed. The fountain was no longer frozen but began to dance, and the tinkle of its waters joined the chiming music, and the air in the room vibrated with energy and life.

The little bird turned to look at the Queen on her throne, and she too was changing. The white frost was gone from her skin, and she was beginning to flow. Warmth and color spread throughout her body and she began to smile, and that smile warmed the land and melted the ice, and signs of new life were everywhere. There were gurgling streams, burgeoning buds on branches, new green shoots pushing up from the warm brown earth. Then the beautiful Queen spoke, "Oh, thank you little bird! I have waited so long for you to come and release me. I thank you with all my heart. Now, will you drink from my fountain, for it was you who made it flow again?"

The little bird flew to the fountain and drank, and as she did, a song rose up within her. A song so beautiful it touched the hearts of all who heard it. She had found her voice at last! She flew out into the woods and sang her song, soaring high, her heart light. And as she flew there were answering songs, few and faint at first, but then growing stronger and swelling the sound so that all the land was full of glorious music.

Thus it was she found her heart's desire and lived in peace and joy.

Joan Bailey is a teacher turned storyteller who was born in England. She loves to tell traditional tales as well as her own *Tales of a Lancashire Childhood*. She has told stories and given workshops for both students and adults around the world.

Blue Performing in the Spring of 1977

Ahhhh!

Ruth and Blue

Dan Barrett

She Pokes His Rib,
He Shouts IT Out!

That Old Butterfly
Rockin' The World!

Dan Barrett produced and directed the audiotape, *Brother Blue, True Life Adventure Stories* for Shambhala Lion Editions.

A young Blue performing - 1970's

Ahhhh!

My Initiation

Bob Barton

He sat there gazing up at me, large expressive eyes filled with anticipation. This was my initiation as a circuit rider on the storytelling trail.

Blue never missed any of my sets that week. He was always there winking, smiling, showering me with every ounce of encouragement he could. All of our behind the scenes chat centered on storytelling. I knew he was teaching me everything he could without ever appearing to do so. I had told one story earlier in the week that I was not comfortable with, and my discomfort was obvious to everyone. Later in the week, in a gentle off-hand manner, Blue managed to tell me to drop the story. I did.

As I observed Brother Blue very carefully that week, I grew to respect him more and more. His passion, his commitment and his talent impressed me greatly. Yes, he was a great showman and could ham it up with the best of them. But he could also touch people in a way I had never witnessed before. Looking back on that summer, I think what impressed me most were the stories he told one on one to people who sought him out. Whatever it was that perplexed them, Blue addressed with a story that was often improvised on the spot.

I also learned that there was another dimension to Blue, and that was Ruth. Gentle, patient and wise, she was his guardian angel. And in the words of Christopher Marlowe she was "the passionate shepherd to his love."

A native of Ontario, Canada, Bob Barton became a professional storyteller after a career in teaching. His books include *Telling Stories Your Way: Storytelling and Reading Aloud In the Classroom* and *Story Works* (with David Booth), *The Reindeer Herder and the Moon*, *The Storm Wife*, *Best and Dearest Chick of All* and a retelling of Paul Gallico's *The Smallest Miracle*.

Ahhhh !

The Road Taken With Blue

John Basinger

I told a story at the Corn Island 20th, that I hoped would be boffo. It
was a short piece wherein the character, Chester Behnke, after years of
puzzling over Robert Frost's existential challenge to the twentieth
century—his poem, The Road Not Taken—finally feels, deep in the
Iowa countryside, a moment of incipient satori that ends in a poem
springing full blown out of his head: his answer to Frost's challenge. I
gave my story my confident all. The audience response reached the level
of polite, this being Kentucky. On the bus back to the storyteller's
motel, Blue leaned over to me, stuck his head inside the cloud I'd
wrapped around myself and asked me to repeat Chester Behnke's poem.
I did so:

> Two roads converged in an Iowa wood
> and having traveled the one, long I stood
> And looked up the other as far as I could
> Waiting for what? My alter ego to arrive?
> Unless he'd already come from somewhere
> Waited awhile for me and left. I searched
> For signs of his presence but didn't know
> What they were. Things seemed normal for the place:
> Washboard roads, dusty weeds, an empty bottle,
> A box. Then perhaps he'd not yet come.
> But the picture didn't change: washboard, weeds,
> Bottle, box. Read either way they seemed the same.
> I listened for sound. Nothing rising or falling.
> I tasted the air. Nothing lingering there.
> Then I thought, "No, I'll go on! If he is ahead,
> Perhaps I'll overtake him. If he is to follow,
> Perhaps he will come." I'm telling all this

Ahhhh!

With a sigh, here, ages and ages since
That two roads converged in an Iowa wood
And that has made absolutely no difference.

"Yes!" Blue said. "Yes!" And warming to his task, began, by analysis, to weave the piece into the canon of English language poetry. Somewhere between Edgar A. Guest and Ogden Nash would have been good. But he did me better than that. Then he asked to hear other poems and responded avidly to each one, finding in them triggers to his own feeling and thinking. By the time we'd reached the motel, the cloud was gone. Here, in appreciation, is a stanza from a poem he didn't hear that day:

The sudden flutter of a butterfly
Caught his eye. Nearly falling it flew,
Flickering white across a heaven of Blue.

John Basinger is active as a performer and director in storytelling, theater and poetry venues. He has had a long association with the National Theatre of the Deaf, NSA/N, and the slam poetry movement. For the past decade he has been learning and telling John Milton's "Paradise Lost", and recently presented the entire work over a three day period for which he received a Homer award.

Blue talking with Rob Evans in Harvard Square during the 1970's

Photo: Jerry Howard

Ahhhh!

The Teacher

Jeanine Pasini Beekman

There once lived a teacher who was renowned for his goodness and wisdom. He traveled the land dispensing gifts, and always gave to others exactly what they needed. To some he offered laughter, on others he bestowed tears. He left whispered confidences with huge gatherings and raucous shouts with small ones. Wherever he went he always left part of himself, and his gifts seemed cloaked in an azure light of otherworldly hue.

The teacher was so intent in nourishing others, he seldom paused to eat or sleep himself. Some thought him foolish. More thought him holy. Because of this, students came to him from far and near. Many came in search of knowledge; others came to learn compassion. Some came to sit quietly in his presence, and a few came in hopes that they, like their master, would gain certain entry into Paradise.

One day, a new student presented himself to the teacher. The young man listened and watched. He studied and learned. He modeled every action on that of his teacher, certain that his good works in this life would merit him ease in the life to come.

After several years of study and service to others, the young man's effort was rewarded with a dream. He stood in a radiant land which bedazzled all his senses. At first he stumbled, but, when he became accustomed to the brightness, he moved with ease and made out fragrances, then shapes, then sounds. The vision was of such unearthly beauty, the student was certain he had been blessed with entry into Paradise. And so he had.

In the distance, he saw a shimmering light the color of the sky and heard the joyful voices of his friends. The young man rushed toward them, anxious to join the leisure his life on earth had earned. But when he reached them, the student saw that his friends were not engaged in

Ahhhh!

30

rest and contemplation or frivolity and games. To his surprise, they were employed exactly as they had been on earth. And no one worked harder than their teacher.

In confusion and anger, the student approached the holy man. He said, "Teacher, is *this* our life in the world to come?" The teacher smiled his radiant smile and nodded. "Teacher, is *this* our reward for doing such good works on earth?" Again, the master smiled and nodded. "Then, Teacher, if we are to work this hard, we might as well remain on earth as enter into Paradise."

The holy man smiled his gentle smile, danced a few steps, and took the young man's hand in his own. "My angel child," he said, "in all the time you've spent with me, have you not yet learned the truth of the life I lead? Look closely, and you will see that the workers are not in Paradise; Paradise is in the workers."

And so they were. And so they are.

Winner of the 1991 John Henry Faulk Award for storytelling, Jeanine Pasini Beekman has been a nationally known professional storyteller since 1975, enthralling audiences of all ages with her lively and dramatic retelling of literary stories as well as traditional tales.

Brother Blue, a popular and much-loved storyteller, appears regularly on The Spider's Web.

Photo: Dorothy West

A 1970's publicity photo for The Spider's Web on WGBH radio Boston.

Ahhhh!

A Tribute to Brother Blue
(a.k.a. Hugh Hill and Ruth Hill)
Robert A. Bennett

Brother Blue, Hugh and Ruth together, as I always see you: I nominate you to be inducted in the HALL OF FAME of African-American Mentors. Webster's Dictionary says that a mentor is a trusted counselor or guide, also one who is a tutor and coach. Brother Blue, Hugh and Ruth together, by your colorful and distinctive dress, by your actions and performance, your narration and poetry, your props (I love your use of chains), by all these, plus more, you truly fulfill the office and vocation of mentor.

Two great, yet quite different African-American mentors come to mind, though this title is seldom attributed to them. These are Frederick Douglass (1817-1895), a forceful and passionate agitator for black freedom and empowerment after Emancipation, and Howard Thurman (1900-1981), a mystic striving for universality, yet whose preaching and writing gave underpinning to the civil rights revolution at the middle of the Twentieth Century. Brother Blue, I see your role as storyteller in the tradition of the mentoring—guidance—given to black folks and the whole nation by Douglass and Thurman. Though their (and your) calls are rooted in the past history and experience of the ancestors, their (and your) perspectives are always directed toward the present and future. This is a vocation based on the injunction: "Never Let Your Memories Be Greater Than Your Dreams."

Narrative, telling the story for the benefit of others, especially for future generations, is what you share with Frederick Douglass and Howard Thurman.

The Life and Times of Frederick Douglass chronicles his story from slavery on the Eastern Shore of Maryland, and in Baltimore, to a life of service as a free person to his people and nation. Among many other

AHHHH!

things, he was an advisor to Lincoln and served as envoy to Haiti. His newspaper in Rochester, New York, aptly titled "The North Star," in more ways than one guided his people toward freedom. His was a voice, in print and on the stage of oratory, which mentored folks then, and still stirs up the conscience and the will to action. Brother Blue, I take this to be your calling as well.

Howard Thurman, preacher and mystic seeking to encompass universality, left his mark at Rankin Chapel of Howard University in Washington, D.C., The Church for the Fellowship of all Peoples in San Francisco, California, and more locally, as Dean of Marsh Chapel at Boston University (1953-1965). One cannot begin to appreciate, let alone fully understand, the profundity of the African-American religious tradition— its deep spirituality—without the mentoring guidance of Thurman's seminal works in the 1940's: *Deep River: Reflections on the Religious Insights of Certain Negro Spirituals* (1945); *The Negro Spiritual Speaks of Life and Death* (1947); and *Jesus and the Disinherited* (1949). It was the last of these which so moved Martin Luther King, that he kept it, along with the Holy Bible, as his constant companion. *Temptations of Jesus* (1962), selected sermons from Boston University; Marsh Chapel, gives deep insight into Thurman's philosophy and theology under the phrase, "The Gothic Principle in Life." Like the gothic arch, whose deep rootedness in the earth allows it to soar heavenward, so human existence in its earthboundness, its rootedness deep in life and humanity, is given the stage, the platform, from which it can soar beyond itself. So, Brother Blue, keep telling the story, keep rattling those chains, for therein you follow the tradition of the great mentors before you and who will follow. Welcome to the MENTORS' HALL OF FAME!!!

A graduate student in Harvard's Near Eastern Language Department, Robert A. Bennett met Hugh and Ruth Hill in 1965. Having taught Hebrew at the Episcopal Divinity School, and pastored local Episcopal congregations, he co-pastored his last congregation in Central Square, Cambridge with his wife, Marceline Donaldson. They still delight in running into Blue and Ruth in Harvard Square.

Ahhhh!

Zusia

Carol Birch

This story epitomizes the vision and power of Brother Blue's life and teachings and begins:

When the Rabbi Zusia entered the synagogue his face was ashen. He looked so stricken that one man asked: "What's troubling you? Are you ill?"

And Zusia answered: "I've had a vision of what the angels will ask me when I die."

"No wonder you look upset," said another, "to think of *death*."

"No. It is *not* thinking about death that troubles me.
I am troubled by the question the angels will ask."

Silence.

Finally someone said: "What will they ask you?"

"They will *not* ask me why I didn't lead my people like Moses!"

"So?"

"They will *not* ask me why I didn't have the wisdom of Solomon."

"So. What will they ask?"

"They will *not* ask me why I didn't have the patience of Job.
No, the angels will look at me and say:

Ahhhh!

Zusia, in YOUR life
there was ONE thing *YOU could have been*, that
NO ONE ELSE Could Have Been...

So

While YOU Were Living, Zusia,
WHY WEREN'T YOU ZUSIA?"

Brother Blue reminds us that we won the race called Life
the Minute We Were Born!

We slid across our own finish line, secured our place as...a winner.

Because He does not look at us and say: I was hoping for more.

Brother Blue reminds us, and each child he touches, our very presence
is The Gift.

On TV, you'll see the commercial:

"Mary, now that you've won the Gold Medal, what are you going to do?"

She says: "I'm going to Disneyland!"

Meaning, now that I'm a winner,

I'm going to play more in life.

Brother Blue answers the question: how do we live as winners?

With Love

To Play

To Play with the Love

to see Others, and Ourselves, as Complete and Unique.
In his words: Beautiful.

This Story is The One he tells everyday in different words and ways: Zusia, be Zusia.

And we say: Thank you, Brother Blue, for being Brother Blue!

A respected teacher and producer of award winning recordings and books, including *Who Says? Essays on Pivotal Issues in Contemporary Storytelling* , Carol Birch is a recipient of the NSN Circle of Excellence award.

AHHHH !

A Thank You for You

Judith Black

(A segment from: "The Turkey Rebellion of 1699")

All the other birds parted the way, making room for Wild Turkey who danced and flew and skidded towards the deep hole in Mother Earth. He slid to a stop, seeing the little one caught in what could easily be his end. They all heard the humans nearby, approaching to claim their prize.

"Look to the sky little one. Trust the spirit of the sky to guide you. Dig your little claws into the earth and fly little one. FLY!"

Little Waddles cried up in abject misery "I can't. I'm not strong enough."

Wild Turkey opened his wings "Little brother, you are the butterfly, you are the spirit, you are life. Come up to us. Just dig your claws into the side of earth and climb. You can do it." Wild Turkey lowered on his claws as far as it would go. "Come on Little Brother, reach for it. Reach for the sky." And as if the older bird's soul created a lifeline, the small turkey began, one claw at a time, grabbing at the earth.

"Yes, little brother, you are strong, you are the one, you are the king, ascend your throne and put on your crown of light…" The smaller bird continued, his complaining replaced by an intention that could no longer be broken.

Without Blue, where would we find our heroes for our stories, for our lives? Without Ruth where would we find Blue?

Thank you both for:

• The story you told Solomon when he was just ready to exit the womb. He's 6'3" now, playing lineman on the varsity football team, and there is some of you in him.

Ahhhh!

- Thank you for shaking hands with William Shakespeare.
- Thank you for being the living embodiment of what you preach.
- Thank you for being the kind of listeners that draw out the best that any teller has to give.
- Thank you for reminding us that G-d lives in everything and everybody on this earth.

Judith Black first heard Brother Blue regaling the citizens of Cambridge in a busy Harvard Square street, where bit by bit the chaos of the world fell away and what remained was the sacred connection he gave us to G-d through stories. She is also a storyteller who, in dreams, would like to touch that place he lives in. She was inducted into the National Storytelling Network's Circle of Excellence in 2002.

Blue & Solomon Black, Judith's son - 1970's

Ahhhh!

David's Birthday

Jacob Bloom

It wouldn't have happened if it wasn't David's birthday. You see, for his twenty-fifth birthday, David wanted nothing more than to have an excellent meal together with a few of his closest friends. Naturally, when he asked me to join him, I wasn't about to say no.

And so Linda, Ingrid and I met David at the Cafe Budapest, a Hungarian restaurant where the elegance takes your breath away. We fit right in. We may have been poor working people, but we each had one fancy outfit for special occasions, and we were wearing them that night. We made our choices from the refined menu, ordered them from the gracious waiter, and engaged in droll conversation about how different this place was from any place we'd ever been. We chatted long after the waiter discreetly left the check on our table, and when David excused himself to go to the restroom, Linda, Ingrid, and I grabbed our chance.

David had made it clear that he would pay for his own meal and that he just wanted the pleasure of our company. But as soon as he was out of earshot, the three of us looked at the check and started figuring out whether we could afford to pay for his meal as well as our own. We emptied out our wallets, and sure enough, when we added together all of the bills in our wallets, plus most of the pocket change, we had enough to cover both the bill and the tip.

David returned and was surprised, then insistent about wanting to pay, and finally grateful when we refused to let him. We left the restaurant and came out into a beautiful September night, deciding to take a walk.

There is a curious lightheadedness that comes over you when you are dressed rich and have no money, especially if you are with friends. We strutted off into Boston's Back Bay singing "We've Got Elegance." We danced down Boston's poshest street four abreast, arms around each others' waists, doing the Salty Dog Rag.

Ahhhh!

We came to an old stone church, and outside its open door we were accosted by a very strange looking man who tried to talk us into coming to the church. He was a tall black man, dressed all in blue, with bells and other strange decorations sewn onto his clothes and rainbows painted on his face. We stopped, and tried to figure out if we should listen to him or run.

Our confusion only lasted a few seconds, for I realized that this was something I had read about in the Free Events section of the newspaper.

"It's Brother Blue. I've heard of him. He does storytelling at this church every week, with no admission charge. I've been meaning to get here someday. Let's go in."

We went into the church's chapel, and sat down in the first row of seats. It was a slow night for Blue, for we were the only ones there. It took us a while to get used to the way that this strange looking man talked. The first things he did were to take off his shoes and socks, put a large book on the floor, put one foot on the book, and tell us that he was going to let the stories flow up through his feet and come out of his heart. We stayed, and listened, and enjoyed. Unfortunately, David had to get home early for some reason. He said goodbye after the first story and headed for the Arlington Street subway station, but the rest of us stayed and listened until the end. And, at the very end, Brother Blue passed the hat, asking for whatever we wanted to give.

And there we were, dressed to the hilt, looking the height of elegance, feeling very much that what we had heard deserved ample compensation—but with less than a dollar between us. Brother Blue must have been very disappointed that night.

But then, maybe Blue was used to it. Because Blue hasn't just told stories in prisons and for the poor. Blue has also spent a lot of time in places like Newbury Street and Harvard Square, trying to give something to people who thought they were too busy to stop and listen, trying to give them a story that will open their hearts and enrich their lives.

So Blue understands about people who look rich on the outside, but who are poor on the inside.

I hope he wasn't too bothered by us people who looked rich on the outside, but were broke.

Jacob Bloom has lived all around Boston, went to school out west in Worcester, studied theater, then sold plumbing supplies, toured Europe with two dance performing groups, calls square and contra dances, and has stories to tell about all of it.

Ahhhh !

Knee Deep in Story

Joan Bodger

Blue!

He annoys the hell out of me. Always has to be "on." In the middle of the street he's suddenly struck with an idea. He has to tell me *now*. Has to tell me by *dancing* his idea—in the middle of the street, yet. Could get us all killed. Is he oblivious as people turn to stare at us? I'm stuck here, with this exotic bird bending toward me. A capering cockatoo, taller than I am, but much, much thinner. Thin! He doesn't eat enough to keep a bird alive. A blue cockatoo festooned with balloons and red and yellow ribbons. His cheek bones are so knobbed you could hang your coat on one of them, your hat on the other. I wonder if there's native American blood…African, we know about. With that legal name, Hugh Morgan Hill, there must be Welsh. (In a movie, he played the part of Merlin.) No matter which what. Prick him, and the blood runs blue. He's a world class aristocrat. Cosmic class *holy*.

Ruth Edmonds Hill is Blue's wife. I have known her for twenty years. Ruth, the opposite of ruthless, therefore compassionate. I am reminded of the Ruth in the Bible, choosing the journey with her obsessed companion. A sojourner, yes, but never a follower. She has a life of her own, as intellectual and scholar.

> There is an old woman, lives under a hill,
> And if she's not gone, she lives there still.

She's always there, his muse, sitting near the front, where Blue can see her. Enigmatic, part of the scenery.

But now let us again consider Blue. Blue as shaman, Blue as powered by butterflies, his familiars. Shamans in South America, Mongolia, Africa, Australia, the American plains, Celtic Britain, all wore feathers—

AHHHH!

feathered headdresses, feathered cloaks—to indicate their ability to be
transported to another plane, bring back prophesy to the people, to king
and court. Blue, transported, soars on the jeweled wings.

Let us now consider Blue as fool. Of *course* I looked it up! From Latin
follis, meaning bellows, or windbag. O how the mighty have fallen! The
fool in medieval courts carries a pig bladder on a stick, to make rude
noise with. His costume—layered, scalloped, fringed, ruffled—is all that
remains of the feathered cloak. He capers, like a bird with a broken
wing. He is the only one who can tell off the royalty, although he must
veil his shamanistic prophesies in a whirlwind of words, in jokes, stories,
and parables.

Jesus, according to Carl Jung, is a trickster hero. Let us consider Blue
as a trickster, wise and foolish. Sly (did I mention he is *Doctor* Hugh
Morgan Hill, his degree from Harvard?) and truthful, tale spinner, street
rapper, ordained minister. As Anansi reincarnated, *he tells the myth that
lies, the lie wherein lies the truth.*

Let us now consider Blue as man at play, or playful man. Story, which
is a form of play, is his chosen profession. Years ago, on first looking into
Johan Huizinga's *Homo Ludens*, I learned that play, by definition, con-
notes choice. As listener, as teller, we choose to enter the game: *Cric?
Crac!* Story is a cosmic game, framed by *"Once upon a..."* Not now, not
the future, not historical time, but time beyond (outside of) time. Not
only the beginning, but the story's end, too, is often edged, sometimes by
a bit of nonsense, to remind us that we're *just playing.*

Blue and Ruth have chosen a hard way to live, a hard way to *be*, yet are
graceful and elegant in everything they do. They do for the love of
doing, which makes them, in the best sense, aristocratic amateurs. Yet
they are professional to their fingertips. They stay attuned to those who
share the boards. They listen, which is rare among storytellers.

*Overcome, Blue springs up to tell the teller and tell the audience what he felt,
thought, experienced upon hearing the story.* The audiences gapes. Who is
this old windbag? Are they fools to let him get away with being so
outlandish? Fearlessly, courageously, he allows, chooses, gives himself
permission to be outlandish, to be transported out of this world. Knowing that Ruth Hill, steady as Silbury, holds the string to his balloon.
Listening to him, I marvel at how brave, generous, sensitive, perceptive,
professional, sweet, acute, and passionate his is. How he does love a
story!

Ahhhh!

I am standing in the street with Blue, annoyed as hell for being here. Feeling foolish. Afraid I'm making a spectacle of myself, afraid that I'm going to be hit by a car. Instead, I am struck by an epiphany! I am here only because I chose to be here. I would rather be here—*now*—with Blue and Ruth, than anywhere else in the world. *Standing knee deep in story.*

Joan Bodger taught children's literature and storytelling at Bank Street College in NYC, and was a regular reviewer of children's books for the New York Times. Her work in Canada included helping to found the Storyteller's School of Toronto.

Ahhhh !

Dear Brother Blue and Ruth: Soul Mates of Enlightenment

Gabriella Britton

Many years ago I saw, heard, experienced Brother Blue for the first time, immediately realizing I was in the presence of a living saint, a holy man, a genius, shaman, griot-poet and storyteller. Magically creative and visionary, his work that day, and many times thereafter, gifted me with a spiritual awakening, an enlightenment. As he danced, spoke, sang and wove his *Butterfly* story and *Miss Wunderlich*, I actually saw light emanate from him and felt it enter my spirit and heart. I went into a vision-trance state while standing in the sunshine on Brattle Street, feeling uplifted, transfigured, and ecstatic. This had been a time of hardship in my life, but also a time in which I was spiritually open and receptive.

At a later time I stood gripped, transfixed, listening to his amazing inner city *Ugly Duckling* and *King Lear.* (I had just lost more than a few beloved people.) When Brother Blue passionately intoned "never, never, never again!" welcome tears of grief streamed down my face. He can make you laugh all your laughter, cry all your tears. He is immediate, improvisatory, his stories full of messages that are true to universal realities *and*, at the *same* time, unique to current realities and injustices.

Brother Blue's perfect soul mate is Ruth Hill, beautiful, brilliant, and infinitely balanced. She is saint, genius, creator, and innovator, in tandem with *her* soul mate, Brother Blue. Ruth's scholarly research on women of color and the original women of N.O.W., among other projects, have opened the doors from his-story into her-story. It has been work filled with many obstacles and challenges, met with a steady combination of wisdom, humor and compassion.

If ever I met true soul mates, they are Brother Blue, (Hugh Morgan Hill) and Ruth Edmonds Hill. Everywhere they go, they make this difficult world a better place, whether they are taking the stories to the

Ahhhh!

streets, to the prisons, or to wherever the suffering is most.

God bless you, dear Brother Father Grandfather Blue, and Sister Mother Grandmother Ruth.

All my love from the bottom of my heart, the deep of my soul and the spirit-mind you always enlighten,

Gabriella

and your goddaughter, Khadijah (a graduate again).

After raising amazing now-grown children while waitressing, working kitchen-prep, factory, housecleaning, cabdriving, community-volunteering, Gabriella Britton still works in retail, dances, writes, and takes classes in Flamenco, drumming, acting, pottery, and life-drawing.

Ahhhh!

The Importance of a Name

Kevin Brooks

All I did was get up and talk about my name. That's all. I don't have a long name nor an exotic name. But the first time I got up to tell a story at the Bookcellar Cafe in Cambridge, all I did was talk about my name. No big deal. Brother Blue, however, in his own special way, helped me to see the big deal. As soon as my meager piece was over, Blue got up and told me and the assembled group that was soon to become my family, just what a big deal it was to talk simply about myself, with no pretense or fanfare. He saw beneath my shy, clumsy layers to a place deep down, deeper than I had ever mapped myself. When I finally sat down after Blue's comments, I knew that some link was born between this man and me. I knew that he had established something complex, because he is complex. What he did and continues to do is exactly what he says, which is to touch from the middle of the middle of him to the middle of the middle of me. But he didn't just do this for me. I saw him do the same for each and every other person that got up to tell that night, and every night following. Blue empowers people with his listening and elevates them with his praise.

Through those initial visits to the Bookcellar group, my storytelling world was born. I was hooked. I went often and got up to tell every chance I got. Meanwhile, in my academic world at MIT, I was working with lots of very bright and technical people, trying to merge my love for writing and story with the power of the computer. It was a very different world, influenced primarily by those doing narrative deconstruction rather than the architects and construction artists of my storytelling world. For about two years I kept these two worlds as separate as I could. I didn't want to mingle the soft rocking caress of storytelling with the harsh deconstructionist analysis and cold computational structures of my academia. Until one day I saw an open slot in my department's

Ahhhh!

colloquium series calendar, and I thought, "You know, why not. Why not invite Blue!"

I talked to Blue and Ruth about it and they agreed. Arrangements were made, the date was set, and all looked well. As the date approached, I thought more about what I had done. You see, most of the other monthly colloquium speakers were scientists or engineers of one type or another. They were leading theorists and practitioners, people pushing on the edges of their field, helping to define the future in their own special ways. While Brother Blue is much the same, pushing on the bounds of the human heart and mind, telling stories for no other reason than to change the world, he represented a departure from the norm for my lab. The butterfly images on his face and clothing, for example, a departure. The balloons and ribbons tied around his arms and legs, a departure. A black man standing up in front of one of the world's most prestigious, predominately white, technical institutions talking about the power of love and story, big departure! This man, who by this time I had considered my adopted father, was going to stand up and speak to people who I was afraid would be unable to listen, unable to absorb a message for which a mathematical equation did not exist. "Would this work?" I thought.

It fell to me to make a poster advertising the event. Posters would be hung all over campus to help ensure a good turnout. But what to say? Come see the storyteller? No, not enough. Black man scheduled to change the world on December 11th at 4:30pm? No, might give the wrong impression and too sixties. The poster ended up including a full body picture of Blue along with his full name, Dr. Hugh Morgan Hill (I thought that might offer people some legitimacy before they had their minds blown.) I quoted what he and others had said about his work, like the middle of the middle line and how many have called him the world's greatest storyteller. But I also prayed, "Lord, let this work. I don't know what exactly to ask for, but please just let this work."

The day came; the pre-arranged taxi dropped Blue and Ruth off in front of my lab. A modest crowd of 50-60 people was assembled in the auditorium, and I was nervous. Would they get it? Everyone looked so serious, everyone except Blue. I hoped that by the end of the allotted sixty minutes, these hearts and minds of technology would melt just a little bit. My advisor introduced him and Blue was on. Actually, Blue was really ON. Blue did his version of Romeo and Juliet, bringing on stage a women sitting in the front row, who by the end was charmed

Ahhhh!

beyond belief. He told a brief version of his signature story about the caterpillar that didn't know himself until he changed into a butterfly. And Blue took questions from the audience with kindness and creativity until the time was up. The audience was stunned. Those technical hearts and minds I had worried about so much melted five minutes after the start. The world didn't stand a chance; everything changed that day.

When it was over, after struggling to pull Blue from the throngs of people who came up to him, I took him and Ruth up to my lab area where we had a vegetarian dinner waiting. It was storytelling group night, and I had to get them through dinner and on their way to the Bookcellar by 6:30. But when Blue is on, he is on! And the last thing his overflowing energy allows him to do is eat. Surrounded by graduate students, Blue launched into his version of King Lear, as told to him by his old friend Will, accompanied by a large cast of characters, including Ella and Nat King Cole. Nobody ate. Nobody breathed. We all just watched the master.

I learned something that day about the power of storytelling. Yes, Brother Blue is a powerful storyteller, no doubt. But the most valuable lesson that Blue has taught me is that to tell a story is perhaps the most powerful thing anyone can do. Blue taught me that it is the story itself that can pierce any shell, academic or otherwise, and reach the waiting heart beneath. It is the teller's job to simply launch the story on its way. Governments and cynics can scoff all they want to, but Brother Blue shows us by example that to tell a story changes lives, and when you change enough lives, you change the world. Blue has certainly changed my world. I am thankful that God brought Blue and Ruth into my life.

Kevin Brooks is a Boston area storyteller who learned how to tell stories starting in 1994 by simply watching Brother Blue and those who Blue "enlisted" stories out of on a weekly basis. He performs personal stories from his urban childhood and challenging parenthood, which somehow strike universal and cross generational/cultural notes.

With a Ph.D. from the MIT Media Lab, by day he applies narrative construction and understanding to computer interface design.

AHHHH!

Brother Blue

Michael Brown

Ungainly and loquacious
light patterned skin and showy clothes,
his poems and gestures flow
with a hesitated swing
like the butterfly's wings
that don't spread and close
with even motion,
but hitch halfway
as if to say,
I can't show you all of this at once:
catch this hint
and blink before the whole thing
opens
and closes fast.

So often when we are young
we write out of depression.
We're lucky if we ever learn
to use our craft in celebration.
How much more than to give expression
to the soul,
the butterfly that flutters in others.

Lately,
I write what I care most about—
those good feelings I trust
in the best part
of my heart—
I feel a soft bright dust
as though a blue butterfly's wing
has touched a dark compartment there.

Ahhhh!

48

Michael Brown is a professor of Communications at Mount Ida College; by night he's a poet, and on Wednesday nights, he's the Master of Ceremonies at the Third Rail Lounge in Cambridge, hosting the increasingly popular Boston Slam.

Many Slam Poets have come and gone, but the one constant at the Boston/Cambridge Slam is the smiling face of The Godfather of New England Slam, Michael Brown.

Ahhhh!

A Heron Feather and a Rainbow for Brother Blue

Joseph Bruchac

When I close my eyes and whisper his name, it is always easy to see Brother Blue. Slender, a little stoop-shouldered from carrying the sky on his shoulders, buoyed up by a rainbow of balloons, his graceful hand raised up, he is about to tell a story. Can't you see him, too?

Aside from my own immediate family, few people stand more clearly in my memories. Here's one of them. I'm at the Sharing the Fire Conference. I've just finished doing a presentation. Brother Blue walks up to me, his wife, Ruth, by his side. Perhaps, I think, he's going to shake my hand and say, "good job," as others have done. Instead, he falls to his knees and touches my feet with his forehead. "I kneel before a master storyteller," he intones in that unforgettable, resonant voice of his.

That act of gentle and humorous homage was, at one and the same time, extravagant, graceful and a wonderful combination of generosity and showmanship. No one else could have pulled it off as Brother Blue did. (And I hope to God no one else tries!) I felt honored, amused, and a little awed. Though my own tradition is a bit different from Blue's, I felt he deserved the same respect from me. So I stood there and accepted his praise. When I caught Ruth's eye, I could see that she approved of my response. There was a look on her face, too, that I'll never forget. Love, pride, and a sort of "Oh, my! There Blue goes again!" expression. Plus the watchfulness of a mother lion watching out for her cub! It was a memorable moment.

Memorable? Then again, maybe memorable is not a big enough word to describe Brother Blue. We need a new dictionary for him, one more completely kinesthetic. Or perhaps a whole parade of praise singers, those peripatetic minstrals of West Africa whose job it is to improvise songs in celebration of not only the great and the mighty, but also any

Ahhhh!

person they meet for the first time on the road. I had such a group of Yoruba praise singers, equipped with gourd rattles, two-throated bells and hourglass drums perform such a song for me one day in a small Nigerian village. Blue's brothers. Can't you see how he, too, is the sweet-throated keeper of an ancient tradition?

There's now a good number of us storytellers in America. So many that it's easy for us to say we're storytellers these days. But there weren't so many of us seeking the sky when Brother Blue began, when he stood up, wings spread wide to show he was, indeed, unafraid to make a fool of himself by trying. After all, when you first take flight you may fall. Has Brother Blue ever suffered from a fear of falling?

One of the reasons we are so many is because of examples such as his. And then there is generosity of spirit that Blue embodies. Maybe you've seen it as I have. A storytelling festival like our big jamboree in Jonesborough. And there Blue is, in motley costume, Ruth right beside him—unless she's gone off to find something to eat for Blue, knowing that when stories are being told, he might just about starve himself to death if she didn't watch him. It isn't even a year when he's on the program to perform, but he's there. And what is he doing? Hour after hour, he is sitting on one of those hay bales in the Swapping Ground, listening to fledgling storytellers, encouraging them, cheering them, helping them find their wings. Fly, baby, fly! Can't you hear him?

I have a feather on my desk. It's from the wing of a great blue heron. It's a sacred bird to my Abenaki people. Its color is that of Water and Sky, those two great gifts from Ktsi Nwaskw, the Great Mystery. The heron has the power to travel between worlds, to walk the earth, a bit stoop-shouldered in its stride, to plumb the depths of water with its beak, finding mysteries hidden from ordinary human sight, and then to rise on wide and majestic wings to pass in slow majestic flight across the sky. If you have ever seen a great blue heron take flight, you know what I mean. And you know why I say that heron feather is for Brother Blue.

And here's one more thing for my friend, colleague, holy fool, and teacher. It is a story I've heard in the Northern Plains among the Assiniboine people and others. I've also read a brief version of it in a small photocopied and stapled edition of stories told by the children of Fort Belknap in Montana. It goes like this:

Long ago the wildflowers were sad. Though their lives on earth were bright with beauty, when they died, their petals simply dried up and fell

Ahhhh!

off, and they were gone forever. So they spoke to Wakan Tanka, the Great Spirit.

"Why is it," they said, "that the spirits of the people are able to walk the Sky Road after they die, while we flowers simply wither away at the end of our lives? We offer beauty to the world. Is it not right that we, too, should be able to continue after our lives are ended?"

The Great Spirit saw that the flowers were right. Such beauty as theirs should not be lost. So the Great Spirit commanded a great wind to blow. It lifted the fallen petals of the many-colored flowers up higher and higher, spreading them in a great arch across the sky. So it was that the rainbow was made from the petals of wildflowers. And so it is to this day that the rainbows made from the wildflowers can be seen, reminding us that true beauty—like stories told from generation to generation—can last forever.

A heron feather and a rainbow of wildflowers for you, Brother Blue. Wlipamkanni, wliwini nidoba. Travel well, and I thank you, my friend.

Joseph Bruchac is a writer and storyteller whose work often reflects his Abenaki Indian ancestry. His poems, articles and stories have appeared in over 500 publications, including *American Poetry Review*, *Cricket*, *Aboriginal Voices*, to *National Geographic*, *Parabola*, and *Smithsonian Magazine*. He has authored more than 70 books for adults and children, including *The First Strawberries* and *Keepers of the Earth* (co-authored with Michael Caduto), His honors include a Rockefeller Humanities fellowship, the Hope S. Dean Award for Notable Achievement in Children's Literature and both the 1998 Writer of the Year Award and the 1998 Storyteller of the Year Award from the Wordcraft Circle of Native Writers and Storytellers, and the 1999 Lifetime Achievement Award from the Native Writers Circle of the Americas.

Ruth and Blue in The Museum of Comparative Zoology, Harvard - April 1972

Ahhhh!

Reflections on our Times with Brother Blue and Ruth

Betsy and Dave Bueschel

They are beloved, gifts in our lives. They have blessed us with a new sense of wonderment. They were always giving us cause to wonder much about things, about other people, about relationships, and about what is truly important in our lives. They did this in such wonderful ways.

We are fairly typical white suburban folks who live in an old stucco house up north of Chicago in Winnetka. About fifteen years ago, Betsy was the first of us to encounter Brother Blue. She was an aspiring minister in seminary then. As part of her field studies, she attended a storytelling course where Blue was cited and discussed. Later, we both met Blue through an introduction by Chuck and Mary Sue Willie, friends to both of them. Chuck and Mary Sue are Betsy's brother-in-law and sister.

Blue and Ruth always travel around the country by train. When they came through Chicago, we would connect whenever possible. They stayed with us in our home, and we enjoyed many hours of friendship— eating together, catching up, sharing views, philosophizing, always learning from them. On several occasions, it seemed that we inspired Blue (that seemed easy). He would rise up and burst forth with a story, sometimes old, sometimes new.

One time, he wanted to give a spontaneous tribute to our niece, Mary Sue and Chuck's daughter, Sarah Willie. She was in the Ph.D. program in Sociology at Northwestern University then, preparing for a career in higher education. As part of their visit, Ruth and Blue attended one of the classes that Sarah was teaching.

It was, of course, Blue at his best. We have never seen otherwise. He consented to our videotaping this moment. With the butterfly inked to

Ahhhh!

his right palm, the streamers, balloons, tambourine, and harmonica, it was a magnificent and longer tribute than we expected. We were all absolutely delighted and again humbled by his heart, soul, and creativity.

God bless Ruth and God bless Blue. There are few precious, magic life moments such as these. We feel affirmed by them. We are in wonder of them.

David and Betsy Bueschel live in the Chicago suburbs. They met Brother Blue and Ruth through Betsy's brother-in-law when visiting his home in Concord some years ago. Since then, the Hills have become part of their extended family.

Blue Performing in August 1977

Photo: Ed Nute

Ahhhh!

Tribute for Ruth and Blue

Milbre Burch

A walking stick of a man, dressed in blue,
wearing a beret, bedecked in bells and colorful, curling ribbons,
with butterflies painted on the palms of his hands,
opens his arms and the stories fly out.
We are enveloped by the music of his language,
wrapped in grace, humor and the unexpected,
bundled up in a free floating poetry that is spun around us,
warm and wonder-full as a cocoon or a welcome embrace.
Standing on a street corner, in a church, on the stage,
he raps his own life story and ours, gives thanks to God,
wears his wounds like blessings and his blessings like wings,
chases Shakespeare through the air with his quick tongue.
When he sees the woman seated in front, smiling, shaking her head,
lifting her hand to give him the sign to wrap it up, he does.
Every tribute to him becomes a tribute to her,
because they've shared a faith and a life and a love of words.
She is his lifeline, the source of the energy
that radiates from his face and his heart,
the nectar sipped by all Blue's butterflies,
the gentle breeze that gives him direction and flight,
and also the leaf held out to him, fragile but enduring,
beckoning him to return to earth once more.

An internationally known performer, an award-winning recording and teaching artist, published poet and writer, Milbre Burch is a storyteller in every sense of the word. She "grew up as an artist" in New England where she first met Brother Blue and Ruth Hill. Milbre Burch was inducted into the National Storytelling Network's Circle of Excellence in 1999.

Ahhhh!

A Bottle of Blue Sunshine

Kendra Crossen Burroughs

I first encountered Brother Blue in Penn Station in New York City, where I had gone to meet a friend coming by train from Boston. Oddly, I did not stop and think how extraordinary this tall, handsome man, dressed completely in blue, looked. As he awkwardly wielded a huge, colorful duffel bag in rainbow stripes, I just spontaneously asked him if he would like some help with the bag. Blue laughed with delight at the offer of assistance coming from a small woman. We fell into conversation quite naturally, and I discovered that he knew the person I was meeting at the station, a street singer with whom he had often shared performance space in Harvard Square. Now Blue was rejoined by his wife, Ruth, and they chatted with me as if we were old friends, because by that time we were! Several months later I moved to the Cambridge area and had the chance to enjoy Blue's performances. Now and then I'd run into him on the street or while shopping. I noticed that Blue always seemed to be "on," able to ad lib a performance at any time and in any place. At the same time, he really listened attentively to others and made them feel as if they were the most interesting people he could talk to at that moment. Brother Blue is one of a kind. He should be bottled and distributed!

Kendra Crossen Burroughs is a freelance book editor and writer living in Myrtle Beach, South Carolina. She is the author of *Bhagavad Gita: Annotated & Explained* (2001) and *Selections from the Gospel of Sri Ramakrishna: Annotated & Explained* (2002).

Ahhhh!

Learning to Fly With the Bluest of Ease

Derek Burrows

When I was a child growing up in the Bahamas, I remember watching our TV in the living room. We had to look through what looked like snow because our reception came in from Miami and was never good, and we would twist those antennae every which way trying to find something we could see clearly. One of my favorite types of programs to watch were circus shows. I loved seeing the trapeze artists at work. I was amazed by the feats they performed, flying through the air, grabbing onto bars and others' hands, and sometimes I would find myself breathless, watching them fly without nets to catch them. I wanted to learn to fly the way they did and do circus tricks; the closest I got to it was doing cartwheels, badly, and somersaults and back flips. I practiced these on the grass in the front of my house—falling constantly but cushioned by the thick mat of carefully cultivated turf, my mother's pride.

I came to Boston in 1974, and one summer I was walking through Harvard Square and heard and saw a strange-looking man. It was Brother Blue, and true to his name he was dressed in blue with balloons and streamers hanging down and his beret on his head, and he danced about barefoot. I remember the growl of his voice, "I have to take off my shoes. This is holy ground. Whenever stories are told the ground is holy." I remember the first time I saw this as he removed his shoes and socks and rested them near his wife, Sister Ruth, and began telling stories. I was enthralled the first time I heard him. Words flew around the heads of people, under buses and into stores. Sounds of music and stories intermingled with cars and students bustling by. He seemed like a magician doing sleight of hand, and every time you thought you knew where something was, it changed. People seemed drawn to him as crowds gathered wherever he stood.

Ahhhh!

When I first saw Brother Blue I didn't understand what he was doing. I felt like I was watching television and the reception was fuzzy. It was strange seeing this grown man in Harvard Square decorated with ribbons and pins dancing around and singing words and playing his little harmonica. Occasionally I passed by him and listened to his words wondering about him. People gathered as he ruled the stage we called the street, and some stayed for a long time while I moved on to get my coffee from Coffee Connection and read my book.

As the years went by, I rediscovered a part of my heritage. I started telling stories. I always loved storytelling and recalled the nights sitting outside my grandparent's house listening to people talk ol' talk and sing songs. I felt it in my blood. As I began my career as a storyteller, people would occasionally ask me, "Have you ever seen Brother Blue?" and I would reply, "Yes I have, he is, uh, very interesting."

One day I remember walking through Harvard Square, and I passed Brother Blue and decided to stop and listen. I watched him as he did his Brother Blue thing. I observed people passing and looking; some laughed and moved on, and others stopped and stayed. As I listened to him I found myself transported back home to the islands where people talked old story and sang songs and danced in the evenings around the fire. And standing there I began to hear for the first time. The words that Brother Blue used didn't make sense to me in any traditional form; these words were flying and dancing with the wind and teasing the senses of the listeners and coaxing reluctant spirits to wake and play. These words were not meant to be read but lived and experienced and seen in the mind. I had somehow thought, as I passed Brother Blue performing, that he was making it up as we went along. He just seemed to be pulling things out of the air and not making much sense in the process. But I could see that he knew what he was doing. I had seen many storytellers over the years of living in Boston, but this was not just a storyteller. I was in the presence of, this was, a trapeze artist traveling through the air with words and sounds and movement. I watched him tumble and roll and reach out, holding onto a thread of tradition only to let go and fly some more. I marveled at what this performer was doing, and the only safety net sat there in front of him, Sister Ruth. She as always was there, solid and grounded and ready to catch him, and this seemed to give him the courage to fly higher and go further every time.

Over the years I have gotten to know Brother Blue and Sister Ruth. I enjoy seeing them at festivals and on the street in Harvard Square. I still

AHHHH!

stop to listen every time I see this artist perform. I think about his work and how he has affected me. At times he made me laugh, and other times made me cry. He has become a great teacher to me for so many things, but mostly about letting go and playing and daring to fly as high as you can dream.

Born in the Bahamas, Derek Burrows has been telling folktales, myths and legends and has performed with the International music group, Voice of the Turtle for many years. Derek is the recipient of a Massachusetts Artist Foundation Fellowship for Storytelling.

August 1977

Photo: Ed Nute

Blue Performing 1978

Photo: Les Schwartz

Harvard Square - The Blizzard of '78

Photo: Lisa Hirsch

Spring 1977 - Boston Common

Photo: Ken Martin

Ahhhh!

Miles Away, or Dr. Seuss on the Loose

Len Cabral

Every Who down in Whoville
The Tight and The Loose
Were singing the loss
Of
Miles and Seuss
Miles was
The Cat in The
Hat
He would think of a lick
He would think it up quick
He would practice that lick
until he was
Sick
and with that
Trumpet he would
Play Play Play Play
Through the
Who Night
until the
Who Day
He would
Play Play Play Play
Play Play Play Play
And all the Whos down in
Whoville
The Who girls and Who boys
knew that this
Sound

Ahhhh!

was a lot more than noise
A lot more than
Sound—
It was Round   It was Square It was Down   It had Flair
as it
Bound
Bound Bound
Bound
Up the Down Stairs...

Len Cabral is a great grandson of a Cape Verdean whaler. He has been an author and teller of tales for over 25 years, working at colleges, schools, museums, festivals and libraries across the the country. Len is a husband and father of two daughters. Len Cabral was inducted into the National Storytelling Network's Circle of Excellence in 2001.

Blue & Ruth - photo taken at Jordan Marsh, Boston

Ahhhh!

Words

Magdalen Cantwell

Once there was a woman who had no words. Many years ago, an evil witch had stolen them from her. No matter how much she begged, the old witch would not give them back. The child grew up to be a sad, sad young woman. "Why are you sad?" her father would ask. "You have so many gifts...music, dance...people always ask you to play and sing." And so it was. But each time the young woman played, while the listeners were happy, inside she became sadder and sadder. One day she became so sad that she could not sing or play anymore.

"I cannot do this anymore!" she cried in anguish.

"Wait!" cried her father. "You will play someday. I know you will. Perhaps, if you travel to a distant land, it might help you forget your sorrows. As you journey, and with time, you will unravel the mystery of the lost words." She knew her father to be a wise man. He too had traveled the earth.

As was the custom, her parents invited her to choose a treasure bag for her journey. She picked a bag that was soft and velvety on the outside. However, when she opened it, there was nothing inside. "It is empty," she wondered out loud.

Her father laughed. "You chose wisely, my dear. You chose the bag that is easiest to carry. Why, no one will try to steal a treasure they cannot see. Only you will know that it is there." And he begged her to look inside once more. This time, to her parents' joy, she found the treasure.

"It's hope!" she said. "You have given me the greatest treasure of all. People can take away words. They cannot take away hope."

And so she left that land and traveled day and night, north and south, from one end of the earth to the other, in search of her words. She traveled for many years until she met a wise man who said, "Stop your

Ahhhh !

lonesome travels. Your words are wherever you are. Let me bring you to the wise king, the keeper of the Spirit and the Fire."

When the king asked her if she had a tale, she responded, "Why, yes. Everyone has a tale." But when she began her story, first one way, and then another, she wondered if the king would like her tale. She told her tale as if it did not belong to her, as if they were someone else's words.

The wise king said, "You have the voice. You have the words inside. Tell from your soul." The woman wept and wept. She said she could never dig into her soul. What was to become of her? She would never belong.

She remembered then…the gift from her parents, the gift of hope. Every week she returned to hear the wise king's tales. One day, she said that she too had a tale to share. To her surprise, everyone listened. From then on, she told tale after tale. Very soon the words were hers. Time went on. One day, the wise king said to her, "You don't cry anymore."

It was as if he knew why…

Native Irishwoman Magdalen Cantwell, a learning disabilities specialist/storyteller/musician, leads workshops for parents and educators using storytelling to enhance language, reading, and writing skills. She treasures Brother Blue's guidance to "tell from the soul" and Sister Ruth's bell to remind us that it need not be an epic.

Ahhhh!

When Blue's On

Richard Cambridge

Of the many encounterings of Blue, this is the one I would like to
recall, when he featured recently at Squawk Coffeehouse:

He was on tonight, in a visceral way. Before words—
in utterings and mutterings, the Guts of God—
he groaned forth the nature of killing in man.
What courage to let go and let God's Spirit shape you !
Blue became moist with the tears of God as he shimmied
and shaped in the Potter's Hand the form of grief
of killing by the hand of man.
What a humbling thing to see—the way Blue abandons
himself into the whirling wheel of God.
This is the great thing one can do.
This is what it means for Blue.
What does it mean for you?

Richard Cambridge is a co-founding member of the performance troupe "Singing
with the Enemy," whose piece, ¡EMBARGO!, brings awareness of the devastating
effects of the United States' 40-year economic blockade on the people of Cuba. The
troupe performed in Havana, Cuba in 1998 at the first U.S.-Cuba Friendship Conference. Richard curates the Poets' Theater at Club Passim in Cambridge, MA.

Ahhhh !

Uniting Nations

Mitch Capel

In a hotel room on a rainy day in Boston, I was flipping channels when there appeared a handsome man adorned with the most beautiful butterflies and covered in various hues of blue. I knew instantly who he was. Emanating from this man was genius unlike any I had heard or seen before. Brother Blue transcended from a street corner through the electronic medium a kindred spirit sort of connection. Even though I caught only a glimpse of his being and heard the tail end of his story, I'll never forget the sense of familiarity and healing I felt.

A few months later, I flew to Oakland to attend the National Association of Black Storytellers (NABS) festival. There I met Dr. Hugh Morgan Hill (Brother Blue) and his beautiful wife, Ruth Hill, who in his own words, "saved and maintains" his life. I was inspired by their words of encouragement and mesmerized by Blue's presence, delivery, rhythmic style, and spirit. He was Al Jarreau, Jimi Hendrix, Paul Dunbar, Richard Pryor, and Mahatma Gandhi all rolled into one!

The following year I was featured in New York at the NABS festival along with Brother Blue and a few others. However, at one of the venues, The United Nations, Brother Blue was not on the program list of tellers. Thinking it inappropriate that a man with his ability to bring people together was not being given the opportunity to "unite nations," when introduced, I told *one* story only and then yielded the remainder of the time to Blue. I'll never forget the look on his face. Later, as I boarded the transportation for tellers and attendees, Blue reached in his jacket and removed the most beautiful butterfly pin of all. As he handed it to me, he turned and announced to everyone on the bus that if he had a son, he would want him to be just like me!

In the years since, I've had many opportunities to break bread, tell stories and share magical moments with Brother Blue and Sister Ruth in cities all over the country. In Myrtle Beach a butterfly landed on Blue's

Ahhhh !

shoulder precisely at the moment he said "Ahhhhhhhh!" At the Annual Retreat Jamal Koran and I co-founded, Blue taught me the true power of the spoken word. I took Blue with me to the Very Special Arts festival for physically and mentally challenged children, where I had been telling annually. The children were literally climbing out of their self-constructed shells within five minutes of hearing Brother Blue begin to tell. Had there not been a ceiling over that room, I'm positive a few would have flown away.

I still have that butterfly pinned to my "Junebug" hat...and even though some fourteen years of wear and tear have made it physically challenged, it still remains the most beautiful and meaningful pin out of the 147+ pins and buttons on my "Gran' Daddy Junebug" attire. That butterfly possesses the spirit of Brother Blue, which I try to infuse into all the stories I tell. It represents the spiritual connectedness I felt with Blue the first time I saw him transcending that hotel room TV on a rainy day in Boston so long ago. And when neophyte tellers seek advice from me on how, what, where and which...Brother Blue is usually paramount in my response.

Writing and acting since the age of 12, Mitch Capel studied speech and theater at North Carolina A&T State University and at Howard University. Capel is a life member of the National Association of Black Storytellers and co-founder of the National African American Storytellers Retreat.

Blue Performing at the Hans Christian Andersen Statue in Central Park

Photo: Ruth Hill

AHHHH!

Brother Blue in Memphis

Judy Card

Brother Blue tears down the walls
Steps into the break room of Memphis City Hall
Says to a woman with long red nails and a short black skirt
Do you know you're so beautiful
She's astonished and isn't sure of the deal
He says it again sincerely, the sparkle of his
Butterflies finally reaching her eyes

Brother Blue tears down the walls
Steps into the Memphis Brooks Museum of Art
On a cold wet day with Ruth at his side
You can't come in here like that, says the restaurant hostess
Blind to the magic she's seeing, the chance she's been given
In that case we won't, he replies
Until his host the board member returns
From parking the car and in a wave of power
Shifts the balance

Brother Blue tears down the walls
Steps into a limo to accompany the
Memphis Hoodoo Mafia to pour libation
at the home of W.C. Handy's birth
Sacred on top of sacred

Brother Blue tears down the walls
Steps into the courtyard of the
National Civil Rights Museum
The Lorraine Motel where Dr. King died
He bursts into tears for the grief
And the beauty of the universe

Ahhhh!

And gives us new ways of looking
At our hometown history

Brother Blue tears down the walls
Standing in a house moving to the beat of a drum circle
Of women and men, black and white, from Senegal to Memphis
Honoring all by his presence and vision

Brother Blue tears down the walls
Telling his stories, playing his harp, ringing his bells
And reaching our hearts so that
We'll tear down the walls long after he's gone.

Born in East Tennessee, Judy Card dances, drums, tells stories and bakes cornbread in Memphis. She cofounded Delta Rising Storytellers and co-produced for six years *Pass It On*, a storytelling program on WEVL Radio, in Memphis.

Brother Blue at *Africa in April* - April 20, 1997, Memphis TN

AHHHH!

Sleepers Awake!

Victor Carpenter

He points his finger, and a heart expands in response. This "street cat" (his name) touches the core of life and dances in a rhythm of hope into the lives of those to whom the finger points.

A shaman! A mystical seer of truths which he wraps in fantasies of dance for those who have eyes to see, ears to hear, souls to expand and grow. The child in each is moved by the wonder of another who recognizes it and calls it forth. Discovery! Sleepers Awake! Open yourselves to a wider world of possibility, music, laughter, and yes, tears. Blue understands. Blue knows the color and the wounds of life. No neat knowledge here. No bottled, pre-digested recipe. He knows that what ails you, is you. He knows that what will cure you, is you. And he is the chemist/alchemist to draw out the hidden pain and sorrow from your soul in healing, hopeful, happy harmony with the great flow of life and love.

Hail Blue! Maker of magic mime; poet of possibility; creator of the luminous, transcendent moment. We express our love in return for the love which flows from your wellspring of creative power and truth.

A graduate of Harvard University Divinity School, Victor Carpenter has published articles and reviews in a variety of printed media. He is also the author of the 1982 Minns Lecture, "The Black Empowerment Controversy and the Unitarian Universalist Association." He is married to Catherine Anne Larrabee and they have three children.

Ahhhh!

Standing at the Crossroads

Chris Cavanagh

Nineteen years old and feeling a little lost in a world that seemed to be doing its best to persuade me to choose bland options of career and citizenship, I stumbled, hardly of my own will it seemed, into the timeless space of a folk festival. Green trees and blue sky above me, I wandered amidst vendors, stalls and—seeing beadwork, instrument making, tie-dyed clothing and food of all kinds—I felt lulled through time to some medieval idyll. Though I was aware that I was no doubt romanticizing an era that lacked both flush toilets and national health care, I was nonetheless enchanted by the fantasy of simpler times.

My imagination conjured jugglers, town fools, food barkers, and preachers.

But all around me was quite sober and quiet, save for the distant music and laughter from the workshop stages a few hundred feet away. My Montreal snobbishness asserted itself with the thought, "Of course it's quiet and sober."

And there in that timeless time I saw a man under a tree. "That'd be the town fool," I thought. He was standing, bent slightly forward and speaking with a passionate intensity that I was sure must be scaring the two enthralled young listeners. I approached quietly, not to disturb (or perhaps to avoid notice?) and confirmed that, yes, he was all dressed in blue, and, yes, those were butterflies on his hat and clothing. I looked around for one of the festival hosts, any clue to assure me that this wildly gesticulating man in blue was an official part of this otherwise reserved event. There was little in my experience of life to prepare me for the wildness I witnessed on that long ago day beneath a tree on a warm summer afternoon.

I recall a feeling of unease as I came closer and closer to this strange tableau. I heard what I thought was poetry, and then I heard enough to

Ahhhh!

hear that there was a story happening there. I don't recall sitting. Nor do I recall how long I sat. Only that a spell was cast that has never let me go. With one ear I listened to the tales while with the other I heard a growing roar as of an approaching storm that pushes a telltale change in air pressure ahead of it. Part of me wanted to run; another part said "Don't you dare!"

Somewhere in the midst of this swirling maelstrom of words and verse and suddenlies and meanwhiles I thought, "This is storytelling? You've got to be kidding." Later I thought, "This is storytelling. How do I learn?"

Listening, I absorbed learnings that would take years to bear fruit. I don't recall the stories I listened to that day. Nor do I recall the words that Brother Blue shared in response to my bewildered questioning. My memory is of being caught in a thunderstorm. Who remembers even the first raindrop of warning? But the fury and tempest make a lasting impression. So it was with me that day: fury and tempest and the thought that I hoped that I could learn to live everyday with the passion that I knew still lived and moved in this world.

That summer day of 1979 at the Mariposa Folk Festival (the last to happen on those enchanted isles) was the cusp of my teenage to adult years. Brother Blue showed me a road that day, and I recognized it immediately. That road would take me across the world and into new worlds. From the Cape of Good Hope, where I watched cormorants dive into the boundary waters of the Atlantic and Indian Oceans, to a foggy mountaintop in Nicaragua, where I harvested coffee to the sound of distant gunfire. And from the deadening ennui of suburban Canada back into my family's past, surviving as they often do, in the most inconsequential of anecdotes. I charged down that road with as much passion as I could muster, living (as I still do) as honestly as possible (not always easy nor possible), savoring the juice of life, sucking the marrow and always remembering the spinning, grinning, blue whirlwind of stories who stood at the gates and, bowing flamboyantly, eyes twinkling with danger and excitement, invited me along. One day on that road I stood up in front of some people, and I told a story. Then another. And still another. One day, further on down that road I told someone I was a storyteller. And so I am.

Once upon a time, in order to begin a new walk in life, a person was initiated by those who had gone before. Once initiated, a person

AHHHH !

(whether weaver, tanner, blacksmith, scholar, monk, or storyteller) followed a path of learning and growth that did more than pad a resumé. (Okay, so I'm idealizing a bit here, but compared to today's world where McJobs are the only choice for many, while still others change jobs and careers as often as they change clothes, the challenge of finding meaningful work has never been more severe. I beg your indulgence in allowing me to stretch my comparison in order to advocate for a world in which all work provides not only income, but also vitality and meaning.) This choice of initiation onto a meaningful life path remains in the world still, though now it must be sought after amidst the deadening demands of conformity to market needs. Finding those who have walked along a path you may wish to follow is itself a journey as filled with luck and misfortune, helpers and detractors as the grimmest of fairytales. The choice of the journey is nonetheless there for those who dare.

Now, as for me running across Brother Blue on that summer afternoon, I suspect it was just dumb luck. But I also suspect that it was the kind of luck that is abundant in this world and in the way that things repeat. Somehow, my Acadian and Irish ancestors (raconteurs and merrymakers, by all accounts) were pushing me along in the direction of that road in order to continue traditions that have been all but forgotten in the 20th and now 21st centuries.

The winding, dangerous, exciting, and ancient road of the telling traditions lies in wait for any who dare to search for it. Obscured by the monocropping of world cultures, (also called globalization), it is a unique challenge today to find the gates to this road. But standing there still, as of old, you will see Enki and Inanna, Homer and Ovid, minnesingers and troubadours, ollaves and shanachies, griots and witches, grandmothers and grandfathers, Legba and Eshu, Mulla Nasrudin and Herschel Ostropolier, Coyote and Tortoise, Alice Kane and Dan Yashinsky, and a laughing, loving, butterfly-bearing, man in blue who beckons for all those who dare follow, pointing to roads of wonder.

Chris Cavanagh is an educator, storyteller and graphic artist who has worked in popular arts production, coalition building, anti-racism, international solidarity, and democratic organizational change. He is a member of the Catalyst Centre, a popular education group in Toronto, Canada where he promotes storytelling in community organizing. He designs "Pippin," the newsletter of the Storyteller's School of Toronto.

Ahhhh!

Listening

Tom Cieslak

Why do you listen to me? I suppose that is the most important question. There is nothing I can say that hasn't been said by countless millions before me. And yet, when I stand and speak, you listen. The timbre of my voice quavers a little as I start, but confidence builds with experience, and before too long there isn't the slightest trace of hesitation. My story. My story. A little triviality that I need to expunge so that my mind can get on to the greater problems facing me. A hindrance, an obstacle to clear thought that bugs me and pesters me with the details it feels it needs. And the truth is, that as much as you say you need my story, I need it even more, despite the fact that it's a triviality. The house of my world is built upon such trivialities. As I continue to weave this illusion of reality, this fantasy world, this fantasy life, this possible alternative to the here and now, you sit with attentive and sympathetic faces. Somewhere along the way I strike a chord with her or him, and I can see the flicker in the eyes that tells me that this fabrication of my mind was not a fabrication to them but a tangible event from their past. To hear me speak the words, to open that door to their souls, is a confirmation that she or he is (are) not alone. An incident or a person from a life that I am totally unfamiliar with has made an impression on my soul and found its release through one of my stories. What I considered just a silly word game has importance. If not to me, then to you, because you listen to me. And in my turn, I will listen to you; I owe it to you to listen, and you owe it to me to teach me the trivialities of your mind because one day, you will hit upon a tangible event in my life and show me that I am not alone. This is what Brother Blue has taught me.

Tom Cieslak is "a malodorous little creep who lives in a cardboard box on the side of the road emerging only occasionally to scrape the moss off his bottom." He prefers stories to writing autobiographies.

Ahhhh !

Blue Ribbons
Karen T. Craddock

Blue—like ribbon that floats firmly yet effortlessly in my sky reflects vibrance of sunshine and wisdom of moonlight through a satin voice. Clarity in his esoteric narrative poetically speaks to my soul and often reveals me to me. The sojourn I am on feels closer to resolution when his fatherly, gentle insight and soulful spirit embraces. He knows Truth and sings so with the muse and majesty in his story.

I have been so blessed to have Brother Blue and Ruth Hill come into my life. They divinely appeared about five years ago in such a knowing and comforting way that has proven to be a guiding light in my life. Having grown up in Boston, I vividly captured Blue in my memory as a fanciful piece of my childhood tapestry, and his re-appearance was warmly familiar. This remarkable couple embodies a dialectical essence of perfect harmony. Ruth's steadying grace and Blue's effervescent zest wonderfully dance together with such a refreshing humor and powerful love that it is an honor to behold. I am forever grateful for these gift givers.

Karen Theresa Craddock does research and development work at Education Development Center (EDC) in Newton, MA, and on the beliefs and practices among African-American families, the role of personal storytelling and narrative expression in relation to identity development among African-American children, and issues around cultural diversity in effective program implementation. She and her sons, Clark and Coleman, live in Medford, Massachusetts where she enjoys and learns from the unfolding narratives in their lives.

Ahhhh!

The Listener

Donald Davis

The first time I met Blue was in 1981. Jackie Torrence and I were at an event in Georgia where Blue was also to perform. I had never seen Blue at that point.

Prior to the event, Jackie and I were being interviewed by a television crew. The interview was being held in the yard outside the auditorium where we were to perform later.

The camera was on Jackie and she was answering a question that had just been put to her by the reporter. All of a sudden, the camera left Jackie and began focusing on something in the background that had caught the camera person's attention.

The reporter stopped, annoyed, and looked around to see why the camera operator had left Jackie. Then we saw it. Blue was simply walking across the lawn, looking like Blue! No self-respecting camera operator could resist swinging the camera aside to take in this great show!

What a wonderful character and long-term friend I met on that day. How I have come to respect his work and, more than that, his loving personhood.

While Blue is remembered well for his stories, there is one special thing about him that storytellers everywhere have benefited from. His listening! In Isak Dinesen's book *Out of Africa*, there is a chapter in which Denis Finch-Hatton is introduced. The description is that there are always stories when Denis comes…because…Denis is such a good listener!

I have never met a more helpful and exquisite story listener than Brother Blue! Every person who ever wants to tell a story deserves to have him once in their front row!

Ahhhh!

Blue takes in everything, catches on before anyone else does, and shows you such supportive response in his listening that you cannot fail! To have him in the audience is assurance of successful telling. What a helpful and nourishing listener he is.

While many talk about the power of his telling, his greatest influence on me has been to help me learn to give more attention to helpful listening. Knowing what his listening has done for me has modeled for me a vision of what helpful listening is like. I thank and bless him forever for that.

Donald Davis grew up in the North Carolina mountains hearing traditional and original family stories. In his life as a storyteller, he performs his own original work as well as preserving the traditional tales of his family. Donald Davis, along with Brother Blue, was inducted into the National Storytelling Network's Circle of Excellence in 1996.

Photo: Ruth Hill

Ahhhh!

A Preacher and a Prophet

Ossie Davis

Brother Blue is a storyteller, the kind my father was and my mother, only better. They were amateurs occasionally indulging what some would call their hobby. Brother Blue is a stone professional. The difference is amateurs tell stories for the fun of it, sometimes at parties simply to entertain, or to put us children to sleep.

Brother Blue is more a preacher and prophet. Telling stories is the work of his existence. He does it because he has to, and because he knows it will save children's lives. Save them from television; save them from dangerous movies; save them from destructive images of themselves; save them to be black warriors and not only children. We grown-ups need stories too. Stories to remind us where we came from. Stories that tell us where it is we must go. Stories that remind us we are family.

Just thinking of Brother Blue gives me an appetite. I wonder what became of Brer Rabbit? High John the Conqueror? Stagger Lee and John Henry? I'll bet Brother Blue can tell you! I'm so glad he still makes house calls.

Ossie Davis is an actor, writer, producer, director, and award-winning author of several children's books, including *Escape to Freedom*. He has appeared in numerous movies and starred in two television series. Several of his plays have been produced on Broadway. Ossie and his wife of 50 years, Ruby Dee, received the Screen Actors Guild Life Achievement Award and published their joint autobiography, *With Ossie and Ruby: In This Life Together*, in 1998.

Ahhhh!

Blue Man

Leeny Del Seamonds

At Len Cabral's invitation, I attended my first Sharing the Fire. It was 1992. I sat in the Dining Commons early Saturday morning sipping a cup of coffee and picking at a muffin wondering, what am I doing here? Though no stranger to performing, I was new to storytelling. I didn't know a soul at this conference, except for Len, a little, and wasn't sure he'd have time to visit with me when he arrived.

Voices entering the room caused me to look up and see attendees marching in two by two, full of anticipation and excitement. Ants arriving at the company picnic. Everyone looked busy and happy, as they reunited with their buddies. I envied those ants, feeling a bit lonely and unsure of myself and wanted to join their feast. The surrounding tables were starting to fill up with a buzz of activity and camaraderie. I buried my head in my program, pretending to mull over the workshops, but their laughter and excitement prevented me from concentrating, forcing me to look up and observe the room. Oh, how I wanted to be part of this flurry of activity. Maybe I should have stayed home.

A flash of blue caught my eye at the next table. There sat a tall slender man bedazzled and bedecked in all his glory, decorated with butterflies and sporting a dapper beret. An African king? A colorful beatnik? A jazz musician? Perhaps all three, I thought. The cherubic woman sitting to his left smiled at him, and her kind face lit up. I recognized my grandmother in her eyes and wanted to hug her. But the couple was busy talking to the entourage sitting around them. I was fascinated by this unusual man and must have been staring at him, because suddenly he looked up from the crowd, and our eyes met. I was slightly embarrassed but smiled at him. He smiled back and nodded. And then I saw it: Blue's twinkle. His twinkle started from his toes, flowed up through his heart and shot right out of his eyes at me. I smiled even bigger, as

Ahhhh!

did he. I knew in an instant that I had known this Blue Man before, in another time and place. Then he did something unexpected: he pointed at me with his right index finger, then wagged it back and forth, while nodding his head, as if he recognized me too.

Blue could tell I was all alone in unfamiliar turf, so he beckoned me to join him and Ruth. I happily obliged and pulled up a chair at the end of their table. Introductions were made by all, and I felt welcome. When Brother Blue asked me what my background was, I replied, "Theater. I'm an actor and director turned storyteller." He giggled and wagged that finger at me again. "I knew it! I could tell this lady is a singer, a real entertainer. She's a young Ethel Merman!" I didn't know what to say, so I began a comic rendition of "There's no business like show business", as several others joined in. Everyone laughed. I started to feel at home. In one kind gesture, Blue had invited me into his home: the storytelling community. Throughout that conference weekend I saw Brother Blue again several times, mostly from a distance. Each time I'd glance through the crowd at him our eyes would meet. We'd smile, and Blue would nod and wag his finger at me, mouthing the words, "Ethel Merman!" It always filled my heart and carried me throughout the conference.

It's been nine years since that first STF conference, and every time I see Blue (which isn't as often as I'd like), we share that ritual: smiling eyes/finger wagging/head nodding. But Brother Blue no longer mouths the words Ethel Merman at me. He simply allows the silent words to speak for themselves.

Ah Blue, you will always have a special place in my heart. Your warmth and tremendous generosity is incomparable. You welcomed me into your storytelling community like a proud papa. I will forever be grateful that our paths have crossed again in this lifetime. Aaaahhhhhh.

Leeny Del Seamonds is an internationally known actor/director/performer of Hispanic, original, and World stories spiced with mime, a cornucopia of characters, and love of people. With a twinkle in her eye and fire in her heart, Leeny encourages listeners to feel positive about themselves and rejoice in human and cultural diversity.

Ahhhh!

A Note for Brother Blue

Pawel and Ingrid Depta

We are overjoyed that you have undertaken the task of long overdue recognition of Sister Ruth and Brother Blue's lifetime of achievement.

Indeed, they both have been like family to us. They took part in two of the most important events in our lives: our wedding celebration (1970) and the baptismal ceremony of our son, Alexander John Paul (1980.)

It is difficult to imagine a more self-less, inseparable, devoted to each other and their life mission couple, who, over the years have contributed more to the community at large than some of the famous teachers at Harvard.

Sister Ruth and Brother Blue exemplify to all people what marital devotion and dedication to others mean.

Ahhhh!

The Whirling Vortex

Jeanne Donato

Brothers Blue's voice sparked into the evening's dark, challenging us to reach inside and soar with our story. "Come!" his voice trumpeted. "Come and stand in the sacredness of it all!" he commanded as he ever so gently led us one at a time to stand. There, supported by whirling waves of encouragement, Brother Blue brought forth another and yet another storyteller. And so he continues to this day, birthing storytellers into the world, leaving a legacy of courage, faith, belief, and love borne on the healing wings of laughter.

This energy is balanced by a quiet, unobtrusive calm. His reality is lovingly nurtured with patient wisdom, as one would tend a flourishing garden. And we are struck by the incredible strength that supports not only Blue, but all of us with love—Ruth.

Thank you, Blue and Ruth, for all the giving; for the love of story; for all the evenings of storytelling; the hours of listening, talking, encouraging, and inspiring us.

Jeanne Donato, MEd, is a professional storyteller, speaker, author, educational consultant/kinesthesiologist, and co-author of *Storytelling in Emergent Litercy: Fostering Multiple Intelligences.*

Ahhhh!

Ruth's Gifts
Jeanne Dreifus

As ephemeral and will-o-the-wisp as Brother Blue can be, Ruth is wonderfully solid, dependable, and inspirational as well. Her management of Radcliffe's "Women of Courage" exhibition brought us all together in Memphis, Tennessee in 1987. We at the University Art Gallery at Memphis State University (now U. of M.) were thrilled to have this impressive collection of portraits of prominent African-Americans. Ruth gave the opening address, and Blue, floating around the periphery of the gathering, brought the meeting to its feet in a closing piece. I have always been delighted when they have returned to Memphis, for Blue to read to the children, out of his continuing source of mental books and his wondrous supply of magic, engaging our Memphis Public Library children. He has also applied his arts in the "Africa in April" celebrations in W.C. Handy Park on our Memphis Beale Street.

Ruth, you are truly to be admired, not only for your own work of elevating the lives and images of "Women of Courage," but for being one yourself. It takes all kinds of energy and intensity and love to bring us all the best of Brother Blue.

Jeanne D. Dreifus, Radcliffe '52, worked closely with Ruth Hill to bring the exhibit of "Women of Courage" to the Memphis State University Gallery in1987. Jeanne served as an alumna trustee of Radcliffe College 1981-1985. She and her husband, Jed Dreifus, a fellow Harvard alumni, were hosts to Brother Blue on several occasions while they were in Memphis.

Ahhhh!

82

Dr. Dave Colling
Jane Dreskin

After many years in research and industry, Dave (a metallurgical engineer) turned to his real love—teaching. In the college classroom a natural inclination toward storytelling emerged. But it wasn't until he found Brother Blue's story circle, where there is always loving permission to tell whatever you want, that he blossomed. Here he shared his passion for history, science, and the materials that make up the basic things we take for granted.

One week it might be the history of the Ferris Wheel and the story of Mr. Ferris. Another week the story of Hephaistos, the Greek God of metalwork. His listeners journeyed with him to the building of the transcontinental railroad, and the brutal history of rubber and its slave trade. We learned about the Mayan Creation Myth and the Periodic Table.

"Brother Blue has been a constant supporter from the time I told my first story at the Bookcellar Cafe," Dave wrote. Brother Blue has a unique and uncanny ability to grasp the essence of a teller. Be it in many words or few, he gives this gift to each teller. In Dave he saw the sweetness, the passion, the teacher. And so did the listeners. Dave was among the many tellers who we were privileged to watch come into his own voice, with his own niche among the tellers. When Dave died, many people commented that his stories got them interested in things they never expected to learn about. They said they looked forward to what "Doctor Dave" would come up with next. None of this would have happened without Brother Blue.

Jane Dreskin is the wife of the late Dr. Dave Colling.

AHHHH!

Tribute to Brother Blue

Jane Dreskin

Over 20 years ago, I was told a story, the first anyone told me as an adult. She was in her late 40's, alone raising two teenagers. I was in my late 30's, finishing my training. She had grown up in Lithuania, and had come with her family seeking freedom. She and her brother, not yet teens, did not find freedom. The neighboring kids called them "DP's" (displaced persons) and chased and beat them. She went on to become a public defender (later a judge).

Over some time, she told me her story. One day she asked if I would like to hear her favorite story. I was surprised and eager. No one had ever asked me that before. "This is my favorite story; it's from Lithuania," she began, and told me the story about the Light Princess. In her telling, a virtuous and childless elderly couple were finally blessed with a child, a daughter. She was the answer to their hopes, and they gratefully loved her and her one "flaw." She was so light, she would fly away unless moored with a cord. The only place she was free to be untethered was in the water, and so they made a small pond for her in their meager yard.

As the couple approached the end of their lives, they hoped for a companion, a husband for her. Many suitors came and were attracted to her loveliness and virtue. But they soon fled upon learning that she lacked the substance to stay present. One day, a young man came and stayed. He helped her old parents with their chores and grew to love the light princess. He asked for her hand in marriage, and she agreed on one condition. He would have to dive down, deep down, all the way to the bottom of the small pool, in order to live with her.

At this point in the story a sudden terror overtook me, as a terrifying thought overtook my mind. She's telling me that I will have to die, to

Ahhhh!

give up everything, to help her. I couldn't make that sacrifice. I barely heard the end of her story: that the young man agreed, and in doing so freed her to love untethered.

I began encountering this story many times, from different countries, including George MacDonald's *The Light Princess*. The terror remained in the background, holding me at a "safe" distance.

Many years later, my husband (Dave Colling) and I went to First Night Boston for the first time. We went to the African Meeting House on Beacon Hill to listen to someone called Brother Blue. I had never seen him before; Dave recalled him being in one of his kid's grammar school more than 25 years before. I didn't understand what I heard that night. It was like listening to a great rabbi when I was a child. He had such a huge mind and spirit that took off so quickly, and I was left far behind.

Not long after that First Night, Dave and I found our way to Brother Blue's and Ruth's weekly temple for stories, people, and truth. As I experienced this wonderful man and his wife, behind his intellect, his moves, his music, his poetry, his prayers, I felt myself in the presence of ultimate integrity. I have heard him say so many times that he would give his life for stories, for a person, to change the world. And I believe him, and I believe that he has done just that over and over and over.

I keep returning to the Light Princess, as first told to me by a Lithuanian women I once knew. Since becoming a part of the storytelling community inspired so much by Brother Blue, that terror is disappearing, and I am deeply grateful to him for this. My way of living his message is to listen with my whole heart and mind to the stories I am told and to tell mine as honestly as I can.

Jane Dreskin had been a storylistener for years. She tells stories in local venue, and daily in her work as a healer and psychiatrist. When she asks "can I tell you a little story" it's like magic—the heart and ears open.

AHHHH!

Brother Blue

Susan Dubroff

At the Charlestown Working Theatre
you and Ruth sit in front of us,
your blue beret, its butterfly pins
for the soul, you know—
your scuffed shoes, limp clothes,
you carry too many bags and bundles
to be classy, though it's what
you accuse us of for agreeing
to give you a ride home. Afterwards,
the director of the spunky,
street clothes Hamlet
rushes out to ask you eagerly,
You Blue?—thumps your hand, listens hungrily
to your enthusiastic praise.
In the back seat you're no bent Boston man;
you're a child on your mother's knee.
Your wife explains to you why we
can't let you off at the Red Line.
Want to hear you finish Ham's Blues,
moan for Ham and that little Ophelia,
throw in some Muddy Waters.
When we've dropped you off
and we've turned our arms and fingers high
in the jaded Cambridge air.

Susanne Dubroff's poems and translations have appeared in *The Great River Review*, *Ships of Fools, Curious Rooms, The Bitter Oleander, Luna* and *The International Poetry Review*. In 1994 her first collection of original poems, *You and I*, was published.

Ahhhh!

The Day of Brother Blue's Doctoral Dance

Arthur Dyck

"He was a riot!" That is what we sometimes say about a performer who greatly stirs and moves his audience. On the day that Brother Blue performed the drama he had prepared for his doctorate, he was not only a riot, but he competed with one. I know. I was there.

That performance took place at the prison on Deer Island. At the time, the police were trying to quell a prison riot there. To receive attention at such a time, to draw an audience at such a time, was a considerable feat in itself. But Brother Blue did it, and he did it superbly. Many prisoners gathered to see and hear his drama. While Brother Blue performed, there were, from time to time, prisoners who ran behind the seated audience, through the large auditorium, disappearing into the halls of the prison. Despite it all, Brother Blue gave an outstanding performance filled with dance, and story, and beautiful poetry. The prisoners were not only delighted, but inspired. They were moved to transcend their present conditions and envision a better life.

After the performance, Brother Blue and I were escorted by police to the main prison exit. On both sides of the hall leading to the exit, two long lines of prisoners had formed on either side of the hall; all eyes were turned on us. I must have looked somewhat fearful before walking between the prisoners, forming what looked like it would be a gauntlet. One of the prisoners, a tall handsome African American, said to me: "Don't be afraid, no one will hurt you." I stepped boldly between these men just behind Brother Blue, as they clapped, and cheered, and reached out to shake our hands or just touch us. Clearly Brother Blue was their hero that day. His intelligence and empathy, expressed in dance, song and storytelling, had melted their hearts, lightened their loads, and moved them to joy and kindness.

AHHHH!

When we walked to a waiting bus, we saw that the prison was surrounded by a whole host of police officers. This riot was a serious and dangerous one. The accounts of it in the newspapers the next day confirmed that.

What Brother Blue did that day was something of a miracle. It launched his calling. Above all, he had visited Christ in prison, and many of the men there somehow felt it. It was a day I will never forget. By the grace of God, Brother Blue made it all happen.

Arthur Dyck began teaching at Harvard Divinty School in 1965, and he is on the faculties of the Divinity School and the School of Public Health and a member of the Center for Development and Population Studies. Pilgrim Press released his book on physician-assisted suicide, *When Killing is Wrong*, in April 2001.

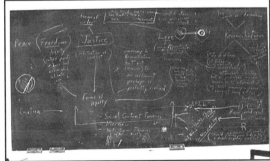

Blue and Ruth in Arthur Dyck's office 1971

Ahhhh!

For Brother Blue

Rex Ellis

I wanted to add my voice to the many who I am sure will respond in
honor of this renaissance man. Brother Blue has been an inspiration for
me in many ways. First, as a mentor with wonderful bits of advice and
encouragement. Second, as a respected and thoughtful elder who has
provided council to those of us who have served on the board of the
National Association of Black Storytellers. Finally, as a performer,
evangelist, soothsayer, and Jazz aficionado who had taken risks with his
work that few of us are emboldened enough to do. He not only displays
his heart in its rawest form to anyone who will accept it, he also lays
himself bare to those who would misunderstand and malign what they do
not understand. But in his inimitable way, he continues to love, prick,
challenge, and stretch us. His admonition has always been the same to
us all: to love beyond our thoughts, see beyond our eyes, and accept
beyond our capacities.

Rex M. Ellis is a teacher, historian, storyteller, and the Director of the Center for
Museum Studies at the Smithsonian Institute in Washington D.C. Prior to his work
with the Smithsonian, Ellis directed the Department of African-American Interpreta-
tion and Presentations at the Colonial Williamsburg Foundation in Williamsburg,
Virginia. He is also the author of *Beneath the Blazing Sun: Stories from the African-
American Journey* and *The Ups and Downs of Being Brown*. He was inducted into the
National Storytelling Network's Circle of Excellence in 2001.

Ahhhh!

Threshold

Rob Evans

After meeting Brother Blue for the first time, it took about four months before I finally conceded that, okay, maybe Blue *wasn't* Jesus.

It was touch and go, though. No, *really!*

After all, the Lord was known for his stories, his power, and his ability to transform the hearts of those who knew him. Not to mention his surprises. His original departure could not have been more surprising. He said he'd be back, but who could presume to guess the hour or the manner of His coming? Returning as a dancing Black street storyteller would be just his style.

I met Blue on a summer's afternoon in 1975, after having avoided him countless times as he held forth in Harvard Square. I was a student in divinity school, working full-time as co-director of a drug detoxification ward at a local hospital, and volunteering almost all of my weekends with a prison-counseling program called Thresholds. The Thresholds Program trained local volunteers to go into jails and prisons to teach a method of decision-making to help inmates sort out what happens next with their lives.

Blue was the keynote speaker for the Thresholds annual convention held at Harvard Divinity School. If you are reading this, you know what Blue can do with an audience. You can imagine how he captured our hearts as thirty or forty sat on the floor at his feet. You can see our faces as our adult masks began to melt away, the way they always do when Blue tells stories.

That night was the annual party of the Cambridge Hospital Department of Psychiatry. Our detox program was run under their auspices, set up under a grant from the National Institute on Drug Abuse to compare the results of Thresholds volunteers with those of psychiatric nurses and

Ahhhh!

mental health workers. About a dozen of us were going from the Thresholds convention to the party at the house of John Mack, who chaired the department. We were led to expect a no-holds-barred, raucous blow out.

I was curious to see this crowd at play. From my work in the detox program, it had become clear to me that psychiatrists were the current holders of the keys to the kingdom. They held the face cards within the mental health establishment. They declare you sane or not. They can lock you up or let you out. Pretty heady stuff. I seriously considered medical school as an alternative to wherever divinity school was taking me.

We prepared for the party by getting deeply stoned. Instead of a rock concert, though, we walked into a refrigerator. The other guests were uptight, and seemed offended by our very presence. They reacted to us with silence or, worse, with verbal attacks. We were challenged to justify the Thresholds program, our faith commitments, and the very fact that we were there at all.

We soon found an out-of-the-way porch and held our own party. We drank, we smoked some more, and we laughed. After a couple of hours, out of the corner of my eye I saw a middle-aged man motion to a younger guy as if to say, "Watch this. " As he walked over to us he began to fake being drunk. He focused on a friend sitting next to me.

It might have seemed like simple harassment from a hard partier, except for two things. I had enough training in the art of the psychiatric interview to recognize that this guy was good. I also knew my friend well-enough to know that this "drunk" was going for the jugular, poking at my friend's weak spots, the secret and embarrassing things, and slicing away the protective social layer of his personality to get at something raw and tender underneath. Every so often he would glance at his young friend to make sure this toady was taking in the entire performance.

This night had everything to do with why I stopped smoking dope. When stoned, I would become The Watcher. All input, without the ability to respond. This was like watching vivisection. And there was nothing I could do about it. At last, someone went to get our host. John Mack sized up the situation in a glance. "Miles!" he said, "Cut it out!" Had he seen this before? The "drunk" sobered up immediately and yelled back at John to stop spoiling his fun. We were on John's home turf, however, so Miles and his protege backed down. That's when I

Ahhhh !

learned that this guy was not only a psychiatrist, but that he actually ran a psychiatric hospital.

So there it was: as sharp a choice as ever I saw. Blue on the one side and Miles on the other. I was deeply rattled (though maybe you had to be there). I sat up all night shivering at this new view of the continuum between Good and Evil. Good was *much* gooder, though much less powerful according to most social and economic yardsticks. Evil turned out to be casually malicious, technically superb, and at the top of the pecking order.

I had a choice to make, so I made it. I started hanging around Blue and Ruth in earnest. In those days, Blue would hold forth on a Sunday afternoon on the lawn of the Gutman Library on Brattle Street. I have always been a drummer, and I could hear the rhythms and patterns in Blue's stories. I bought a second-hand tumba drum and showed up with it one Sunday afternoon. I was soon a regular. I learned to lay down a beat for Blue to dance upon. In those days, Blue would tell stories in the Chapel of Emmanuel Church on Newbury Street on Sunday evenings. My drum and I went along for the ride. I bought an old VW beetle and soon I *was* the ride.

That was also the era when Blue would close out the day at WBUR radio station with a live story at 2am. I went as often as a full-time job/ full-time student schedule would allow, which turned out to be pretty often. Twice a week, Blue would then walk down Commonwealth Ave to WBCN to tell stories on Eric Jackson's all-night jazz show at around 4am. I was the young white guy with the big drum slung over his shoulder walking beside Blue in the middle of the night. Those slow walks were treasures to me.

I have seen Blue perform miracles in the years since, whether he was Jesus or not. Normal, everyday miracles like turning a room full of veteran drug addicts into open-faced children with a new sense of hope. More dramatic miracles like roaring a lion's roars in Danbury prison to turn an aggressive heckler into a brother. I have seen him story the dying into a state of grace. I've seen him tell stories to my children in the womb, just after birth, and all the way into college. I've seen the countless miracles he has brought to my life through his kind wisdom and unfailing support.

Then there are the miracles he has brought into his own life. Especially Ruth, the Angel God sent to look after his Fool. Together, they taught me that in marriage, two people really do become one. His

Ahhhh!

students always seem miraculous to him. You, reading this, may well be one of those miracles yourself.

Even if Blue turns out not to be Jesus returned (I figure I'll never know for sure), there has never been any doubt who Blue serves. He invites us all to a higher calling and deeper, purer stories. John's gospel ends with the most marvelous verse: "But there are also many other things which Jesus did; were every one of them to be written, I suppose that the world itself could not contain the books that would be written." And so it is with Blue and Ruth. This tribute is just the beginning of the stories that we could, and will, tell.

Rob Evans is a vice president with Cap Gemini Ernst & Young where he leads the Transformation Consulting discipline in the Americas. He is proud to have been Brother Blue and Ruth's driver and drummer for the past 28 years.

Watercolor by: Ann Hoban

Ahhhh!

Hugh "Brother Blue" Hill

Roy Fairfield

I first met Brother Blue when he came to my office on the Antioch College campus on a raw day in February, 1971. He was interested in the possibility of transferring to our year-old Union Graduate School (UGS), hence was checking out its possibilities. He carried with him the shackles his grandfather had worn during slave days, also his father's trowel that he used as a mason. He explained the symbolism of each. I believe that I told him of both the risks and the opportunities that UGS presented, since we were obviously bucking a powerful tradition embodied in the doctoral programs of Harvard, Berkeley, and Tulane. He made it clear that he was more interested in an experiential Ph.D., rather than the narrower academic programs he had encountered at both Harvard and Yale. He soon matriculated and attended our next colloquium, held on the Skidmore College campus in Saratoga Springs, New York. From those days until this very moment, he has been a living presence in my life, as well as in the lives of so very many people in the UGS and the larger world.

At his colloquium both he and Ruth endeared themselves to their fellow and sister students. He performed at the drop of a hat and presented his plan for completing UGS. He was a vital part of that rich personscape that once characterized any gathering of UGS learners. For whatever reasons, I forget, he chose me as his core faculty member (a role comparable to Chair of a traditional Ph.D. committee but one that included being a facilitator of learning, father/mother confessor, encourager of Creative Doing as well as Thinking.) Hence, I visited him in Cambridge and did everything in my power to encourage him to push on for the doctorate…feeling/knowing that it still could be an empowering step in his life. At a meeting in a restaurant just off Harvard Square, we outlined a potential program on a placemat, one he says he kept long

Ahhhh!

beyond his receiving the degree. And so has been our relationship.

As a member of his committee I applauded his choice of site for his Terminar (graduation seminar); namely, Deer Island Prison in Boston Harbor.

Entering our first prison was a bit scary for my wife, Maryllyn, and me; but filled with curiosity and eagerness to learn more, we cheerfully boarded the bus that took us from Cambridge to the prison gates and walls. Having to wait for permission to enter was anxiety-producing, but our apprehension was somewhat modulated by the fact that Blue had served an internship at Deer Island and was providing the leadership that his committee needed. Once in the prison, we wound our way up the steel staircases, past men shouting from their prison cells, reached the chapel, where, during the quiet moments, we could hear the mournful cries of seagulls and the waves crashing on the island shore. Blue had it well organized: TV cameramen and reporters were present, also musicians, and a gathering of friends. But little did he or we know, there would be a "rumble" in the middle of his graduation performance that day.

It seems that some prisoner had been found with white powder, presumably drugs, hence the wardens checked every cell in a "rumble." His program was broken up when a bleeding prisoner was thrust into the chapel, and he sat down amidst Blue's committee. Not long after, the prison wardens stopped the meeting, gave us warning, and summoned all of the women in the room to move quickly down the winding steel stairs where prisoners, banging their bars, were subjecting the women to wolf whistles and cat calls. Not long after, Blue and the men in his party were shepherded into our bus and whisked through the prison gates past a squadron of police officers and TV newsmen and other media. We breathed a sigh of relief; at least we were not hostages…on this, the day of the infamous prison break and fire in Oklahoma. Soon we were on our way to the Harvard Faculty Club in Cambridge.

Once there for luncheon, Blue showed us that he was in complete charge of *his* graduation. He'd not missed a beat and continued with his presentation. During lunch and the presentation, we were witnesses to powerful outdoor pyrotechnics, one of those flash-bang thunder storms. I thought that it was significantly symbolic: the location, the occasion, Blue's performance. He demonstrated the Hemingway definition of courage, grace under pressure.

Ahhhh!

And so has he lived his life during the three decades I've known him. He's taken his stories into every media known to humans. He has carried the storytelling tradition all over the United States and Europe. He has carried his message to some of the main thoroughfares of the world, but also to some of the out-of-the-way places. He's spoken to both proud and humble, and even amidst prize-winning and much PR, with great humility.

During his tenure in the Union Graduate School, I sometimes felt self-conscious and squirmed a bit when he "pinned my star" to an imaginary constellation he held high over his head. Somehow I didn't feel that I was such a star. But I continue to see that star as part of the "cosmic" communications which he and Ruth continue to send to Maryllyn and me from every point in the compass. And though we do not keep any kind of chart of his activities, it's a rare year when we do not receive at least one postal card, in both his and Ruth's handwriting, expressing his feelings for us.

I think they will not mind if I quote from some of their many cards: from Oct 6, 1996 from Jonesborough, Tennessee—Ruth: "Blue received a Circle of Excellence Award from National Storytelling Assoc for commitment and contributions to story-telling;" Blue: "We've come to the glorious end of a wonderful storytelling festival—singing, poetry, drama, guitars—In the telling, thought of you, Roy, with thanks and love…singing from the heart and mind." From Philadelphia, Oct 14, 1996—Blue: "…thanks for your letter, your poetry…Love and grati-tude…" From Washington, D.C., Dec 17, 1996, where Blue had taped a Christmas show for a Black Entertainment program—Blue added, "Most Beautiful Brother…Thank You for You…Your student ever…" From Oregon, March 6, 1997, where Ruth reported giving a talk on her oral history projects and Blue added, "…your mind and heart got me thru graduate school and your poetry shed a light that lifted the darkness…" The postal cards continue to arrive from many points of the compass; I treasure each and every one of them. It makes me feel connected to the storytelling tradition and one of its best practitioners.

Hugh "Brother Blue" Hill was an important person in the evolution of the Union Graduate School. Not only was he a vital and living role model in the vast wasteland of traditional doctoral education, he put flesh on our faith that it was possible to evolve a more humane approach to doctoral learning, and that experiential and theoretical learning could

Ahhhh!

work hand in hand. During those early and tentative years of UGS, Blue manifested in person what no amount of rhetoric or journal articles could ever express so well. Also, he was helpful, as example, in our struggle to shape the criteria for guiding and evaluating artistic projects.

Henry Adams once observed that "a teacher affects eternity." I am honored to have been a part of the teaching that he has done to contribute to that eternity.

Roy Fairfield is a Maine native and a historian, novelist, and poet, the author of thirteen books, including *Get Inspired!!*. He has been a professor at Bates, Ohio, Antioch and Hofstra Universities and at Fulbright and Athens Colleges. Roy was one of the founding faculty at Union Institute & University. He was a Peace Corps trainer for West African units, and President of the Maine Appalachian Club.

Photo: Rick Booth

Blue at the University of Florida, Gainesville

Ahhhh!

Papageno in Blue Feathers

Eliot Fisk

The first time I met Brother Blue I was just running out of a hotel in Cambridge and for some reason he was just passing through from the opposite direction. I had just played the Berio *Sequenza XI* as part of Luciano Berio's Norton lectures at Harvard, and as I remember, was charging out of the Hotel to get somewhere in a hurry. A dignifiedlooking man with a white turtle neck shirt and an elegant pair of trousers approached me and complimented me on my performance. We chatted about our mutual dreams of changing the world, about problems of race in America, about how we had to persevere in the face of enormous obstacles. If God was looking down, he certainly had a good laugh at these two Don Quixotes comparing notes on their individual ways of charging at stone windmills! Little did I realize how rare it was to see Brother Blue in his Dr. Hugh Morgan Hill get up…ever after I have only seen him dressed in blue ("my blue rags" as Brother Blue describes his version of Papageno's feathers!) with a butterfly pin or two attached wherever it or they may fit. Indeed, this gentle man, who walks this earth as the nearest thing most of us will ever see to a living Shakespearean "fool," seems to have just stepped out of the pages of some writer's fantasy. If Brother Blue hadn't existed, someone would have had to dream him up, but fortunately for all of us, he has beaten the novelists, playwrights and poets of the world to the punch and created HIMSELF!

Perhaps what I most admire about Brother Blue is his courage, his courage to choose vulnerability, simplicity, and naiveté in an age when these attributes are in such short supply. And it's not that Blue doesn't know different! He's read all the sages, and he can quote them to you. But instead of adding to the piles of unread books and position papers gathering dust on the back shelves of libraries, he's taken his P.h.D on the street. His laurels are the smiles of all the people he's charmed, his prizes are the light he's brought into the lives

Ahhhh !

of his fellow humans and his reason for being is to "be" in the way
Buddha or any of the great visionaries simply "was." Don't think that
Blue's a pushover though! We did some very toney work together down
at Disney World in Florida, but we also have occasionally done some
tougher stuff. One time we were in a sort of half-way house for children
with impossible, dysfunctional families somewhere in the Boston area. It
was a miserable, rainy Saturday night, an insult to the very idea of
"Saturday night"! In fact, we could hardly convince our cabdriver to
take us to that part of town where we needed to go!

I have played in every imaginable type of place, but this had to be the
toughest…These were kids who were passed from their real families to
this half-way house Blue and I were about to enter, a sort of holding
place when the abuse gets too bad. The courts regularly move the young
people who pass through this facility around, and despite the efforts of
their counsellors, their lives are impossible, and they let everyone else
who comes anywhere near them know it and feel it. There had been no
preparation whatsoever for our visit. Not surprisingly, the kids were
restless and un-receptive. At one point they were making more noise
talking and being smart than I was playing. Suddenly, Blue, who had
been sitting quite meekly off to one side, jumped to his feet and, shaking
with indignation, defended me, let them have it, silenced them dead in
their tracks: "This man," (he meant ME!!) "is the greatest guitar player
in the world, I said, IN THE WORLD!! What are you doing treating
him like that?" I was as surprised as anyone by this outburst. Yet it was
what Martin Luther King, a great hero of Blue's and mine, would have
called "militant" non-violence at its finest.

Every once in a while some film or book or article crosses my path and
I realize just how famous Blue actually is: in the best sense of the word, a
real street legend. And he lives up to both parts of that phrase…despite
the two P.h.Ds (Yale *and* Harvard, but I forget which one he earned
first!) he is still a man of the stree And, legend? Well you won't meet
anyone who more deserves the title. Blue and Ruthie keep me informed
by those charming little postcards that arrive from all corners of the
world, from wherever this American Papageno has been making magic
out of the air itself.

And I can just imagine Ruthie starting those postcards with some
actual information about where they've been and what they've done
there and then handing them over to Blue so that he can send his so
touching and heart warming lines, "Beautiful Brother of the soul…"

Ahhhh!

And, even though I'm so bad about writing back, those little postcards keep right on coming. How many anguished moments of my life have been lit up with hope by those little missives! And I think this is at once Blue's sort of immortality and the great message of the work of art that is the life of this genuine *Lebenskünstler*.

What more is there for us to do this on this "*cammin di nostra vita*" then search for those fleeting moments of joy and to try to pass them on to others? Martin Luther King spoke of it on the last full night of his life, in that great address that he gave on the 3rd of April, 1968, and which has gone into history as the "Mountain Top" sermon: "I just want to do God's will." I think that's what Blue is trying to do too. And his unique, fearless, creative way of doing it is what makes us all want to give him a big hug and say once again, "We love you, Brother Blue."

Upon receiving his M.M.A. from Yale University, guitar virtuoso Eliot Fisk founded The Guitar Department at Yale School of Music. He is Professor of Guitar at the Mozarteum in Salzburg, Austria. He also conducts numerous master classes and residencies throughout the world. His repetoire spans a wide range of music, from contemporary works to his own transcriptions of works by Bach, D. Scarlatti, Haydn, Mozart, and Mendelssohn. His CD's include "Vivaldi Concerti & other Works," "Paganini: 24 Caprices," "The Latin American Guitar," and "Mountain Songs: A Cycle of American Folk Music," among others.

Guy Davis watercolor of Muddy Duddy - 1984

AHHHH !

Professor Hill

Hugh Flick

I have known Brother Blue in a number of different contexts but what I would like to share is my experience of him as a teacher. I used to teach a number of Folklore and Mythology courses at Harvard and was always somewhat frustrated that most of what I taught could only be experienced through written texts or scholarly articles. There were a few video documentaries that I presented to give the classes a sense of the way the performance itself is an important dimension of traditional folk literature. When I approached Blue about giving a performance and lecture in my folktale course he immediately agreed.

Although I had heard Blue tell stories many times on the street, I was not exactly sure what he would present in my class, and I purposely gave him no guidelines. Blue arrived at the class in his familiar blue butterfly outfit with his lovely muse/wife Ruth. I didn't give the class much information about Blue, other than his academic credentials and the fact that I considered him the World's Greatest Storyteller. Blue immediately began engaging the class in the storytelling process by walking around the room among the students talking about the healing power of stories. After some fascinating examples of the ways his stories had affected prisoners with whom he had worked, Blue began to tell some tales. He danced, he leaped, he sang, and he whispered as he told of the lonely caterpillar who becomes a butterfly. The class was totally entranced by this time.

Before I realized what he was doing, Blue had put a chair on the desk in the front of the class and was climbing onto it. When I did realize that he was intending to stand on the chair on top of the desk, it was too late to stop him since he had already launched into another of his tales. Ruth also had a horrified look on her face, but she was more used to such actions than I was. If Blue had simply stood still, there wouldn't have been any problem, but, Blue being Blue, he was swaying, hopping, and

Ahhhh!

waving his arms as part of his performance. It was tempting to close my eyes and pray, but I couldn't look away as the chair crept closer and closer to the edge. Just as I felt that the chair was getting too close to the edge, Blue, near the end of his story, gave a small dance step, which catapulted the chair and his body off into space. Somehow Blue landed on his feet like a cat and just kept on telling the tale. As soon as he finished the tale, the class broke into appreciative applause.

Blue's performance/lecture did more than anything else in this course to help the students understand the dynamics of folktale performance. Blue continued to be a valued guest lecturer in my classes until I left Harvard, but I was careful not to leave any empty chairs near to desks in the classrooms where the classes were held.

Hugh M. Flick, Jr. is the Dean of Silliman College and a Lecturer in the Religious Studies Department at Yale University. He earned his Ph.D. in Sanskrit and Indian Studies at Harvard University. He has also taught in the Folklore and Mythology Program at Harvard University.

Blue performing at Memorial Park School in Fort Wayne, IN

AHHHH!

The Journey to Cambridge

Libby Franck

For me, the journey to Cambridge to attend one of Brother Blue's Storytelling Sessions has always been a magical one. I don't go frequently, but the times I have attended have affected my life in a profound way.

Wherever his Open Mike is held, Blue is able to make the space sacred for the listeners and the tellers. One must prepare for the adventure, but also expect to encounter the unexpected. He allows each teller to do inspired work. He creates enchantment in the air around the storytellers, but of course it is Ruth who keeps us all grounded on the earth. They are living examples of how to live one's life. We, as cloud-dwelling storytellers, must have someone to keep us grounded or figure out a way to do it ourselves.

I draw strength from the fellowship found there—being a part of the company of tellers, seeing old friends, making new ones. I am very much aware of participating as a teller or a listener, and each role has equal significance. Tellers will never have a better audience.

If you get to tell that night, there can be magic in the air which allows you to do some of your best work. And then there is Blue's response to each story and its teller, the depth with which he listens to and appreciates each nuance of the told story and the special blessing he bestows upon each artist designed to help each one of us grow. The flip side of this is that the next time you tell in another place, to another audience, you must create your own magic, for all storytelling spaces are not so expectant and receptive.

I would like to thank Blue and Ruth for the particular impact my visits to their space, especially at the Bookcellar Cafe, have had upon my life as a person, not just as an artist. When I told the story of my now empty house after my husband died, Blue's blessing gave me strength. When I

Ahhhh!

was the featured teller, I felt I was weaving a spell with more than my stories. Five months later that magic was still in place, and I met another kindred spirit, when he was the feature, who has been sharing my life ever since.

The Boston area is graced by Blue and his lady, Ruth. Once a week they share themselves as mentors, infusing inspiration and encouragement into our community.

Libby Franck had furthered storytelling through her cable TV show, by hosting Natick Art Center's OutSpoken Word open mike, and serving on the LANES Board. Her myths, legends, and folk tales frequently feature intrepid heroines, and she seeks out strong, daring, and unusual women of history to research and dramatize.

Drawing by Guy Davis after hearing Blue perform *Muddy Duddy* on Thompson Island - September 26, 1983

Ahhhh!

One of the Wisest Men
Henry Louis Gates, Jr.

Brother Blue has been a mainstay of Harvard and Harvard Square for many years. As he engaged in storytelling, there existed, just beneath his blue and butterfly costume, one of the wisest men Harvard has produced, far more insightful, compassionate, and truth-telling than many with far more serious reputations.

Brother Blue, like many entertainers, wears several masks. But his have led us to truths that are articulated through a unique dramatic lens, and what Emily Dickinson called "slant."

It has been my privilege to study under the tutelage of Brother Blue. He inspires us with his weekly attendance at the Du Bois Institute colloquia as an African praise singer. His enduring and central message is that we learn with the heart as well as the head.

Blue brings a spirit to this place that has enriched us all. I am proud to be his brother.

Henry Louis Gates, Jr., Ph.D, is an editor, author, and professor who has taught at Yale, Cornell, and Harvard Universities. He is the author of, *The Signifyin(g) Monkey: A Theory of Afro-American Literary Criticism*, *Figures in Black: Words, Signs, and the Racial Self*, and *Colored People*. Since 1991, he has served as chair of the Afro-American Studies department at Harvard University.

Ahhhh!

Thanks for the Awakening

Marni Gillard

During my early years of knowing Brother Blue, our energies intertwined at moments I will never forget. My first memory occurred during a Sharing the Fire conference to which I had brought my twelve-year-old son, Brian, and my younger sister, Maria. They both decided to attend Blue's "Climbing the Mt." workshop while I headed for something else. When they found me afterward in the hall, Brian exclaimed, "Mom, I climbed the mountain!" Excitedly they told me of how some of the people in the workshop had chosen to "climb" and to speak about "mountains" in their lives. One participant had pulled a chair over and stood on it to replicate the feeling of being on a mountaintop. That helped Brian claim his connection to mountains (since at 12 he was still pretty short) so he stood on the chair too. He didn't say anything, he just very slowly made eye contact with the room of people and bowed deeply and regally to the crowd "below" him. Hearing that, I smiled.

I had watched Brian earlier that spring play the part of the Mikado in his school's production of the operetta by the same name. I knew that his silent bow meant he had reached inside himself for that metaphor. Being the Mikado had been a mountaintop experience for him though it isn't actually much of a speaking part. He had made quite a splash as this emperor in his white face and Asian features. I knew it had meant a lot to him to step inside that character's demeanor and his culture. The bow represented more than the emperor's authority: It was a gesture of spiritual belief in another's goodness. Now, with the encouragement of one very special adult, whose demeanor and culture were also different from his own, my son had claimed the power of what he had learned from that character to "climb the mountain" and share himself silently with his mother's storytelling friends.

Later, I watched Blue approach Brian from across a crowded dining room to thank him for coming to the workshop and for claiming his "mountain" self elegantly. I loved watching Blue thank and praise my

Ahhhh!

young son in that way that only Blue can. I basked in the glow of his affection for my son and have always been grateful they connected.

Another time I brought a friend to the Bookcellar. This young woman had a difficult childhood and adolescence and does not open easily to the attentions of others. But right away Blue "read" that my friend was unique and precious to me. His gentle way of being with her made her laugh and encouraged her to put her name in the box as a first-time teller. Later she proudly took the stool and shared some of her original poetry. I had hoped that would happen, but it seemed like a lot to hope for. Blue's uniqueness and his generous and sensitive manner blended easily with my friend's. She has never relinquished her affection for him, nor he for her. He asks me about her every time we meet.

My third memory is really more about me than about Blue. It relates to the magic he casts over our community. During my first experience at a Sharing the Fire Closing Ceremony, the facilitator asked if anyone was willing to share what had been particularly instructive or memorable from the weekend's activities. That year's conference had been especially important in helping to build my confidence as a teller and presenter, but I couldn't think how to express all I was feeling. After a moment of no one saying anything, Blue jumped up. "I just gotta say one thing. But I want you all to hear it, to hear it clear. STORYTELLING'S GONNA CHANGE THE WORLD!!!!!!" I hung on Blue's every word. His incredible enthusiasm gave me permission to claim aloud how much the conference had meant to me. I was still pretty new to STF and a little shy, not to mention tired and feeling more than a little overwhelmed.

I'd never stayed for the closing before because of rider or driver commitments. I live over three hours away from Boston. But that year I stayed to feel the bittersweetness of the closure and to testify to the gathering's importance with my presence. Blue's fervor-filled outburst shook words out of me. I stood up the minute he sat down. I have no memory of what I said, I only remember I began to cry as I spoke. I think I was letting in, for the first time, the *big*ness of storytelling, how life-changing it had been for me. I was also accepting a commitment to this world-changing community and movement. I'll always be grateful to Blue for awakening that consciousness in me.

Marni Gillard, founder of the Story Studio in Schenectady, NY, tells tales and gathers people together to support each other's artistry. Her book, *Storyteller, Storyteacher* and her tape *Without a Splash: Diving into Childhood Memories* encourage others to find the teller in themselves.

AHHHH!

Ahhhh!

Jackson Gillman

Some people, myself included, might be inclined to describe Blue as a man-child. However one cares to color this label—as an example of arrested psychological development, or a perpetually youthful quality of openness and wonder—it would be hard to deny that he retains an irrepressible child spirit. In the *Portrait Series* of Brother Blue, Blue is quoted as saying, "Don't ever ever ever ever let me sit in the front row ever again, don't let me even get near the front row 'cause I'm dangerous. Even if I'm only near the stage I'm liable to jump up there..." As Blue himself would be first to admit, he often just can't contain himself. Sometimes he and others wish that he could, but other times we're grateful that he can't, or won't.

Well, regardless of how one feels about Blue's propensity for taking over the stage at the end of a program, I think I can speak for many performers when I say that I love having Blue in the front row. I don't think that anyone can argue that Blue "gives great audience." So much focused energy comes back that one feels truly supported just by his presence. This effect of Blue's actually runs counter to the view of him as a restless personality. I myself am a restless personality, admittedly, with potential attention deficiencies. I am either totally engrossed by a performance and can give a performer that same sort of hyper focus, or I just might be totally unengaged. As a performer, I might not want to take the chance of the likes of me in the front row, but I'd take Blue any day.

Regardless of the performance, I've never seen Blue give less than 100% as a spectator. This not only takes tremendous self-control, but it epitomizes Blue's enormous generosity of spirit. I was aware of Blue's special gift from my very first experience of him as a focused, supportive workshop leader and audience. I told a personal story that I had never told anyone before. His response convinced me of the power of it, a story that, otherwise, would probably have never seen the stage, by a budding storyteller who had just received a giant, gentle lift from a gentle giant.

No doubt, Blue likes to call attention to himself. But he just as genuinely likes to call attention to others. So much does he crave attention, that I tend to avoid walking by him when there's a group around. I might be subjected to one of his testimonial ambushes, ballyhooing me as the chameleon genius who can do everything. He once pointed out to me that I shy away from him in public. I think he was concerned that I didn't like him. Far from it, my friend, but offstage I can be a very different animal than the one who is comfortable in the limelight when it is my time to shine. Perhaps he just doesn't relate to another performer's inclination towards staying in the shadows till showtime.

And speaking of being in the shadows, a partner of his has little choice but to be in his shadow. (Can you imagine two of the likes of Blue together? Now that could be truly dangerous.) Just as every action has an equal and opposite reaction, the beautiful power of Ruth's quiet rootedness provides an invisible sort of tether that keeps Blue's butterfly spirit from drifting off, off and away…Everyone knows how amazing Ruth is at this, and no one more than Blue himself. He would be the first to sing the saintly woman's praises.

There are two stories that I'd like to recount that have been collecting interest in my memory banks. One is fairly recent, on the occasion of my giving a keynote address at Sharing the Fire. Against his own directive, Blue was in the front row, and I was glad to have his supportive presence. I was very pleased with how my presentation was received and I built in a deceptive cadence, a sort of false ending, if you will. Characteristically, Blue couldn't contain himself and jumped up to add his appreciations. Some in the audience thought it inappropriate for him to tag on his two cents, kudos, or whatever, and were trying to shout him down. I quickly interceded, cut off the audience, explaining that my Swami character would still have the last closing words, and Blue was welcome to take the floor. Uncharacteristically, this was the one time I wanted to hear what he had to say about my work. While he launched into his fullest-blown accolades, I not only allowed myself to take it all in, but knelt at his feet as he delivered it, feeling as though I were being knighted by the King of the Shared Fire himself, with his torch, Excalibur.

Ahhhh!

My Swami ended with some maxims to ponder, the last one being a quote of Sarah Bernhardt's that "it is by spending oneself, that one becomes rich." By that measure, a rich man is Brother Blue. I am richer for knowing him, and I am proud to be accepted in his court.

And finally, the story I always thought would be a wonderful eulogy-type story for Brother Blue, but is much better now as a living tribute to his vibrant presence amongst us. The setting was an early Storytellers in Concert at the First Church Congregational in Cambridge. It was a Christmas program that included Jay O'Callahan. The program was over, but, no, it wasn't. Blue was compelled to still the crowd that was rising to leave. He had "the best Christmas story ever" still to tell.

Quiet rumbles in the crowd no doubt included things like "sit down, Blue, the program is over; you're not on it..." Blue was insistent, however, on getting complete silence before he delivered this best Christmas story ever. He waited; we got quiet. "The best Christmas story ever," pause, then with quiet strength and simplicity:"Jesus."

He may have said something very short like "Merry Christmas" or "God bless you" or "Good night" after that; I don't remember. But I sat, took it in, and realized what he had done. Something essential had been missing from the program of Christmas stories that we had just heard. Ironically, there was no mention of Jesus. Blue saw fit to fix that.

However one might describe Blue—sage, naïf, poet, child, philosopher, fool—it was a moment like this when I just have to thank him so much for being who he is, and say, "I love you, Blue."

If Brother Blue were to write Jackson Gillman's bio blurb, his description of Jackson would be "He is Leonardo—the storyteller who does it all: mime, music, dance, sign language; the magical, protean, chameleon genius—truth dressed in the royal clothes of God's Harlequin."

AHHHH!

Black-Eyed-Susan Filled Day

Diana Gleason and Captain Bob

On July 19,1997, Brother Blue stood with Diana and Captain Bob in the center of their flowerbeds filled with golden black-eyed susans and surrounded by family, friends, and fellow storytellers. He was there to perform the marriage ceremony that would unite the two in love. Captain Bob had been attending Brother Blue's storytelling at the Bookcellar Cafe since shortly after its inception in February 1992. When he met Diana in January 1993, and brought her to the Bookcellar on their first date, she also became a regular member. It was natural that, when they decided to get married, they should ask Brother Blue and Ruth if they had time in their busy schedule for him to officiate at their wedding. They knew that if Ruth wrote it in her book, they would be there. After the ceremony, when the music started, Brother Blue stepped out on to the dance floor—not to forward the cause of storytelling in bringing peace to the world, but to dance—and dance he did! With the verve and passion that he gives to all things that he loves—his arms and legs flying—he tired out partner after partner. Since that day, when Brother Blue sees Diana and Captain Bob, he asks how their garden is. The joy of that black-eyed–susan filled day is a memory they share.

July 19th, 1997

Bob Smith instructs teachers in Orientation Mobility for the Blind at U. Mass. Boston. Diana Gleason is a retired teacher and elementary school psychologist. They reside in Scituate, Mass. and regularly attend Brother Blue's weekly storytelling

Ahhhh!

A Hatful of Peas
Globiana

This is a story about a migrant farm worker. In early Spring, he pushed aside crackling ice-transforming-to-mud and nestled seedlings in chilly earth. On hot Summer days, he gently plucked life when it was ripe.

This year was hard. The weather had been unkind. Few of those hope-filled beginnings had survived. Trudging familiar paths, I sought ready fruit.

"Have you work?"

"You?"

Then the pea field: I marveled at her transformation from moist browns to lush greens.

Oh, yes, I approached. My callused hands were my resume: Able. Experienced.

The foreman issued me the long, canvas bag. I slung its broad strap over my shoulder. Its large pocket lay crumpled at my feet.

"We weigh you in at sunset. Don't be late."

And I began. In the early rays, the long bag brushed lightly along the long, narrow walk-rows, trailing me.

My work is hard. What I recall most of those long summer days are the aches in my back and legs, the cramp of my hands, and deep, greedy thirst.

My methodical path wove ahead and back, again, again. Above, the sun carved its one magnificent arc.

As the sun shot its red rays from the evening-approaching sky, and my bag dragged ever more heavily, the day did not cool. I began my last row, gladdened that I would be moving, however slightly, away from the sun. It was late; I would have to hurry to finish that last row and weigh

Ahhhh!

in by sunset.

I picked rapidly. I watched that hot sun measure my time.

When I looked up to see how far I had yet to go, I saw him. He was there, bent like me, picking peas—picking peas in my row! He had begun at the far end of my row, and, yes, he was picking—my peas.

I picked faster. I flung a handful of fragile green peas into my bag, and plucked more. I looked up. He was closer (and still picking). He looked at me and bent to pick faster, too. He was tossing his peas into his hat. He didn't even have a bag!

Who is this intruder? The nearer he and I drew, the angrier I became. We stole glances at one another and kept picking. Now we were very near. His hat was brimming with peas.

I stood. I took in a deep breath, preparing to tell him that he had no right...and, during that breath, he stood, too. He turned to me, and he dumped the contents of his hat into my bag.

"Now," he said, "you owe someone a hatful of peas."

Globiana has been creating and performing in and around Boston and the world for around ten years. Her work has been described as "...mystical, magical, sometimes disturbing, always provocative..." She feels fortunate to happen to occupy the same corner of the planet-at the same time as Brother Blue and his precious wife, Ruth.

Ahhhh!

Blue Rainbow

Annie Goglia

I know a rainbow
like no other.
He reaches up
like a true blue flame.
Cool blue,
blue Blue.
Blue is more
than blue.

Sometimes
he is purple,
spilling into sadness,
diving
into the twilight
land,
into the shadows
between
night and
day,
between
hot and
cold.

Sometimes
he is red,
red that inspires,
and annoys,
turning us into
wild bulls,

Ahhhh!

114

pricking us on
to
fill up our own vast space,
fight our own just battles,
spread our own sweet madness.

Sometimes
he is yellow/orange,
having lapped up fire,
with all his senses,
filling his being,
beaming, shining, bright,
sun/moon/stars
in one,
the reflection
and source of our heat.

Sometimes
he is green,
green that springs up
shouting, spouting, sprouting,
growing, knowing, showing...

and finally
coming back
to earth,
his Ruth, his truth,
the end and
the beginning.

Annie Goglia, a storyteller who grew out of a poet, has been inspired for many years by Brother Blue's poetic storytelling and commitment to the Boston storytelling community. Her workshops help draw out individual's stories and the rich personal meanings below their surface.

Ahhhh!

The Teller, the Told, and the Tale

Peter J. Gomes

Hugh Morgan Hill and I first met at Harvard Divinity School in the fall of 1967, when we entered together. He was the transforming presence in that place, and emerged as the Brother Blue whom we have all come to admire. He gave us many tears of joy in The Memorial Church in the early days of my tenure. I will never forget his performance as Jesus in one of our Good Friday Passion plays in the 1970's. My late mother enjoyed her encounters with Blue, and he remains for me a living link to her. He has given wisdom to adults and joy to children of all ages. He is, in the words of David McCord, "The teller, the told, and the tale!"

Peter J. Gomes is an American Baptist minister. A member of the Faculty of Arts and Sciences and of the Faculty of Divinity at Harvard University, he was presented with the Phi Beta Kappa Teaching Award in 2001. His most recent book is *The Good Life: Truths That Last in Times of Need.*

Ahhhh!

There's Beauty in You and Me
(for my children Aisha, Uhuru, and Jamaal,)
in honor of Brother Blue

Linda Goss

> I AM!   YOU ARE!   HE IS!   SHE IS!
>
> WE ALL ARE   BEAUTIFUL!
>
> WE ALL ARE   BEAUTIFUL!
>
> LIKE THE RAINBOW IN THE SKY.
>
> LIKE THE WINGS OF A BUTTERFLY.
>
> LIKE THE PEARLS IN THE DEEP BLUE SEA.
>
> THERE'S BEAUTY IN YOU AND ME.
>
> I AM!   YOU ARE!   HE IS!   SHE IS!
>
> WE ALL ARE   BEAUTIFUL!
>
> WE ALL ARE   BEAUTIFUL!
>
> LIKE THE FIREFLIES IN THE NIGHT.
>
> LIKE THE DEW IN THE SILVER MOONLIGHT.
>
> LIKE THE STARFISH IN THE SEA.
>
> THERE'S BEAUTY IN YOU AND ME.
>
> Within our hearts there dwells a special place
>
> Where harmony shines in every race.
>
> Love is born throughout eternity

AHHHH!

117

And BEAUTY grows inside of you and me.

SO INSTEAD OF FEELING BLUE:

WE CAN BE LIKE BROTHER BLUE

OPEN UP OUR HEARTS AND SAY

"I AM BEAUTIFUL EVERYDAY!"

THERE'S BEAUTY IN THE SKY AND THE SEA,

YES, THERE'S BEAUTY IN YOU AND ME.

Linda Goss, storyteller and author, is the co-founder of the National Black Storytelling Festival and Conference and the National Association of Black Storytellers. Her books include *Talk That Talk* and *The Frog Who Wanted to Be a Singer*.

AHHHH!

A Liberating Example

Linda Goss

Brother Blue is my LIBERATOR! Back in the early 70's when I was developing my craft as a storyteller, I constantly had the blues. Some folks didn't quite know what to make of me. I was ringing bells, shouting, making animal faces, and wearing African prints. Thirty years later, thanks to kindred spirits like Brother Blue, I still am. But in those days, sometimes I felt isolated and alone, yet I knew I wanted to tell stories from my African tradition and Southern heritage.

Then, one day, while I was watching a TV show, with Aisha and Uhuru, my daughters, a blue vision of a tall handsome man wrapped up in ribbons, balloons and butterflies *and* holding an umbrella appeared on the screen. He introduced himself as "Brother Blue." To me he was a parade, circus, carnival, and festival all in one. His voice was magical, and his words were poetic. I was enchanted by his jazzy, dangling, zazzy storytelling. The show was called "Playmates, Schoolmates," and it was later cancelled. But nothing could cancel Brother Blue from my imagination.

He changed my down-and-out blue mood to a serene beautiful blue. There are many shades of blue, and the essence of "Blue" is in me and you. When I tell my family story, "The Frog Who Wanted to Be a Singer," I think of different people who have inspired me, such as my mother, father, grand-daddy, Louis Armstrong, Billie Holiday, John Coltrane, and Brother Blue, to name a few. But he pulled that frustrated frog out of me, and gave me the courage to "talk dat talk" and "walk dat walk" in my own unique and special way. It was essential for me to list Brother Blue's name as one of the Esteemed Elders and a major influence on storytelling on the dedication pages in two of my anthologies, as well as to include his stories "The Butterfly" in *Talk That Talk*, and "Miss Wunderlich" in *Jump Up and Say*. I want everyone to know of his beauty and his wonder. Thank you, Brother Blue, sweet soul man, for liberating

Ahhhh!

me.

Linda Goss, storyteller and author, is the co-founder of the National Black Storytelling Festival and Conference and the National Association of Black Storytellers. Her books include *Talk That Talk* and *The Frog Who Wanted to Be a Singer*.

Ahhhh!

From NABS with Honor and Love

NABS, National Association of Black Storytellers,
founders Linda Goss and Mary Carter Smith

The National Association of Black Storytellers (NABS) bestowed upon Brother Blue the first and only "Elder's Chair" award in 1995 at the 13th annual "IN THE TRADITION..." National Black Storytelling Festival and Conference held in Detroit, Michigan. He received from NABS the Zora Neale Hurston award in 1986, and he is a part of our Circle of Elders. Brother Blue and his wife, Ruth Hill, are charter members of NABS and have been featured at and attended most of our festivals and festivals sponsored by our Affiliate Members. Sister Ruth is a former board member of NABS.

Brother Blue is a source of inspiration and a spiritual guide to the members of NABS. We honor Brother Blue because he is the Grand-daddy of contemporary storytelling in the United States. We praise Brother Blue because he is blessed with gifts from the Creator and his ancestors. We respect Brother Blue because he has given of himself by blending his life into his art, his art into his life, and by reaching out to people all over the earth.

Most importantly, we LOVE Brother Blue because he is a kind and gentle being whose storytelling comes from the innermost depths of his soul.

The National Association of Black Storytellers, Inc. (NABS) promotes and perpetuates the art of Black storytelling—an art form which embodies the history, heritage, and culture of African Americans. NABS preserves and passes on the folklore, legends, myths, fables and mores of Africans and their descendants and ancestors.

Mary Carter Smith is the modern griot, the matriarch of Black storytelling. Her extensive repertoire of stories, poems and dramatic sketches has been developed through a recollection of experiences drawn from her native Birmingham, Alabama. Mary is a founding member of Big Sisters International and co-founder of the National Association of Black Storytellers. She is a poet and author of several books.

Ahhhh!

The Sounds and the Colors Dance in the Evening Air: Music & Brother Blue

Jay Gottlieb

I am not a storyteller—At least not in the sense of verbal emission worthy of membership in LANES. As a concert pianist, the cushions of my fingers, which receive all possible muscular and sensorial stimuli, get myriad stories told via musical sounds, notes. In this context, my friendship and collaborations with Blue enabled a verbalization of what was happening musically. And my piano improvisations took Blue's words into the realm of pure sound: a most gratifying synergy. When my mother, dancer and dance teacher came into the "web," beautiful dancers (her students) began to extend into the space Blue and his stories inspired.

The journey began in Harvard Yard one night. Our hero was indeed "a dancing story" in the winter snow. After leaving Harvard and moving to Paris, what we had shared in innumerable venues and radio stations in the United States could now be exported internationally. When Blue and Ruth were in Europe for various storytelling congresses and engagements, I organized an evening with Blue in Paris: a representative selection of his solo pieces, plus our duo improvisation. Even though that was twenty years ago, the crowd present that evening has never recovered from the enormous impact. A French composer who was there, for example, composed a work entitled "Brother Blue." Several lives were changed, despair turning into gleaming hope. And the light seems to have been imparted and permanently placed into each and every person seated at the event.

And so it is for me, privileged to have been touched by the magic of this exceptional being, a catalyst, translator of the highest, invisible threads of the cosmos. Blue may seem to be portraying the "too far to

Ahhhh!

122

go" of which Cocteau speaks, but, with all his eloquence, what is most glorious is the humility and wisdom that informs Blue's enjoinder that the absolute highest cannot be spoken.

Jay Gottlieb received a degree in Music from Harvard, where he also taught. He worked closely in France with Nadia Boulanger, a source of inspiration for Brother Blue's stories. Continuing to perform, lecture, and compose, Jay has been selected to represent the USA through the Arts America Program.

Jay Gottlieb and Brother Blue in Paris

Ahhhh!

They Also Serve...

Stephen Jay Gould

When Ruth, Brother Blue's wife, worked as the head librarian at The Harvard Museum of Comparative Zoology, my son, then a toddler, spent a good deal of time being raised as a "laboratory brat." He and Blue became at least casual pals.

Life has been hard for an autistic person like Jesse. Friendships do not come easily, but the universal need for human contact does not lessen. Disappointment can be especially discouraging, and can easily suppress further effort. During the winter of the great blizzard, schools closed for three weeks around Valentine's Day. Jesse made cards for all his schoolmates, and delivered them to their homes by hand. He received not one in return. His classmates meant no harm; I doubt anyone realized what such a simple gesture would have signified to him.

I still live in fear of similar failures by others to respond (for, to him, "let's have lunch" can only be read literally and concretely, and he will be hurt when he makes an effort, so rare and hard for him, and others then treat the phrase in its conventional meaning of "nice to see you for a moment on the street-car once a year or so.")

Jesse and Blue have always hit it off, for nearly thirty years now. A street encounter—their usual mode of contact—always inspires an animated and antic conversation. One day last year, we ran into Blue just a week before Jesse's annual violin concert. Blue said that he'd love to attend, and took down the information. I "knew" the purely conventional character of such responses, and held no expectations—but I didn't have the heart to tell Jesse that Ruth and Blue would probably not be there.

Ahhhh!

124

They came. Their presence animated an already joyous occasion. I told Jesse later that I had been surprised. And Jesse simply stated, "but he said he'd come." Little things do mean a lot. And little things mark the true treasure of a man. Thanks, Blue.

The late Stephen Jay Gould is the author of *The Mismeasure of Man* and many other works on evolutionary biology and the history of science, and was the subject of a NOVA profile. He was a member of the NOVA advisory board and was a professor of Geology and Zoology at Harvard University, Curator of Invertebrate Paleontology in the Harvard Museum of Comparative Zoology, and adjunct member of the Department of the History of Science. As a scientist interested in stories (his passion was the story of Life on Earth) and equally in the *nature* of stories, he inevitably met and befriended Brother Blue. The mutual admiration among Blue, Gould, and Gould's son Jesse was obvious to anyone who knew them.

Ahhhh!

Quilting Brother Blue

Beatriz Grayson

Thank you for all the postcards you have been sending me from all over the world. I keep them tucked away in the copy of *Homespun* you gave me "from the middle of you." I reread them every so often and wonder if you are still using the quilt I made for you to stand on when you tell your stories. I know Ruth has used it at least once as a cape when she was caught unprepared in a cold climate. No matter what you have done with it (I *know* you wear the sash I made), I have the memory of your storytelling on the (my) quilt-covered concrete floor of the New England Quilt Museum in Lowell. At the time when "Who'd A Thought It—Improvisation in African-American Quiltmaking" was being shown.

Getting to know you in person, having you wishfully commission me to do a quilt for you, working on it, trying to illustrate some of your leitmotifs, was so inspirational, I still carry the experience "in the middle of me." In my work as an art/quilt maker I *know* I can paint my butterfly wings any color I wish; I can reinterpret any images that I see or that come to my mind any way that I conceive, because, as it all comes from inside of me, it is beautiful.

I thank you for your vision.

Love forever and ever,

Beatriz

Beatriz Grayson, a Brazilian-born artist whose work is in national and international collections, has been working for the last fifteen years primarily with fabric, producing high chroma art quilts.

Ahhhh!

Brother Blue & Ruth accepting a sash commissioned from Beatriz Grayson in 1989.

Ahhhh!

When I Think of Brother Blue

Katie Green

I know that Brother Blue is the storyteller. I mean: Brother Blue is THE Storyteller.

You know how it is with life-changing events? It's like this. I will never forget where I was and what I was doing when the radio announcer said, "The President of the United States (JFK), has been shot. Likewise, I will always remember my surroundings when I learned that Martin Luther King and Robert Kennedy were killed.

I certainly don't mean to put Blue in the category of famous assassinated leaders, but the first time I heard Blue was definitely a life-changing event for me. It is right there with the first time I met my husband, Phil, or looked at each of my brand-new babies. Events that change our lives are indelibly etched in our memory.

I will never forget the first time I heard Brother Blue. And I do mean heard, because I heard Blue before I ever saw him.

Even today, more than 20 years later, whenever I think of Blue, I am transported into the back of my vehicle, parked in my driveway. It is early spring, and I am building benches inside my Chevy van, listening to WGBH, planning a camping trip once the van is completed. It is a late Sunday afternoon and Blue's story, "Miss Wunderlich," comes on the radio.

I stop hammering. I sit, unmoving, cross-legged, probably with my mouth hanging open in story trance. My heart beats with the storyteller's as he tells me how Miss Wunderlich could see the goodness in him. The story ends, and I weep for all the children who never had a Miss Wunderlich in their lives.

The following day, I felt renewed when I returned to my class of young children. Blue's story gave me the gift of hope and faith that my time as a teacher had been well spent.

Ahhhh!

Later that year, I attended my first storytelling festival: Three Apples, in Harvard, MA. Blue was one of the featured tellers. He sat in the front row on the right side of the church. I sat behind him, not knowing who he was. He captured my attention before he took the stage as storyteller: A tall, thin man with great energy. He was dressed in royal blue, with colorful flying ribbons. Butterflies danced on his hat, his shoulder, his palms. He sat crossing and uncrossing his long legs, looking back at the audience coming in, and whispering to the gentle lady next to him. She, too, was dressed in the same blue. I imagined that she sewed both their costumes. The woman in me recognized a fellow nurturer. It was clear that they were a solid pair. His lanky arm draped around the metal folding chair in which she sat. She smiled quietly and patted his hand: "You'll be wonderful."

He was wonderful. He was wonder-full. Full of wonder for me. Blue told several stories that weekend, but I especially remember him talking about the butterfly. He told me, and yes, it was me, that there was a butterfly inside me that longed to be free. He said he was a lover, that he loved life, loved people, loved me, and I believed him. I sat listening to Blue at the Three Apples Festival, and when Blue repeated, almost chanting, "I can see into the heart of you," I knew, without a doubt, that he could.

When Blue tells stories, he is too full of the wonder of life to sophisticate his style of telling to that of the dominant culture. Blue's storytelling is completely and uniquely his own. The African-American rap, his own internal rhythm, his personal history, his love for each of us is freely given. We, as listeners, become worshippers with Blue and fly with him on the wings of the beautiful butterfly.

Brother Blue reminds us that the story is holy. It captures, in words, the journey, the experience of life—truly a miracle, when we stop long enough to behold it as it flutters by.

Blue not only captures the essence of storytelling, he gives that energy to others. When Blue told stories to me on that day in Harvard, MA, my life was changed. I knew that I was in the presence of a person who was able to love completely, without inhibitions, unconditionally. It takes a great deal of faith to be able to do that.

Now, so many years later, I have stood in the storyteller's spot often enough to know that Blue was, indeed, telling to me. No doubt my face was like some of the open, spellbound faces I've seen before me when I tell stories. I pray that I can keep that faith in humanity, that love that

AHHHH !

Blue has, alive in me. Blue's telling inspires me to strive to be true to the story, the audience, and to myself, the teller.

Through the years, our paths have crossed several times. I had the privilege of spending time with Ruth Hill as a board member for the League for the Advancement of New England Storytelling (LANES). Blue and Ruth. Ruth and Blue, lovable and even more precious as their steps slow with increasing years, model love to me. I feel blessed to be in their presence.

Blue and Ruth have been running a weekly storytelling event in Cambridge for over ten years. Because I live a fair distance away and have family obligations, I'm not a regular. Nonetheless, I have been there enough to know that the atmosphere at this forum is unique. Blue finds beauty in all the tellers. His unconditional love for story has created a safe place for budding tellers, intellectuals, for accomplished professionals, for timid souls, for all of us who seek to explore our creativity, our humanity.

I teach storytelling to teachers. I want them to be aware that they are storytellers for young people, and want them to realize the power of storytelling. I always show the video of Blue telling "Miss Wunderlich" to the teachers. A few courageous ones have ventured into Cambridge to the storytelling. They come back inspired by Blue and comment on the still, deep calm of the woman next to him. One student observed, "she is like a beautiful still lake." Ahh, yes. If Ruth is the lake, then Blue is the splash! And the story must be the stone. We often think of the story as a butterfly while it's happening, but the image and experience of story are just as solid and lasting as stone.

Katie Green tells stories of truth, folk, and faerie. She believes that storytelling can change the world. She knows that it has changed her experience of it.

Ahhhh!

Out of the Blue:

An Ode to Brother Blue & Ruth

Marie Green

"I do not know whether I was then a man dreaming I was a butterfly, or whether I am now a butterfly dreaming I am a man." -Chuang Tse

His name is Hugh—it means intelligence
He is everyone's brother, akin to our souls
He travels outside his own experiences
He sways to the music others make
The fusion confusion jazz of life.

His aura is blue
The kind of blue when the sun hits the ocean
And bounces back a radiant illumination
That crystallizes the entire scene.

He speaks of love to the lovelorn
He lights, then flutters by
Like the elusive butterfly.

He is the butterfly, and we the chrysalis
Who hope to emerge with the same grace
As his delicate outstretched wings.

How fitting that his helpmate is Ruth
Whose name means friend of beauty.
Together they are an enchantment
The priest and priestess of the muse.

Out of the blue they trance waltz
Across our minds
Yet they embed lasting impressions.

Marie Green, originally from Florida, has been living in Massachusetts since 1994. Storyteller, Girl Scout leader, volunteer with the elderly and in food banks, she is the mother of three adult children.

Ahhhh!

A Song for Blue

Bonnie Greenberg

(to the tune of "Mame")

You send good vibes right into the air, Blue
You move with style and grace of Fred Astaire, Blue
You take a word and fashion it
Polish it with love and extra care.
We all shine just a little more
When we know your listening ears are there.

We're glad that you revived the old yarns, Blue
Now Storytelling has your sweet charms, Blue
You came, you saw, you made a point.
Nothing else will ever be the same.
For those inspired by your words
You can hear us always praise your name.

So when we make a tribute to you, Blue
It's from the "middle of the middle", it's "true Blue!"
Your popularity is a given both at home and round the earth
But those right here in Boston know
Tuesday, we can tell for all we're worth.

To you and Ruth who make it come true, Blue
We think you both belong in 'Who's Who', Blue
And in our hearts you'll always be
Loved for what you teach and what you do
You'll always lead the big parade
You've spearheaded the big crusade
You top the hit parade for us, BLUE.

Ahhhh!

Bonnie Greenberg's compelling storytelling is enjoyed both here and abroad. Her recordings have earned Parents' Choice, NAPPA Gold, and Storytelling World Winners' Awards. She chairs the National Jewish Storytelling Network and is featured in *120 Contemporary Storytellers: A Biographical Directory.*

Watercolor by: Ann Hoban

Ahhhh!

Blue's Oral History

Ronald Grele

Alessandro Portelli once wrote that to tell a story is to take arms against the threat of time. Such thoughts come to mind when one is called upon to tell a story about Brother Blue. I can't remember the exact time I first met Blue, but how unimportant such dating seems, because I can remember so vividly the context and the scene—the set and the setting, as we used to say. Like all mythic characters, a placement in time, as historians think of it, is probably one of the least important parts of the story. Memory is not experienced as a narrative; it is the narrative of experience, as selective a story as needs and passions dictate.

It was a meeting of the Oral History Association. I had known Ruth Hill for many years. She was a presence within the organization; her work well known, her personality clear. There was some sort of a presentation; the room was crowded, the questioning intense, as those things go, and then there was a voice—and what a voice. I remember turning and seeing someone dressed in blue. Were there butterflies on his shirt? I'm pretty sure there were. It was this wonderful black man telling us how excited he was to be among us because we were bearers of a mission. We were collectors of stories, preservers of the memories of the clan, and there could be no higher calling. It was kind of cathartic as the words rolled over us in wave after wave of exhortation and exhilaration. Such moments, because they redefine what an event is, are at the same time stunning and ambiguous. Stunning because they open doors to a redefinition. Ambiguous because you are not so sure you want to go through those doors, unsure as to the horizon that awaits outside.

Since that time, Brother Blue has become institutionalized within the world of oral history. At meetings, at conferences, in private conversation, in all manner of public forums he delivers the same message but always with a new twist, a poetry, and a new gentleness. We are en-

Ahhhh!

134

trusted with stories, we have a mission to preserve and respect those stories, we are cultural workers. It is a message that we have to hear again and again, because it is not the story we tell ourselves about ourselves. That story is that we are analysts, we are problem solvers, we are critics. We are, sometimes we tell ourselves, scientists of the subjective—without respect for story? Does the subjective live without stories? Is there not a pied beauty about what it is we do, and is not that beauty far more complicated and fraught with responsibility than we would like to admit? In a very deep way Blue returns us to those considerations that we tend to forget.

I suppose all historians must, from time to time, be brought back to what is the basis of their work. Traditional historians must love to grovel among old manuscripts that tell of the idiosyncratic lives of people who are not like themselves. Quantitative historians must immerse themselves in the world of measurement and take joy in the elegance of numbers. Oral historians must return to the world of sound and story. The voice is our vocation. It is our calling. It is this sense of the possibilities of story that Brother Blue sets before us. It is an honor to thank him for his belief in us.

Ronald J. Grele is the former director for the Columbia University Oral History office. He is past President of the Oral History Association and author of *Envelopes of Sound: The Art of Oral History.*

Ahhhh!

Toes

Anne Hallward

I first met Brother Blue because of my toes. I was a college freshman at Harvard, and it was springtime. I was sitting in the back of the lecture hall during Harvey Cox's class on Liberation Theory. It was beginning to get warm outside, so I kicked off my summer sandals and wiggled my toes for pleasure as Harvey talked passionately about movements for change in Latin America. A few minutes after the lecture started, this funny-looking guy comes in and sits down next to me. He was wearing all blue, with a weather-beaten beret, and he was covered in butterfly pins. I took note, but stayed focused on the lecture. When class was over, Blue introduced himself to me, and made up a whole story/song about my toes. He was so soulful about my toes, it made quite an impression!

After that, whenever I ran into Blue, we would talk. I learned about his street ministry, about telling stories in the prisons, about making oneself a fool for love. I started to seek him out, to watch him tell stories which always touched my soul. He spoke about racism, loving his teacher, about his brother Tommy. The story that touched my heart was about Tommy, about his brother who could only ask one question, "Do you love me?" And Blue, who travels the streets, looking in people's eyes to find his lost brother Tommy there. Blue always got me to stop, to say, AAAAAHHHHH, this is it, this is the only moment we have, and to look right into his eyes and rest there for a moment.

One day I heard that Blue was sick and in the hospital. I made him a blue teddy bear and went to visit him. I think I surprised him, this young woman with the toes who brought him a bear. We hardly knew each other then, but it sealed a connection between us. I met Ruth at the hospital, and then I understood that it was really a two-person

Ahhhh!

operation, this pouring out of love to any who would receive it. I always look for them now in the Square when I walk through. Brother Blue is a prophet, who reminds me that, no matter how big our differences, love is all that really matters.

With love from the lady with the toes,

Anne

Anne Hallward attended Harvard Medical School and upon graduation became a physician.

Blue performing in Harvard Square

Ahhhh!

Coyote in Ribbons
Bill Harley

I heard about Blue before I saw him. It was winter and I was at a little college in central New York. My roommate came back to the room one night and said, "I saw this guy, and you wouldn't believe it. He was all dressed in…" For the next half hour, he pranced around the room, trying to explain what it was that Blue did. Of course, he failed. I was concerned for my roommate's sanity. Who could be Blue, but Blue?

I finally saw Blue two years later and knew he was the guy my roommate had been talking about. He was in Harvard Square doing his thing. A dozen people stood around watching, amazed, perplexed, concerned, enchanted. He appeared, did his work, and disappeared. Blue works below the radar most of the time, and surfaces when you need him.

Blue is the perfect fool for God. Coyote in ribbons. The Indigo Nasruddin. Sometimes I cannot hear what he is saying, and sometimes I can. It has more to do with where I am than where he is. Fools are fools, regardless of the surroundings. His stories can be taken in two ways, or three ways, or no ways at all. His words are double-edged, meaning more than one thing, like any good story. Blue is not a Pharisee. More than any teller, he is a reflection of your mental state. And that makes him look like a loose cannon, because our minds are untrained. What will he do this time? Here's one little story.

About ten years ago at a storytelling conference, Blue was on a panel with four other people in a workshop entitled "Storytelling and the Religious Message," or something like that. The workshop was 75 minutes long. Each panelist was supposed to talk for about eight minutes, followed by a general discussion. The first panelist sat at his place and talked for ten minutes. That was okay; there was plenty of time left. The next panelist stood up and launched into a Baal Shem Tov story. I was sitting in the audience and looked around. Those who knew what we were in for squirmed in their seats. I, personally, had never heard a

Ahhhh!

Baal Shem Tov story shorter than six hours. I think it is written in some Jewish book of wisdom that no Baal Shem Tov story can be shorter than three hours. Sure enough, the guy went on and on and on. It was an interesting story, if you could overlook the situation, and he did a good job to finish it and leave five minutes in the workshop for everybody else. The other panelists were climbing out of their skins, snapping their pencils, hyperventilating with crossed eyes, since their prepared remarks had just gone in time's wastebasket. The audience squirmed, uncomfortable with the dynamic on the panel. And not only that, we were all thinking, Blue is next. Who knows what he'll do? He could talk for hours. We might never go home.

Blue rose from his seat. We drew in our breaths. He shook his bells.

He shook his head, a no that meant yes. He walked back and forth across the room, then twirled before the dispenser of the Bal Shem Tov story, pointing at him with fate's finger. "That," he sang, "was beautiful." We smiled. "That," Blue crooned, "was a miracle." The panelists stared at Blue. "When you told that story," Blue said, folding his hands in prayer, "time stood still." The storyteller smiled, hesitantly, and nodded, hoping he understood Blue.

"*Tme*," Blue shouted in his signature rasp, *Meant nothing to you!*"

There was a moment of silence. What did he mean? Did he mean what we thought he meant? Who else would have said that? We waited for further clarification. But it's not the fool's job to answer, only to ask. "That," Blue said, in benediction, "*Was a story!*" He shook his head again, as if to say "That's bad," which means "good." He sat down.

We stared at each other, trying to figure out where we were, who we were, what we were doing there together. The workshop ended.

Bill Harley is a storyteller, songwriter, NPR commentator, author, and jack of all trades who works primarily with children and families. He was was inducted into the National Storytelling Network's Circle of Excellence in 2001.

Ahhhh!

The Gift of Blue and Ruth

Ed Harris

Some folks have the gift. They live lives that constantly remind us how fortunate we are to be alive, how glorious a wonder it is to have air to breathe, trees to hug, flowers to smell, animals to care for and marvel at, people to love.

Blue and Ruth are two of these too few folk. Twenty years ago we met and for twenty years whenever I think of them or get a postcard from them, my spirits are lifted and I become a better person; reminded once again that our only reason to be here is to share the love that God has offered us.

Thank you, Ruth. Thank you, Blue, for constantly making this temporal voyage more meaningful, more joyful and true.

Ed Harris has been a theater and film actor for the past twenty-four years. He has received an Obie award, a Tony nomination, LA Critics Circle Awards and three Academy Award nominations for his work. Recently he directed his first feature film, "Pollock." He played King Billy opposite Brother Blue's Merlin, in George Romero's "Knightriders" in 1980.

Ahhhh !

A Musical Reminiscence of Blue

[Rev.] Mark Harvey

Brother Blue and I have known each other for a good thirty years and have shared many wonderful artistic experiences. It's been a privilege to have him call me a friend and co-worker in the fields of creative expression and spiritual nurture. For Blue is really a modern incarnation of an archetypal healer, jester, pilgrim and much more all rolled into one—in other words, a holy man whose temple is the streetcorner and whose calling is to bring much needed refreshment to our imaginations and our collective soul.

I first met Brother Blue while playing an improvisational jazz set as part of the first All Night Concert sponsored by the Jazz Coalition in July of 1970. In the Old West Church sanctuary, only two candles provided illumination and my quartet was playing with eyes shut and ears open. All of a sudden, I sensed a presence, opened my eyes, and saw this wraithlike figure whirling about the platform and altar area. In those days, when such an occurrence took place, you went with the flow and didn't question it—and of course it turned out to be Blue interpreting our wild sounds in expressive gesture and movement.

Ever after, we were brothers in arts, so to speak. He toured frequently with my quartet, in New England and even to New York to Saint Peter's ("the Jazz") Church, where we again shared a vigil on that church's All Night Soul. By 7:00 AM , we were exhausted and taking cat naps in the pews, but when a local NYC TV crew arrived, up sprang Blue and roused the rest of us to join him for a quick shot on Manhattan television.

Some of the most satisfying experiences had to be the times I accompanied Brother Blue with his storytelling, especially late night sign-offs on WBUR, back when they appreciated music and fostered regional artistic happenings. I think it was the story of Miss Wunderlich and the story of a boy who blew a trumpet from his soul that were the best interpreta-

AHHHH!

tions we did, there and in many churches and other venues.

At Emmanuel Church on Newbury street in Boston, we shared in an exciting and intense arts ministry, alongside of the famed Emmanuel Music, the Northeast Kingdom Puppet Theater, and many other fine artists. When my Jazz Celebrations concert series presented the great Mary Lou Williams in her Jazz Mass with the choir of the Elma Lewis Center for African American Artists, there was Blue dancing up a storm on the high altar and sanctifying the words and music for both body and soul.

We don't work together so much anymore, although we shared a John Coltrane Memorial Concert a few years back, and Blue gave a lovely impromptu closing to the Ellington Tribute my Aardvark Jazz Orchestra presented in April of 1999. But every time we see each other on the T or on the street, he reminds me of his grand project to tell the *entire* Bible in stories with music—maybe we'll get around to it someday. Until then, I wish Blue—and of course, Ruth, too—only the very best of wishes and hopes and dreams. It's been great, Blue—so keep on keepin' on, brother.

Mark Harvey is an ordained minster and leads and plays trumpet in the Aardvark Jazz Orchestra. They are now celebrating their 30th season.

Blue as Merlin in George Romero's "Knightriders" in 1980.

Ahhhh!

Blue Time

Linda Havel

Like spirits, words unspoken
hang in the air
and wait.

In hallowed story-space
tears flow.
Life's scrapes and bruises
become tellable
and the children we were
fling exuberant hearts
into that circle of love.
Show Blue cruelty, he sees
love's impending comfort
then flutter flies with a 'ding'
of Ruth's bell.

Like the last prayer in the world,
but you should hear the response...
God's.

Linda Havel is working on the integration of her roles as story-grandmother, facilitator and poet. Her current projects include a Massachusetts Cultural Council Elder Arts Initiative with the local Council on the Aging program "Life Stories on the Move."

Ahhhh!

A Carrier of Stories

Seamus Heaney

Ruth Hill and Brother Blue have been good presences in Cambridge for years. In the environs of Harvard, where the motto could be "Veritas Rule OK," their particular kind of verity has been a great enhancement. True to themselves, true to their traditions, true to their generous impulse, they have borne witness to all kinds of good possibilities in the imaginative and the social life. As a tribute to their commitment to the ancient arts of the storyteller, the ballad-singer, and the street musician, I offer the following brief translations—the first an extract from my translation of the Old English poem, *Beowulf,* and the second my version of a famous lyric by the nineteenth century Irish language poet, Anthony Raftery.

> There was singing and excitement: an old reciter,
> a carrier of stories, recalled the early days.
> At times some hero made the timbered harp
> tremble with sweetness, or related true
> and tragic happenings; at times the king
> gave a proper turn to some fantastic tale,
> or a battle-scarred veteran, bowed with age,
> would begin to remember the martial deeds
> of his youth and prime and be overcome
> as the past welled up in his wintry heart.

Beowulf, lines 2105–2114

Ahhhh!

I Am Raftery

I am Raftery the poet,
Full of hope and love,
My eyes without eyesight,
My spirit untroubled.

Tramping west
By the light of my heart,
Worn down, worn out
To the end of the road.

Take a look at me now,
My back to a wall,
Playing the music
To empty pockets.

Mise Raiftearaí an file,
Lán dócha's grá,
Le súile gan solas,
Le ciúnas gan crá
Féach anois mé
Is mo chúl le balla
Ag seimn ceoil
Do phócaí folamh.

Seamus Heaney is an award winning author who divides his time between teaching at Harvard and living in Ireland. In recent years, he has been the recipient of several honorary degrees; he is a member of Aosdana, the Irish academy of artists and writers, and a Foreign Member of The American Academy of Arts and Letters. In 1996, subsequent to his winning the Nobel Prize in Literature in 1995, he was made a Commandeur de L'Ordre des Arts et Lettres by the French Ministry of Culture. His latest books include: *The Redress of Poetry* (1995), and *Beowulf: A New Verse Translation* (2000).

Ahhhh !

The Parable of Two Frogs

Dudley Herschbach

I have had the privilege and joy of encountering Brother Blue and Ruth many times over the past 20 years or so. Always, I come away grateful for their charming humor, steadfast dedication, and radiant humanity.

Our very first meeting came at a Harvard colloquium on the teaching of writing, held in the Science Center. The final speaker was the notorious behavioral psychologist, B.F. Skinner. True to his convictions, Skinner prescribed a "sure-fire" way to produce a book every three years, displaying his own bibliography as evidence of its efficacy. His prescription was to go every day to the same place at the same time, sit down at the typewriter, turn on a red light, and write for two hours. This would on average yield 100 polished words each session. In the question period, Brother Blue was the first to raise his hand. In his resonant baritone voice, he asked how a two-hour writing regimen could be compatible with family life. Skinner replied that it was easy: he wrote from 5 to 7 AM.

In tribute to Brother Blue, I offer a favorite little parable, one I've often told to high school students and college freshmen. I first heard it from Emilio Segre, an eminent physicist at Berkeley, who said he got it from a Quaker lady in Philadelphia. For the version given here, Gertrude Elion, a distinguished chemist, provided a trenchant improvement that Ruth will surely endorse.

The Parable of Two Frogs

Two young frogs were frolicking in a garden when they spied a curious, gleaming object. They jumped right in and found themselves in a pail of milk. For them it was wonderfully novel, far more exciting than a puddle of water. For quite a while they enjoyed splashing around. But

Ahhhh!

146

then they began to feel tired and looked about for some solid perch on which they could rest. Much to their dismay, they discovered that there was no such perch. They became panicky and tried desperately to jump out of the pail, but the walls were too high and too slick. They fell back again and again.

At last one of the frogs gave up; it decided there was clearly no hope, collapsed, and drowned. The other frog, no less terrified but much more stubborn, continued jumping. Over and over, that frog leapt up and fell back. Finally, the second frog was exhausted and resigned to sinking into the milk.

But then the frog suddenly felt something solid under its feet. A little island of butter was forming. Buoyed by a surge of hope and adrenaline, the frog managed a few more jumps, and in doing so churned a chunk of butter big enough to provide a resting place. It later served as a launching pad that allowed the frog to spring out of the pail and hop away, weary but wiser.

Gertrude Elion pointed out that "the second frog must have been female!"

In kindred fashion, Brother Blue and Ruth have long labored to stir in us wonder, wisdom, and love by a gentle but unwavering wind from butterfly wings.

Note: The tale of two frogs is told (in somewhat different words) by Emilio Segre in his autobiography, A Mind Always in Motion *(University of California Press, Berkeley, 1993), p. 271. He has also published it (in nearly the same words) in an article, "Changes in the Gardens of Science, Wrought by Women," Annals of the New York Academy of Sciences, Vol. 869, 66-74 (1999).*

Dudley Herschbach, Ph.D., has pursued scientific research and teaching for nearly fifty years, chiefly at Harvard University, where he received his Ph.D. His research on the molecular dynamics of chemical reactions was awarded the Nobel Prize in 1986. He has taught many subjects, in both undergraduate and graduate courses, including general chemistry for freshmen—for the past two decades his most challenging assignment. He is also engaged in several efforts to improve K-16 science education and public understanding of science.

Aнннн!

An Angel of Poetry and Hipdom
Joan Hill

I first met Brother Blue on a bus. About halfway through my life I was attending summer classes at the Berklee School of Music in Boston, and was on my way over to Cambridge to the Sunday Brunch at Ryle's, where my son was playing the bass. I was at a crossroads in my life, having (more or less) completed the "housewife" segment, with six children to show for it and twenty-eight years of married life behind me. As I stepped up to the bus, the Angel of Poetry and Hippdom appeared to me! From way down at the other end of the bus came this deep, resonant voice clothed in blue jeans, matching shirt and hat and covered with butterflies and ribbons. He was surrounded by little children holding balloons and hanging on to his every word—as was I!

Many thoughts crossed my mind as we crossed the bridge over the Charles River. Nothing but empty seats between the bus driver and I, at one end of the bus, and Brother Blue with his entourage at the other end—me thought, "Boston is the place for me!" Having come from a tiny, culturally deprived, dry, lonely and (seemingly) soul-forsaken place in Northern California to the "hub of the universe" to expand my horizens and break out of the molds of classical music to the freedom of jazz expression, I was already overwhelmed by "culture shock." And then, suddenly, before my very eyes materializes what I had been seeking inside my own self!

When we reached our destination in Cambridge, I waited until he, and the lady he was with, got off the bus and I introduced myself. Turned out we all had the same name (Hill)! I found out he was a real person; not just a figment of my imagination, and actually had a storytelling class at Harvard Divinity School. He was accompanied by his mate, a fellow angel, Ruth, who "took care of business" while he was on his poetic excursions.

Ever after that I was a "believer" in Boston and returned year after year

Ahhhh !

to learn more and more about music and follow Brother Blue wherever I could find him. During those years, he used to close the WBUR broadcasting day with his stories. I have many of them on tape, as I made it my business to stay awake until 2:00 A.M. to collect as many as I could to take home with me when summer session was over. I remember one time I went to Emmanuel Church to see and hear him, and I was the only audience! Ruth told me the performance had not been very well publicized, so not very many people knew about it, but he went ahead and did his show and I felt *very special* and doubly blessed, because not only did I get to listen to his stories that night, but also had a chance to visit with them and get to know them.

Eventually I moved to Boston, and we continued and deepened our friendship, largely due to our mutual love for another of Boston's legends, Leon Collins. When Leon left the planet in 1985, Brother Blue delivered his eulogy, for which I will be eternally grateful—but that is yet another story!

Although I finished the "Boston" segment of my life in 1993 and am now living in California again, Brother Blue and Ruth are first on my list to contact when I go back to visit. They are with me forever.

ANOTHER STORY

When I moved to Boston in 1980, I met another wonderful storyteller. This one told stories with his feet! I'm talking about Leon Collins. I was blessed to have met him and become his piano accompanist for nearly five years, before he left the planet. Soon after I met him, I discovered he didn't know Brother Blue! How could this be? Two brother birds from the same tree, who didn't know each other? I quickly rectified that. We were planning a party-jam-session at the Piano Factory, where I lived and Leon had his dance studio, so I called Blue and Ruth to come meet a soul-mate they had never met before. It was, of course, instant friendship and mutual admiration. When Leon became weak from cancer, which eventually crowded him out of his body, Brother Blue and Ruth came to visit us in our apartment in Brighton and brightened our lives for awhile, and when Leon left, Brother Blue delivered the eulogy. Among many inspirational things he said was, "when I first saw Leon dancing to Joan's music..."—This gave me a whole new view of what our relationship was about. I had always

Ahhhh!

thought I was "accompanying" Leon's dancing! He also painted a most beautiful visual picture with his words, "Everywhere he touched his toes to the earth a rose rose." He described him as "God, wrapped in brown." He said the light of the universe split up into stars, and one came down to Earth to periodically listen to and realize once again what geniuses those men are.

Even now, when I see Brother Blue at Harvard Square telling his stories, as soon as he sees me he starts tap-dancing!

Joan Armstrong Hill, musician/dancer/writer moved to Boston in 1980 to study jazz piano with Charlie Banacos. She learned to tap-dance from the legendary Leon Collins and invented a system of tap notation by which she documented his choreography. Her books are in the New York Public Library Dance Collection and in the Berklee College of Music. She lives in Berkeley, California, where she continues to play, sing, dance, teach and write.

Photo: Edward Lewis

Photo of Blue performing from Times-Georgian, Carrollton, GA

Ahhhh!

In Metamorphosis...

Lynda A. Hill

"They'll never know who I am," he mourned as they walked on the lawn towards the golf course where he and his brother held the jobs that would see them through college. The Depression era was a harsh time on the lives and spirits of men and women throughout America, but never more so than on the countless number of its Black citizens like Hugh Hill and his family.

For them, the Depression was more acutely depressing for far deeper-rooted reasons than the fight for economic survival. Theirs included the fight for racial equality and more personally, human identity. The crux of this fight was most eloquently and succinctly identified by Hugh Hill's sad refrain to his older brother, "George, the thing that always bothers me is that they'll never know who I am. Just as soon as they see me, they block me out—they'll never know who I am." The battle lines were drawn, and Destiny enfolded Hugh in her sheltering cocoon to weave about him her gossamer threads of purpose.

Fate began to fill his soul with the light of life and his heart with creative expression while, with bated breath, time awaited his emergence when Hugh Hill would rise and meet his destiny—Brother Blue.

Before Brother Blue, as he is most popularly known, he was Hugh Hill, my uncle. Many are the stories about him that my father, his older brother, George, would tell us, my brother and me, as we grew. Stories that, even now, continue to inspire me to reach deeply within my soul for the guts to live up to my own God-given gift of expression and creativity and set free the writer within me. My Uncle Hugh, even before his predestined metamorphosis into Brother Blue, gave me this gift. He gave me the gift of creative freedom when, as a child of six years old, he proclaimed to my mother and father that I was a free spirit, a creative spirit and that it was all right, that it was beautiful.

Ahhhh!

My Uncle Hugh's sensitivity to God, to man, and to life enables him to see and feel beyond the outer accoutrements of the body and into the heart of the true life within. He saw into the heart of me. I was too young to know then how much my writing would become my life's blood and the very nectar for my soul. The stories of his personal struggles growing up as well as his influences in my life, even now remain a source of encouragement and inspiration to me.

To this day, my father recalls that Uncle Hugh (or Brother Blue, as you know him) suffered a speech impediment that was his bane—he stuttered.

During the 1920's and 30's, speech therapy was not available and whatever assistance there might have been was generally well out of reach, and most particularly to, America's black citizenry. His father, George E. Hill, Sr., was a staunch believer in education and the proper use of English grammar. He intended his children to be well educated and well spoken, which intentions had prompted his move into the Italian-American community. The quality of education to be found there far exceeded that of the black communities. In their school days, when racial prejudice was so prevalent in their community, Uncle Hugh and his brothers gave literal meaning to fighting for an education. They had to physically fight their way to school and back home until, at last, their perseverance and academic excellence earned them the respect of their peers. Fortunately, Uncle Hugh's athletic bent gave him a good advantage. But his road toward living up to his father's expectations that his sons be well spoken was blocked by the major obstacle his stutter imposed. Then one day, as fate would have it, his father told him the story of how Demosthenes had developed his orator's voice and fluid speech by putting pebbles in his mouth as he practiced speaking. After his father told him that story, a very determined Hugh went down to the sea shore, put pebbles in his mouth and overcame his stuttering. He played Emperor Jones in their school play.

This demonstration of my Uncle's indomitable spirit made a tremendous impact on me. It became the well from which sprang a lot of my own determination and courage to try.

My father told us other stories, such as how Uncle Hugh, in his desire to please his father, had taken some of his hard-earned money caddying at the golf course to buy a two-volume set of dictionaries and then proceeded to memorize their contents from A to Z. I finally understood how my uncle's vocabulary came to be so extensive and awesome. Need-

AHHHH!

less to say, I was dumbfounded and extremely impressed. My brother and I took to breaking out the dictionary when he spoke. Uncle Hugh, with his sparkling and infectious laugh when speaking in his oh-so-mellow voice, epitomized my father's sentiments about the beauty of the English language and the power of words. I don't know about my brother, but I remained enthralled. He would also speak with such expressive drama that he made the idea of learning new words fun and adventuresome—if only to be just like him. He reminded me of the Pied Piper. I ate it up and reading became my joy.

There were times, however, when as a child my uncle's immense vocabulary and wondrously all-encompassing expressions would overwhelm me; then I would look to my Aunt Ruth, whose steady and gentle quietude would solidify me and I would be able to follow my uncle through his creative journeys. Little did I know then the reality that was in metamorphosis.

My uncle's ability to express himself so profoundly had served him well. My father related to us a story of how, while serving in the Navy during World War II, Uncle Hugh had fashioned his own post-war direction. The end of the war meant that many soldiers would return to the States only to become nomads of change, jobless and without direction. Uncle Hugh was stationed in Okinawa at the time. He had written a letter seeking admittance into Harvard University that was so beautiful that upon his return, Harvard accepted him, sight unseen. He graduated *cum laude*.

These stories that my father shared with us, along with the times he and Aunt Ruth spent with us, increased my admiration for him and my appreciation not only for the might of words but also the power of the pen.

I grew up in the audience of Uncle Hugh's plays and creative works in progress. I remember how I would sit, transfixed, as the prose of his plays and writings would cascade from his mouth while his body danced to an eclectic style of free rhythm that was contemporary-hip in a beatnik groove laced with soulful blues and flashes of jazz. How I wanted to be able to write like he did and deliver my words with the passion, art and evocative expression that he did. He totally participated in them. The music of his stories would draw me into his world.

Sometimes when his cascading images became more kaleidoscopic, my aunt would quietly rein in his high flying spirit and gently guide his flight back closer to earth. I remember how he would chuckle and ask her, "was I getting too far out there?" and my very serenely level-headed

Ahhhh!

Aunt Ruth would answer simply, "yes, Hugh." Uncle Hugh would laugh his sparkling laugh and turn to me, snapping his fingers in beatnik beat and motion and in a conspiratorial aside he would confide that Aunt Ruth was the captain that kept his ship on course. She would not let him fly-y-y-ah-ah too hi-i-i-gh-ah. Then he'd turn to her and ask, "Isn't that right Ruth?" She would shake her head in silent amusement and answer him, "Yes, Hugh." He was right. She kept him centered. They were and still are an unbeatable team—best friends, man and wife, artist and artist/agent, the creative and the practical. They did, and still do, everything together, fully appreciative of the contributions that each gives into their marriage, into his storytelling platform and her historical podium and into each other as individuals and as a team. He always acknowledges and praises how Aunt Ruth's quiet spirit, gentle hand and firm enjoinment, when necessary, enables him to "fly high." Their closeness, their camaraderie, and their togetherness as a married couple and as an artistic team is lodged in my mind and heart as an example of what I would love to enjoy in a personal relationship. But alas, their kind of magic is a rare miracle that neither destiny nor fate bestows easily.

Growing up, I remember Uncle Hugh was always occupied with creating new stories and one-act plays or refining existing ones. But most of all, I remember that no matter how busy he was, he would always take time to read my writings—my verses. He had told my father and mother that I was a free and creative spirit and to let me express it, let me let it out. How I loved him for that, and Aunt Ruth for her softly spoken agreement. For me and to me, everything became right in my world. Uncle Hugh gave me a gift almost as precious as life itself. He gave me the gift of creative freedom, the third dimension of my soul, and encouraged me to use it. He let me know that it was all right to hear music or verses and stories in my mind, but to write them down when I did. Let them out. So I did. I would save them up so that when next they came to visit, I could share my writings with them. I knew he would like them or help me make them better. It still amazes me how he just knew how very important my writings, these verses of a small child were—at least to me, the small child.

I'd wait for him and Aunt Ruth to visit and finally, they'd come. He and Aunt Ruth would sweep in on wings of discovery and story and stir up the sleeping, dormant leaves of routine and order and uncover a sparkling, effervescent world of light, fantasy and wonder. He'd be exuberantly alive—full of life—and glad of it. I would eat up his stories and drink in his laughter and joy. His presence and influence satisfied

Ahhhh!

the deep creative hunger in my soul. I would eagerly whip out my "masterpieces" to show him and he would laud my efforts and show such delight in my writing them. He encouraged me to continue—to never stop writing because "words were the expression of the soul." To this day I write. I write what is in my mind, my heart and my soul in story, song, and prose and during his last visit a couple of years ago, in my adulthood we enjoyed exchanging our stories, poetry and even 'raps' together (my Uncle Hugh is so cool. He stays up with the times.)

My parents gave my body, heart, and mind life when they gave me their loving world, but my Uncle Hugh—Uncle Blue, your Brother Blue—gave my spirit life when he gave me the gift of his literary world.

I look back through adult eyes and can see how fate, by the conditions of life, time, and events both good and bad, had purposefully honed my Uncle Hugh. Through his God-given gift for storytelling, he draws people of all races, cultures and ages under his fantastical wings where they can, free of prejudices, come together and, if only for that one-single-space in time, just be human. In the thrall of his stories, we are all equal, we are all the same, we are all as children. His stories both urge and inspire you to learn who you are, come out of your shell and be that person you are meant to be. From the caterpillar, metamorphosed, emerges the butterfly to take wing in wondrous flight, alive and free, and to share its natural beauty as a miraculous testament of personal growth and evolvement, as destiny would have it do. In metamorphosis, Fate took Hugh's hand. When time and change merged, Brother Blue emerged from his cocoon. He, like the butterfly, spreads his wings of creative expression and literary flight to share the natural beauty, faith, and message of his soul that you, too, can rise and meet your destiny. Thus Hugh Hill, the man, embraced his destiny, Brother Blue. But, Brother Blue was never destined to be God's fool—as he may describe himself—rather God's troubadour fulfilling his ministry through soul-stirring story.

Once he cried, "they'll never know who I am," but by virtue of his courage, his indomitable spirit, his selfless gifts of encouragement and inspiration, whether in person or through his stories, he makes himself known. He is a superbly intelligent, wonderfully creative, dynamic, sensitive, and gentle man—a living testimony to the very ethos of humanity, respect, honor, dignity, and love. Brother Blue is a man among men.

Lynda Hill is Brother Blue's niece. She writes poetry and is currently going back to school.

Ahhhh!

Point of Contact

Alan Hoban

Could not see him, but he was a presence. Never laid an eye on him. Saw a picture on a box. Looked strange, felt phony. Hippy-Dippy. Any mention of his name led to an argument. Ugly argument. How could I criticize what I had not seen. Simple answer. Kept to self.

Did see him, unplanned. He and his wife are framed in the door jamb of a semi-private hospital room. They move closer. They bring an aura of healing power. Standing next to the injured one, I move toward them and past them. I leave the injured one behind, whose response to their presence is immediate and startling. Like all seriously injured, the veneer of learned behavior and other symbols and marks of socialization are absent. An innocent look followed by a noticeable quickening of spirit and alert presence to what is happening now. Swap places with them at the door jamb. Two figures move slowly behind a fabric curtain extended around the hospital bed, machines, wires and tubes. Quiet sounds emanate. Caring, prayer, what? One stays, one approaches. Scans me for something. Shock, peace, what? As this goes on, energy, spirit, some feeling (you label it) fills this place.

Want to see him. He looks like the man on the cassette box. Beret, shirt, shoes are all blue. Butterflies are attached everywhere. Steady, high cheek boned gaze. Soft reassuring words. Search for contact, recognition, connection. Jazz flows, music flows, souls flow. A Blue man, but not a named man is he, who chooses direct contact and interaction with the injured.

Offerings are everywhere in this space and are left behind. The color of healing is Blue.

Alan Hoban's professional life involves providing housing for low and middle income families. His spirit life involves collecting the stories of people he meets all over the country.

Ahhhh!

The Voice, the Earth, the Spirits, the Blues

Ann Foley Hoban

In the beginning was the *voice*. It was a velvet mahogany voice emanating from the radio in twilight. It was 1981. My unborn daughter and I would finally begin to relax and settle for the evening when we heard Brother Blue croon, "Dear Ones..." We listened to the other tellers on WGBH FM's *The Spider's Web*; their stories were wonderful too. But it was Brother Blue's voice, *his* stories, that promised safety and hope, warmth and love, forever and ever, for me and my unborn child.

In October, 1995, Susan Lenoe, a talented actress and beautiful friend, persuaded me, finally, to attend one of her Storytelling "things" at the Bookcellar Cafe in Porter Square, Cambridge. I could resist no longer. It was her birthday, *and* she was the Feature! My girls had swim practice in Cambridge anyway, so "why not?" I thought, not realizing my life was about to change forever. For who should I see there but, the *voice* of *The Spider's Web*, from so long ago, in the *now*, and embodied in blue: blue beret, blue shirt, blue vest, slacks, and shoes. Yes, there he was, and there was Ruth, his wife, his ground, his Beatrice. And so many other interesting tellers of all ages, sizes, shapes and colors were gathered around them, telling their multiplicity of tales.

I was irrevocably, joyfully, captured by the Blues, Brother and Ruth, hook, line and sinker! Immediately my life began to revolve around those Tuesday night gatherings, so full of life, so full of color, texture, and stories. Even so, it wasn't until after a near-fatal accident in July, 1997, that I encountered the full impact of what the Blues were about. Brother Blue and Ruth were at Beth Israel within a day or two of the accident, returning again, and again, and again. They prayed; Ruth performed Reiki; Blue told stories and they both rallied the entire storytelling community. They surrounded me with an enormous, loving,

Ahhhh!

healing energy. The speed of my recovery baffled all the medical personnel involved.

I am convinced that Ruth Edmonds Hill, great-granddaughter of Reverend Samuel Harrison, Chaplain of the Massachusetts 54th Regiment of the Civil War, and Hugh Morgan Hill, grandson of a slave, son of a bricklayer, carry the power of the ancestors with them in every step they take, every prayer they pray, and every story they tell. Their erudition is incomparable, their soul life phenomenal. Ruth guides Blue's iridescent flight through the here and now. She is his steadfast beacon of clarity and good sense. Together, they are intrepid pioneers in the worlds of Story and Oral History. Blue and Ruth are of color, texture, magic, courage and dignity.

For Blue dares to exhort us to our highest spiritual potential; Ruth is his quiet and all-knowing accomplice. Blue challenges us. He is outrageous in his praise, in his unambiguous proclamation of the divinity inherent in the work of the Storyteller. For these reasons and many more I name them my mentors. Because of their example I believe if only we listen, with our ears of God to every story we hear as if it were the word of God, as Blue urges, we can, we shall, change the world.

Thank you Blue. Thank you Ruth.

A wife and mother of two young women, twenty and eighteen, Ann Hoban comes to storytelling from a backround in Theater and Art education. Discovering the story a child has to tell in his or her artwork was always her mission. Continuing this mission on a parallel track, Ann currently listens to the stories of her clients, women in crisis, helping them to craft new stories full of renewed personal power and possibility.

Photo: Keiko Morris

Ahhhh!

158

Brother Blue 1969:
Out the Window
Stephan (Esteban) H. Hornberger

For over thirty years—since 1968, I believe—Ruth and Hugh Hill have stood with Nancy (my wife) and myself as elder friends and spiritual guides. Most recently we have shared experiences in our mostly African-American West Philadelphia neighborhood.

In 1969 we shared a few moments of turbulence, as we jointly sought to learn from, as well as to teach, our more elderly colleagues some essential facts of life—Nancy and Ruth at Radcliffe's Schlesinger Library on the History of Women, myself and Hugh at Harvard's Divinity School. Harvard, then, as now, took more from its Somerville, Cambridge, and Boston neighbors than it gave to them. Ruth and Hugh knew this so well that they avoided words to state the facts—better to listen carefully, better to float like a butterfly. In Cambridge in the Spring of 1969 a couple of Students for a Democratic Society members at the Divinity School, myself included—there were only two of us—sought to infuse the spirit of Christ, as taught to us by brother Martin Luther King, Jr., into the non-violent occupation of University Hall in Harvard Yard.

Much to the consternation of the Fellows of Harvard College, our efforts were successful in drawing more students into the action. The Cambridge police were called, and the rest is history. Ruth and Hugh had not agreed with the Administration's clear belief that 'force is a necessary tool of education, better, even, than patience, dialogue and persuasion.' They chose, instead, to cheer on the strike, showing a special empathy with the strikers of Radcliffe and those of the Divinity School.

As a part of the follow-up to the strike, a Divinity School seminar on ecclesiastical politics and piety was broadened in scope to permit Hugh,

Ahhhh!

Ruth, and Nancy to have a role in the presentation of my seminar 'paper.' At the time, I was about to be (or already had been) expelled from Harvard by instruction of the Harvard fellows, only to be simultaneously re-admitted by the Divinity School faculty. The churchly seminar was held in an old building next to the Divinity School library. Hugh was to be my dancer-presenter. Hopping up with me on the seminar table at the appointed time, Hugh proceeded to present my case for the politics and piety of Jesus Christ. When the presentation was over, Hugh flew out the window (a 15 foot drop) into the waiting arms of Ruth and Nancy, leaving me to face the astonished instructor and fellow grad students, as well as the door, through which normal folks exit.

Photo: Jessa Piaia

Blue performing with Neon Grandma at Squawk Coffeehouse

Ahhhh!

Blue and Ruth

Ruth Hubbard

Brother Blue and Ruth
Ruth and Brother Blue
part of Cambridge   I cannot
remember before.

Ruth at the musty library,
musty museum library, full of
old journals and books, heavy tomes
in German, distilled wisdom
of centuries, guarded by pictures
of bearded old men who have
classified us and traced our descent.

Going to meet her,
day's work done, Blue
leaves the Divinity School,
crosses the lawn where
bronze rhinos stand watch.

Blue, Ruth, all of us,
danced on that lawn, exams over,
celebrating spring.

Blue, on top of
blizzard of '78 snow piled
high in Harvard Square
dancing barefoot, telling stories,
those few days when

Ahhhh !

the Square was
ours,   no cars.

Now and again, a postcard
from Leningrad, Nairobi, Rome:
"Thinking of you,
Love, Blue and Ruth"

Ruth and Blue, Blue and Ruth
each day a story, a celebration
together.

Ruth Hubbard and her family (George, Elijah and Deborah Wald) have been long-standing friends and admirers of Brother Blue and Ruth. The Wald-Hubbard family appreciate what Blue and Ruth stand for and have done both in the local community and around the world, and are proud to join in celebrating them.

Photo:Cole Bellamy

Ahhhh !

To Blue with Love

Gould Hulse

Caroline and I, both artists, live in our studio, a one hundred and fifty year old farmhouse on Staten Island, New York.

We met Brother Blue and Ruth while taking his course on storytelling at Omega in the eighties. From our side, it was love at first sight. So, of course, we had to invite them over to our home. (I sometimes feel it was a case of psychic bonding.)

In time, our home became a way station for many of their New York visits. Blue called it a "magical house" and I felt touched. Sitting around our dining room table while Blue did his take on Shakespeare, Ruth would bring out her stack of postcards and begin to fill them in, telling their friends throughout the world that they were here.

"Are you listening?" Blue would ask her if her pen hesitated over a thought. She is his most important audience, and why not? She is the closest to him and also an archivist in the most classic sense, who knows juicy material when she hears it. We have an extensive collection of their postcards tracing their travels through time and America.

It was a number of years before Blue and I discovered we had other things in common. We're veterans of World War II when the army was still segregated. We both served time on New Guinea. We both went overseas with black companies—Blue as a lieutenant in the Corps of Engineers, I as a white artillery officer with a black company of my own, one of the most enlightening periods of my life.

One weekend during a New York stay, I suggested we visit the New Guinea Collection of sculpture at the Metropolitan Museum of Art. We found on arrival that that particular section had been closed due to a shortage of guards.

Here was my chance to use the power of Blue's name. Storming down to the front desk, I informed them that they had the honor of playing

Ahhhh!

host to the internationally known Dr. Hugh Morgan Hill of Harvard, more widely known as Brother Blue, and this was a special trip to study the storytelling traditions of New Guinea as expressed in their totem sculptures.

The whole scene changed. An apologetic young man got on the phone. A guard was summoned. Blue in his beret, butterflies and all, Ruth, Caroline and myself, in our mufti, were given a private view of the storytellers of New Guinea, watched over by an attentive museum guard who followed Blue's every word with rapt attention, not typical of guards. After all, Blue was telling a story.

After five years in the army in World War II , Gould Hulse pursued the fragile life of an artist in 1945, first as a book and magazine illustrator, then as an educator and director of The Newark School of Fine and Industrial Art. He is an architectural and furniture designer in the process of completing a forty year project for publication.

Photo: Keiko Morris

Ahhhh !

Brother Blue and Ruth Too!

Geofftree Hurley

Allow me to tell you how I feel about Brother Blue:

Please come to a bright sunny spring day in the fully blooming Public Gardens, surrounded by a group of adoring children captured in awe by the wonderful butterfly of love. Given in the form of words, words spoken from a tender heart, wearing black skin and rainbow butterflies, with a kind smile and a story. One thing is for certain: if you ever met Blue, you will never forget Blue.

Having said that and knowing it is the truth, how can I say anything more without mentioning Ruth. Blue's guiding light makes sure that he eats and goes home to sleep at night! Otherwise the rose would have frozen in the snows a long time ago.

"Love is the only forever thing," one day I heard Blue sing. This is how I want to be, in the forever ring of love, with you and you and of course dear dear dear Brother Blue and Ruth too!

Geofftree Hurley is a landscaper in Plainfield VT. He grew up in the Boston Area and met Blue by chance.

Ahhhh !

Town Meeting on the Year 2000
Gus Jaccaci

We are living in a time when all humanity is transforming from a world powered by light and electricity to a world powered by soul and love. On the leading edge of this global renaissance there are soulful heroes of the human spirit like Mother Theresa, Nelson Mandela, Desmond Tutu, and the Dalai Lama. They are world souls.

Most of us barely know we are souls, and those that do wear theirs on the inside. But there is one world soul among us who wears his soul on the outside in splendid array and inspiring grace. He is a great pioneer of the evolving human soul and spirit, dancing us all awake to the heaven within and around us. He is young forever—Hugh Morgan Hill—Brother Blue.

Brother Blue is in the business of human evolution. He is the Chief Evolutionary Officer of every street corner that is our church. There is no prison or cathedral, palace or slum beyond the reach of his story of our eternal and inevitable return to divine grace, to love.

Evolution prospers and works among us when the young get wiser earlier and retain their youthful creative suppleness longer into old age. Behold Blue! We are surely evolving here in heaven. Behold Blue!

How is he possible? Behold Ruth! Behind the soul pioneer there is a soul saver, a compassioneer. Behold Ruth. With biblical loyalty she carries the book of his soul in the library of her heart.

Thank you, Dear Ones.

August Jaccaci works with leaders throughout the world who want to envision and architect an ideal future for themselves and their enterprises. Gus is co-author of the recently published book *Chief Evolutionary Officer - Leaders Mapping the Future* and author of *General Periodicity: Nature's Creative Dynamics*.

Ahhhh!

Food for the Soul

Eric Jackson

It has been a joy to have heard Brother Blue tell stories for the last 30 years.

Upon first listening, some of his stories are seemingly just playful and fun, but with a little reflection on our part, we can see facets that reveal themselves, shining rays of light here and there. Other Blue stories are "bread" that he must share with all who hear his voice. Not sermons from a pulpit, but still Blue serves food for the soul. In this time that we live in, just the fact he would take time to share bread is commendable, but he does that one better by "serving" the bread with a story. And Brother Blue also seems filled with music as he sings a phrase, scats a line or chants an ostinato riff, all done with the idea of getting the story across, which might be improvised on the spot.

From the griots of West Africa and the toastmasters of the African American tradition, Brother Blue continues a tradition. But he also brings the "traditional" knowledge of the west, having attended Harvard and Yale. Perhaps it is because his vision was shaped on several continents that he tells his stories so well.

All who have heard Brother Blue should feel fortunate to have been enriched and touched by the work of a true master craftsman.

Thank you Brother Blue!

Eric Jackson has been heard nightly on 'GBH 89.7fm for more than 20 years. Jazz with Eric in the Evening has been voted radio's Best Jazz Show by readers of The Boston Globe. Musical artists from Wynton Marsalis to Ornette Coleman and Dizzy Gillespie have appeared or performed live on Jazz with Eric in the Evening.

Jackson is the author of *Essays in Black Music*, a 35-part chronology of African American musical history, which aired on 'GBH 89.7fm in 1975. Jazz with Eric in the Evening debuted in 1981. He lectures on the history of jazz at the Longy School of Music and has taught a course on the history of African-American music at Northeastern University.

AHHHH!

Blue's Prayer

Stephen Jenkinson

Brother Blue, clearly, is a genius. The older, less cluttered meaning of genius is closer to 'guardian spirit,' or 'a wiser part of you that you have managed to stay close to.' This older part knows you better than you know you, and it remembers, when you don't, why you were born. Blue's genius knows him very well, and it keeps him informed. When I ask him how he's doing, the answer is, "Man, I am blessed. I found what I was born to do." Blue is an advocate for the idea that you were born to do something, and that you can find what that is. He's also adamant enough about it that he's daring you to do the same—and he hints that every day spent ignoring or forgetting this is spent sadly.

Brother Blue is a genius of tragedy, especially. He is one of tragedy's best poets. To the extent that any man can, Blue has mastered tragedy, its sound, its cadence, its footprint, its breath. He advocates tragedy, though you have to spend a lot of time with him before you see it.

Any lover, any real lover worthy of the name, anyone who is 'a natural lover, cover to cover,' loves tragedy. Blue loves tragedy so purely, so intensely, so well. I recognized long ago that he was a master of praise; he has lifted praise to a high, pure art form that would make the Irish claim him as one of their own. Praise swells in him, overflows him, carries him on out over the face of the world. As praise master he is almost irresistible. His praise is high, lyrical, fierce—and tragic. It's only with my own aging that I've come to recognize that he is tragedy's poet, too. Hear him tell his own stories—Once I had a Brother, especially—and you'll know how true this is.

Blue's genius is to subtly and searingly embrace the twins of praise and grief. He makes room for both, invites both into the house of his heart. His best stories hold grief and praise in an aching embrace. His own stories say: if you love someone or something, love also that they will fail

Ahhhh!

you, leave you, die before you. Love the impossible frailty of the whole damn thing; then you're loving. Love how unlikely it is; then you're loving. Your arms have got to be that big to be in this world. Blue's praise has grief all the way through it, and his grief has praise, all the way through.

Blue and I have had many big times performing together as we've done over the years. But there was a private moment that still stays with me.

One day years ago, in between performances, Blue and I did the unlikely thing of seeing a matinee film. It was David Lynch's story of *The Elephant Man*. At the film's end, unforgettable to me, David Merrick sings his final, triumphal surrender to this world, his holy embrace of how sweet and how impossible it all is. After living a nightmare of deprivation, he is in awe of finally having friends, and he is grateful, grateful beyond measure, and it is for him enough that he lived long enough to have friends. Once outside I was chattering on about the film and Blue was, strange for him, silent. I finally asked him, "Well, what did you think about it?" He paused a long while then looked a long time at me and said, "My heart is broken and I never want it to mend."

It took me a few years to see that this wasn't a film review; it was a prayer. It was the welcoming of a broken heart. I think that for Blue, a broken heart is a kind of guarantee that no amnesia, no passage of time, will heal over loving this world. He is one living example, so precious, that brokenheartedness makes this work lovable. Blue's prayer for himself is that he can, over and over, drink the tears that are in all things—and he has shown many people how it's done. Of his many gifts to me—and they have been countless over our twenty year friendship—this prayer has been the most precious and the most trustworthy. Of all the things I love him for, I love him most for that.

Stephen Jenkinson earned a Master's degree at Harvard Divinity School, and a Social Work degree from University of Toronto. He now maintains a private practice and has a particular interest in the spiritual dimension of dying.

Ahhhh!

Breathing Together
Jennifer Justice

Introduction

The first time I heard Brother Blue tell his epic Butterfly story, it literally blew the breath out the top of my head, leaving me open to a limitless star-filled indigo sky of inspiration and possibilities. It took several personal encounters with Brother Blue and Ruth to fully understand how this remarkable team accomplishes their healing work together. Quite simply, Brother Blue knows how to breathe with an individual or an audience until the heart center opens and we are moving in a wider universe, no longer constricted by our own fears and scars. Ruth provides the ground from which Blue takes us flying, and the combination allows us to realize the universal greatness inherent in each individual soul. My thanks to them are endless, and I hope the following story expresses some of that appreciation.

Breathing Together

In the spring of 1994, I was doing student ministry as a chaplain at a large Catholic hospital in Lowell, Massachusetts. Though it was my first placement, I was assigned to the intensive care unit. Like many beginning spiritual care-givers, each day I asked myself, "What comfort could I possibly offer these people during the most agonizing moments of their lives?" Not being Catholic, I didn't even know their spiritual language. One day, however, I learned the secret of healing.

As I was doing my rounds at the hospital that morning I met a young woman. Her husband was in a coma that had come on suddenly for no apparent reason. The woman was standing beside her husband's bed, stroking his hand, his arm, his head. The man's body was still to the

Ahhhh!

core. His skin was shrunken like a tight wrapping on his bones. The small room was only a curtained cubicle with a rolling bed, but it was suffused with light.

Tears were streaming down the woman's cheeks. She was breathing fast, in a panic. I sat quietly in a chair at the foot of the bed for several minutes, breathing slowly. "Do you think he knows I'm here?" the woman asked. "I'm certain of it," I replied. The silence stretched comfortably between us. Finally she turned to me. "How do you know?" "Because," I took her hand in mine, "the love pours from you like air. If it's possible for him to live, he will." We rested hand in hand for a long time. Nothing else was said. Finally, the woman returned to the task of supporting her husband's struggle with her devoted touch. She was calm and I went on to my next call.

For several weeks I had been visiting with an elderly woman, Mildred, as her husband grew weaker from a series of strokes. We both suspected he was not going to recover and return home. Each day he grew notice-ably weaker and opened his twinkling blue eyes less often. I visited frequently, listening to stories of their long years together and the love that was so obvious between them. Mildred seemed glad of my visits, but determined not to share her desperate sorrow. On this day her husband's breathing had shifted and, as I entered the room, the doctor had just told Mildred it wouldn't be much longer.

Mildred kept a constant vigil at her husband's bedside. When I en-tered the room, she gave up her place to me and rested in a cushioned chair while I held his fragile hand. She hadn't been sleeping much and I asked her what she did during the long dark hours. "I pray to Saint Anthony." I had no idea who Saint Anthony was, so I queried her on his significance. Saint Anthony, she recounted, had been her favorite Saint in childhood days, because he was the Saint of lost things. Mildred looked helplessly at me as the tears began to flow. "I've lost my hus-band," she said, "and I want him back." We held each other in sorrow and love as she sobbed out her broken heart.

Finally, the long day ended. I walked across to the parking garage. There was a thin middle-aged woman with black hair and brown eyes waiting at the elevators. As the doors opened, she remarked, "Thank goodness you came along. I hate to ride these things alone. If you hadn't come, I would have had to walk up four flights." "I'm glad I was here, then." I answered. We entered and pushed our floor buttons, (hers, four; mine, five). We waited in silence.

Ahhhh!

As we approached the fourth floor, I advised the woman, "If you ever do get stuck in one of these things alone, just remember to keep breathing." The elevator came to a halt. The doors slid open. The woman walked though them. Before they closed again, she turned back and told me, "Thanks, I will, but it's always easier when two people breathe together."

© Copyrighted material, previously published on *Breath of Life, Parables to Nourish the Spirit*, CD, Moon Star Series, 1986.

Jennifer Justice has been a storyteller for nearly two decades. An early member of Storytellers in Concert, The Three Apples Storytelling Festival, and Sharing the Fire, Jennifer helped launch the revival of storytelling in New England. She is a Unitarian Universalist minister.

Photo: Keiko Morris

Ahhhh!

Uses of Air

Caroline Kandler

Performing his syncopated stories
on a night framed roof, our friends and neighbors circling him,
Brother Blue's caterpillar continues to question
his 'to be or not to be' fate, his appeal

lights us like fireflies becoming butterflies
with his solo style, Ruth acting as recorder and time teller,
while Brother Blue raises the story roof.

The next day, Blue, in his blue and butterfly regalia,
and Ruth, packed and ready to move on, leave us
two blue balloons, each signed with their names
and their affection, long blue ribbons attached.

He says, "I'm leaving my breath with you."
She says, "I blew up the balloons."

Two blue autographed balloons on an extended visit,
centered on the sofa for three days
until Yasmine and Steven come to play

a toss-the-balloon game, a keep-it-in-the-air game
as-long-as-you-can game and when they leave
each takes a blue balloon trailing blue ribbons.

At the top of the hill, they release the balloons which rise,
traveling the skies, eternally blue.

Caroline Kandler lived her life participating in the visual arts, dance, storytelling, performance art, and poetry. She was a published poet and recognized artist. As an architectural designer of homes and schools, she particularly enjoyed designing libraries.

Ahhhh!

True Blue

George Kaufman

I've known Brother Blue for some fifteen years, but I need to start the story of how we met by the fib he printed in the Omega catalogue. Omega is a retreat facility that offers courses you can take on weekends or during the week. My wife and I had been drawn to a program described in the catalogue that was printed just beneath Blue's face wreathed in dreadlocks. The workshop description subtly drew us in with the provocative title "Storytelling: the Art of Praying Slow."

It was a great title, and Helen and I signed right up. The only problem is it wasn't true. By the time we finished the weekend, I realized it had been a program about telling *your own* story. That's quite a bit different than a program in imagination and style, where the dominant theme is just storytelling.

By the time we realized the not so gentle change in format, we were knee deep in the experience. I've taken a lot of programs over the years, but I've never experienced one where the facilitator could make the space we were in that safe that fast. With Blue, storytelling was a religion, and religion is practiced in sacred space. As Blue made the act of storytelling holy, we became devotional students. The outpouring of personal experiences was extraordinary.

Over the next few years, Blue and Ruth, Helen and I became friends. I was fascinated by Blue's unwavering intention to the task of transformation through storytelling. It was his Job, his lifetime Job, and Ruth and Blue honored and respected the work that went with such a Job.

During the time Blue and I began to learn more about each other, I lived in a small community in Westchester, New York. We had spoken about a marriage between storytelling and public broadcasting. But where to start? We agreed that some video of Blue performing would be a good place to begin. The existing tapes that Blue and Ruth had col-

Ahhhh!

lected didn't show off Blue's talent. We needed to create something new.

I mentioned to Blue that perhaps we could create something in my home town of Irvington, since it hosted a replica of the intimate Ford Theatre in Washington, D.C. If we rented the space for a Saturday night, we could fill up to six hundred seats and film an evening of Blue's storytelling.

Blue agreed and I created a Blue trifecta for the weekend. On Friday night, Blue gave the graduation speech to the Irvington kindergarten. On Saturday, Blue performed at the Irvington Town Hall. We hired a folk singer to be our opening act, and sold tickets to an evening of storytelling for *grown ups*. On Monday, Blue was my guest to the 8:00 AM senior honors English class at Irvington High School.

On Friday night, Blue (who is never childish) was magically childlike, as parents and children were mesmerized by his tales. Speaking from a stage, Blue invited the children into his magical world of wonder. Dressed up in butterflies and balloons, Blue captured their imagination and won their hearts.

I still have the flier for Saturday night. After a short description of Blue's career, I quoted him and said:

"Every time I tell a story, I risk all on that deep feeling, trying to do something real from the middle of me, moving in the spirit, trusting with my life. For my work is like that old jazz musician; blowin' an old song but blowin' it ever new."

The afternoon before the show, fierce rains pelted down. Doggedly, the April deluge continued as show time neared. If I were telling tales instead of offering tributes, I'd say that the lines for the show went around the block twice. And every time it rained harder, the crowds cheered and passed free cookies and tea back and forth.

If I were from the local paper, I'd just say that the crowd outside Town Hall that night was surprisingly large and well behaved. I'd say it was unusual to see so many umbrellas bobbing towards the entranceway for storytelling.

But this is a reminiscence, a recalling with affection. As I go back ten years in memory, I choose to recall that night in the spirit that the writer Isabelle Allende uses when people ask her what possibly could be truer than the truth. She replies simply, "A good story." That night, Brother Blue was a very good story. The umbrellas were out in numbers, and the theatre was almost filled to its 600 seat capacity.

Aggie Griesar was billed as a Teller of Tales, Singer of Songs. Her

AHHHH!

enthusiasm was infectious and her stories warmed hearts and enlivened spirits. She opened the door to our imagination and left it ajar for Blue's entrance.

Blue gave us a night of Shakespeare and a dash of the Indian Jataka tales. Over the years, Blue had converted all of Shakespeare's tragedies to thirty minute street rap renditions. As Blue walked onto a bare stage, he wove for us the human losses in Othello, the stripped loves of Romeo and Juliet, and the agonizing disappointment of Lear. Blue's small harmonica—his harp—pierced the silences between his words and filled the stillness with a sense of impending loss.

It was a happening captured on film and a moment of connection between the artist and his art. Hours after the show ended, Blue's family and mine basked over the gift he had shared with our community and the resilience of storytelling as art.

Blue's connection to Irvington deepened—because storytelling is his life, not his job. On Sunday, Blue found a busy corner in our small town, and for an hour or two regaled those wandering to or from their homes with casual, lighter tales. It was Blue's Sunday sermon. His pulpit. And those who listened, lingered in the magic space of storytelling.

Before Blue left on Monday, I had arranged for him to speak with our high school honors English class. The teacher made a brief introduction and the space was his for an hour. Blue seemed strangely out of place. In a room full of button down shirts and khaki pants, he was outrageously dressed in blue. Butterflies were painted on his hands. Even before he spoke, Blue had taken off his shoes. It was both an act of respect for the room, and a freeing of his feet to be used for syncopation.

The body language of the students was not encouraging. They evinced an attitude that melded distrust and distaste. Irvington's future leaders had been euchered into attending a class that violated their standards of dress and threatened their code of behavior. Expressionless and without animation, they prepared to endure an hour of childish prattle, and hunkered down for unremitting boredom.

Blue asked what they were reading. "Romeo and Juliet" came a snarky reply. Few students in the room thought Blue knew the play or the author. "Great play," said Blue, "great play. Romeo was only fourteen and Juliet just thirteen. Younger than you guys." Then Blue challenged the class. "How many of you studs are ready to live for love?" All hands shot up, and the girls in the class nodded appreciatively. "Cool," said Blue. "How many of you studs ready to die for love?" Not a hand

Ahhhh!

176

twitched. No heads nodded. And the girls realized the limits of affection.

"Maybe you want to hear about love and jealousy," offered Blue. "They don't mix well. My main man, Shakespeare, knows all about that stuff. Listen while I tell you the story of Othello and his lady Desdemona." And Blue spun tales, stomped his feet, breathed fire into the Shakespeare tragedy, and captured the hearts of young students distrustful of anything they didn't create or control.

That morning, just for an hour, Shakespeare came alive through Blue's energy. Blue left to cheers, just as he does on stages, in supermarkets and festivals. As we walked out of the classroom together, I thought that if Willie is Blue's main man, Blue sure is mine.

George Kaufman is a lawyer, writer, storyteller, and teacher. He serves as Vice Chair of the Omega Institute for Holistic Studies, an educational retreat facility in Rhinebeck, New York. George and his wife Helen live in a co-housing facility in Saugerties, NY.

Photo: Cole Bellamy

Ahhhh!

Flying
Joseph Keane

It is not so often that I have to venture into the city anymore. Being so busy running one's own business does not afford one many opportunities to stroll around the city. There are times when I have to take on that trip, and when I do I try and make it productive by doing as many errands as I can.

Well, I remember this one particular fine day when I tried to do it all. I had been productive and efficient, completing all twelve items on my list by my five o'clock deadline. Yes, five o'clock and I thought I was done until the most important task of the day came back to me...sales tax due...and I had missed it. "Oh, no!" I proclaimed, placing my hands on my head and looking up into the sky between the rising stacks of concrete. I had forgotten to do the most important errand and I was most annoyed and stressed at myself. As I stood there staring skyward in frustration, I saw something floating down from the sky above.

I looked at it and thought to myself, "a leaf of autumn all too soon." Was time itself to pass me by? A withered leaf from a tree...but no, as it fell towards the city floor I saw that it was not a leaf, but a butterfly falling...floating from side to side with no movements in its wings—just falling towards the ground. As it fell, it came so close to me and as I looked at it pass me by, I heard it say, "enough of that."

"What?" I said, "Did you say something?"

"Whey, enough of that, I said," said the butterfly to me. As it kept falling, I followed it down to the ground. In a state of shock, I thought that I had heard a butterfly speak. And when it landed, I lay down on the pavement and looked at it closely. Again, it looked me straight in the eye and said, "Enough of that." I spoke to the butterfly on the ground and told it I knew exactly how it was feeling and then I asked it where it came from, and so the butterfly told me its story. It looked at me with sadness in its eye and told me it had emerged from a cocoon all the way up in a sheltered

Ahhhh !

wood in Canada. At first, life was sweet and all it did was flutter from flower to flower enjoying the pollen, the colors and the scents. It did not matter where it flew for there was sunshine and flowers aplenty. Then one day, as it was fluttering from flower to flower, something started to happen, and it felt compelled to go and leave the flowers alone. It started to fly and flutter on and on, searching for something it did not know, but somehow knew. For days it flew, down over Vermont and then had to fly so very high over the mountains of New Hampshire and still it flew and flew until it could take no more. And high above this place it said, "I can't fly no more...my muscles are tired and my wings can't keep me in the air. I know something is calling me but I can't go on no more."

And "then and there, I stopped," said the butterfly. "And I started to fall and fall, not knowing where I was until I came to you." It told me it had given up because it was so tired from fluttering in the air and so lonesome for the sweetness of the flowers. "And that's what brings me here," it said.

As I lay there on the pavement, I told the butterfly my story and why we are all driven so. "Oh, it is time for me to go," said the little guy. I asked why did it have to go. And then it said to me, "I am a great monarch butterfly—that is what I am—and I have to go find a home and a friend, go where all the monarchs go, as it's now I am rested and took time with you." It looked at me with its big eyes and a little smile as it flapped its wings so lightly, and again it said, "Yes, I know, I am going to where all the monarchs go." I watched it flutter its wings and rise up higher and higher than all the buildings around and heading south toward Mexico...where all the monarchs go. I got up off the ground and with new found strength and lightness, continued to take on the work to be done each day and I remembered that, I too, am searching for a home and one day will go where all the monarchs go.

The first time I saw Brother Blue, I was new in the country and I thought he was nuts...out around Harvard Square. At that stage, I had never told a tale. I visited the Bookcellar Cafe one evening and heard the tales told by Brother Blue. He inspired me with his foolishness and truth. I learned from him that words do not always have to be chosen when we speak, and that this is when we trust that God is speaking through us. He set a seed, and a few weeks later I told my first tale. And from that tale, so many tales have been spun in the search for truth and beauty, just like the butterfly.

Joseph Keane writes of himself, from sacred well to sea. Connecting the ancient cultures of Ireland and journeys deep into the Earth to find that we are worth more than all the gold in the world.

AHHHH!

God Is Blue

Paul Keens-Douglas

Yu know what I love about God?
Yu can talk to him anytime.
Jus' close yu eye, throw back yu head,
An' God right dey wit' yu.
If yu look good yu could see Him.
God is a cool, blue place deep inside yu,
A light, like a glow, comin' right up,
Yu could sense it,
Like when yu divin' deep in de water.
God, God is always dey for yu,
When yu stump yu toe yu bound to bawl,
O'God..O'God..O'God..O'God..O'God-o!
When yu mudder beat yu, yu bound to bawl,
O'God..O'God..O'God..O'God..O'God-o!
Even when yu don't believe in God,
Yu bound to bawl , O'God..O'God..O'God-o!
Yu know when yu does sense God?
Is when yu lift yu eyes, yes, lift dem,
Just slightly, just slightly,
Above de cars, de smoke, de noise, de people,
Above de roof-tops, de wires, de trees,
De headlines in de papers,
Up to de clouds, de clean blue, an' yu does sense God.
If yu look good, yu could see God,
Somewhere just where de light blue begin to get dark,
Yu does see de same place yu does feel inside yu.
Yu know when yu lie in bed at night,
An' yu say how yu so glad God invent bed?

Ahhhh!

An' yu remember yu didn't pray, yu didn't say thank God?
An' yu wonder if yu have to get up an' kneel down to pray?
An' yu jus' close yu eye, an' yu know God right dey,
Jus' between yu eye an' yu forehead,
A kind of dark blue.
An' if yu squeeze yu eye tight yu could see stars an' planets
An' far-off places.
Jus' beyond yu eye, if yu look real hard, yu could see God,
An' yu know what? God is blue!
So close yu eye...take ah look...see? is true!

Mr Tim Tim in the storytelling world, Paul Keens-Douglas is one of the best known raconteurs and social commentators of Trinidad. His company, Keensdee Productions; Ltd, puts on the annual Carnival Talk Tent and Tim Tim Show. Based in Trinidad, he has published several books, albums, recordings, and travels extensively as a performer and motivational speaker.

Ruth watching Blue perform in Harvard Square

Ahhhh!

Brother Blue at Emmanuel

Alvin and Doris Kershaw

During the 1970's and 1980's, at Emmanuel Episcopal Church on 15 Newbury Street in Boston, Brother Blue was a colorful participant in many church services and programs. We remember how generously and enthusiastically he gave of his time and talents. The importance of the arts in a full worship experience was emphasized at Emmanuel during this era. It was ideal that Brother Blue enhanced many of the services with his objective insights and artistry.

One such service I remember vividly was a traditional Parish Family Christmas Eve service, held in the beautiful Leslie Lindsey Chapel. That year Brother Blue presented the time-honored "Mary had a Little Lamb." His performance was original, relevant, and delightful.

We will also always remember how much Brother Blue treasured the support and inspiration of his beloved "Ruby-Dooo," Ruth!

The late Alvin L. Kershaw was rector of Emmanuel Episcopal Church, 15 Newbury Street, Boston, Mass. from 1963-1989. Upon his retirement he and his wife, Doris, moved to Louisville, Kentucky.

Ahhhh !

Brother Blue Praise Song

Baba Jamal Koram, The StoryMan

Storm clouds swelling up
Blowing winds full of butterfly wings
answering a storyteller's call to be
Reborn.
Cocoon-like.

Wrapped in the warmth of a
Blue Brother's Love

You be God's boy
Mama Ruth's man
You be a wind walking warrior
reaching for God's outstretched hand
"Come, son. Let me show you the universe."

"But daddy, can I take my friends..."

"Sure, boy. But the only way they can come
is if they rock to the be bop
rhythms made by the flaps of butterfly wings sending
out spiraling songs singing rays of sunshine shining
out soul breaths with they bad self. Unh!
Tell them to come on, my flowering child."

And then one day,
Blue blew into Berea to talk to Baba Jamal
and they sensed God talking to the spirit wind walking

Ahhhh!

rain dancing
fire throwing
carrying seeds
yam planting talking 'bout
Papa's got a brand new bag
And we called out to the spirit who said,
"Hey sons, my talkative ones, look in my bag
Got a few look like you with ample hue reaching out
for the chosen few..."

Blue cried out, "What else do you want me to do?"

And God yelled back, "Keep on soul copping and
be bopping Blue!"

My Blue Brother
You a power sign thrower
at a peace convention
Scattering Holy water words just trying to
Help somebody help themselves get on the
good foot

You a muse done paid his dues to sing the blues in all
its Hughs from hope to eternal light
the fight
be to maintain
the name of
GOD
whoever said life had to be hard
we just have to BE
We just have to BE
We just have to Be - Bopping
NO STOPPING
Just dropping the name of Brother Blue on you.

Brother Blue
let me take you
to

AHHHH !

184

the Baobab tree so you can feel the
energy of heavenly praise
to cling to in your
quietest of days a rest home
for Keepers of the Tome

Let me share Africa roots with you
medicinally speaking no weeping it's
just the willow in we
only a shade of difference no defense for the pain of the
crossing
It's your world
'cause you God's boy
turning perpetual pain
into healing joy
YOU healer YOU.

We love you.
You butterfly man
We love you.
You king maker
Spirit shaker
Sorrow taker
Boston beatitude baker in Harvard Square
What you doing up in here?

Dey be moon dancers there
Dey be moon dancers there
Dey be absorbin' day trippin waterbearing wind
        walking fire throwing love
making
moon dancers there
Dance on Blue Brother
Dance on Blue Brother

Ain't it the truth Ruth
The truth in Blue
The Ruth in Hugh

Ahhhh!

The chosen few
claiming you
trying to catch
a little messianic light
shining through
Ain't it the truth Ruth

Dance on Brother Blue
You be-bopping Blue elder
Broken soul welder
magical mind melder
You creating, flirtating, storyteller
You
storytelling son
You
storytelling daddy
You
grand storyteller
You blue man spirit yeller
You brother man
You brother blue man
You Brother Blue!

I GOT MY EYE ON YOU

Baba Jamal Koram, The StoryMan, touches the hearts, minds and spirits of listeners of all ages through the stories and songs he shares and the beat of his drum. For over twenty years, he has told stories that cut across cultural and generational lines to soothe and delight the souls of listeners. Baba Jamal represents the best in African American Griotic tradition.

Ahhhh!

Squirmin' with Blue

Pam Kristan

I have old messages in me, ready to spring to attention that say, "if you want to be loved, you have to be polite," and "public display of emotion is brazen, shameful, disgusting, disrespectful, and even subversive!" Everyone who's been in the company of Brother Blue might see an internal challenge a-brewin" there for me. Blue's weekly storytelling session is balm for my soul, but like good medicine, it doesn't always go down easily. Blue calls up those old messages in me, and I squirm. Why? Because he does exactly what, when I admit it, I want to do.

Blue unabashedly tells how extraordinary he is—how he loves so hard, how he hobnobs with the elite and ministers to the prisoner, how his whole soul goes into everything he does. I squirm. Yet because of Blue, I've revived a Scandinavian solstice tradition called the Yule-brag, where everybody boasts about whatsoever comes to mind as long and as loud as they choose. Once a year? feh! We get to experience the power of a soul being out there for everyone to see every single week, and by his example we're encouraged to do the same.

To stories short or long, monumental or mundane, polished or raw, he invariably exclaims to the teller, "That was *great!!!!*", with all the considerable enthusiasm he can muster. I squirm. How can it ALL be great? Yet I know, deep in my bones, that it's true. Every one of us is, as Blue says, a supergenius, nonpareil. Often when I return from Tuesday night's telling there's his phone message with the most delicate, discerning comment. Within his enveloping encouragement is careful insight.

Blue goes on and on…and on and on. He says the same things over and over. That used to make me squirm. [We regulars ought to make a compendium of The Sayings of Blue.] As my truth becomes clearer to me, I hear myself saying the same things over and over, and if allowed,

Ahhhh!

will go on and on ... and on and on. What Blue says is true. It's all that needs to be said. We're wise to listen and let it sink in whenever we can.

Blue goes too far, regularly, as a practice, prefacing his excesses with "if you don't mind ...". Of course, even if we did mind, we'd welcome his being on-the-edge. He stretches our ability to accept and to love. He calls us to be present, listening and loving, even when those old messages spring forth. So, what else do we have to do?

Pam Kristan has been telling tales of her adventures, dreams and musings at Brother Blue's for close to a decade. One glorious Columbus Day she brought Blue and Ruth to Eastport, Maine to share themselves and their stories. Pam runs her own business, The Practical Matters, helping people organize their time, space and stuff. Her newest book is called *The Spirit of Getting Organized*.

Ahhhh!

Blue and Ruth, On and Off Stage
John and Nancy Langstaff

Admirable friends, Brother Blue and Ruth,

Our first meeting with you was memorable for us—in 1969 at the home of our mutual friends, Ted and Nancy Martin in Lexington. After dinner, you astonished us with your colorful narratives, your enthusiasm, your energy and your imagination. It was an amazing sharing. Your two familiar figures have given an added dimension to the lives of those of us who live in Cambridge. I have also appreciated, deeply appreciated, the devotion and understanding you have shown of the Revels vision and performance—and I can always sense when you are out there in our audience (your energy and perception is palpable to me on stage!)

Bless you both, and thank you for what you've given to all of us.

John and Nancy Langstaff are musicians, educators, and founders of Revels, Inc. They have published a number of books and made numerous recordings of traditional music, both here and abroad.

Ahhhh!

Around the Table with Blue and Ruth

Warren Lehrer

Blue was excited. So much so, Ruth kept pointing to his unbitten curried egg salad sandwich with her eyes. She'd already cut it into four pieces for him. Eating (like gravity and time), I later realized, is a nuisance, albeit a sacred nuisance for Brother Blue. A train of philosophical inquiry or a story mid-flight should not have to be interrupted by chews and swallows. His enthusiasm didn't have much to do with my wanting to write a book about him—it was more a matter of sitting around a circle at an outdoor cafe on a beautiful spring day in Cambridge, Massachusetts with his wife Ruth next to him, and the birds singing in the trees, and all the people, all those storied faces walking by—and the possibility, the ever-hopeful cloudparting possibility of transformation, of waking the melody inside unsung souls, of bridging the past with the present into the future, of diving head first into the sweaty, gritty, sad, mad, ecstatic truth of skin and song and yearning—out out out into a mysterious but attainable state of grace—it was the idea of what a book could be, of what a life could be, of what that very moment could be, that captured his imagination. He married a librarian, of course, for the access—to the collected wisdom and testimony of the ages. "But now we have to go beyond the book you know. No book can capture the (we don't want to admit it, but no book can get the) whole thing." Blue pictures a huge book with nothing in it. Then a small book called *A Little Nothing*. "You open it up to see what nothing looks like and it erupts. Where have all the great books gotten us?" I'm starting to worry. Doesn't sound like he's into being the subject of a book at the moment. Blue continues, "God is shaking his head at what people have done in the name of the scriptures. Waging all these wars with words. We've fallen under a spell. It's called the idolatry of the written word." Inside Blue's liquid eyes is a dream of something never seen before. "It's time for a

Ahhhh!

new kind of book that has what no book ever had— the living thing. It appears… Maybe it appears one night in a child's crib. The child picks it up and says, Ahhhhh. She opens it and hears laughter. She turns the page and there's a tear drop. It's all in there. The stammering. The smells. The interstices. The book finds its way into a mental hospital. An old man's been in there fifty years. He looks at the book. He doesn't know how it got there. He opens it up. He laughs. He cries. In the winter time, roses come to the book. He takes a whiff. Ahhhh. The book lands in a prison cell. It sprouts golden wings. The thing can fly! Right now a blind man's got it. He's carrying it with him. He can hear the sound of thunder and see lightning too. He reads it with his fingers and toes. What's the name of the book? You can't name it. It's… unutterable. But it's gotta have a name. Okay, it's called, Ahhhhh. When you open it, it's like opening a window. All the animals that ever lived are in there."

I reach into my portfolio and pull out a book of mine entitled *GRRRRHHHHH*, a 464 page picture-laden animal fantasy fugue about the long forgotten but pivotal animals of the earth. Brother Blue holds the book in his hands like it's a giant butterfly. He smells the densely inked volume, then brings the pages to life with his fingers and eyes. He beckons the people at the table next. They must come and see this book. A former student of mine from New York happens to be at the table behind us. An admirer of Brother Blue is at another table. A small crowd gathers around us, experiencing the pages of this odd lyrical book of mine, through the prism of Blue's exalted heart.

"So you want to do a book about me. Alright. If anybody can do it, you're the man. Ask me anything. I trust you. But watch out—I got a battery of lawyers crouched behind that bush over there."

On and off for eight years, I visited Blue and Ruth in Cambridge. Walked and talked. Sat around a lot of tables. They came to New York and stayed with me and my wife. I followed the bright multi-hued path they paved through gray train terminals en route to schools, parks, living rooms, town halls, storytelling festivals, prisons, cafes and hospitals. I watched Blue service his open congregation that is the bleeding thousand porthole world of underdogs, misfits, runaways, the misunderstood—even ivy league blue blood beauties, even the renowned and the famous are welcome—as long as they need to hear or tell a story. I'd watch in awe as the barefoot brahman wandered out between invited pitstops onto the street where nobody knew he was Dr. Hugh Morgan

Ahhhh!

Hill, pioneer storyteller, educator, radio artist, theologian. With no introduction, no lights, no sound, no back-up band, nothing but his body and his heart on his patchwork sleeve, the world becomes theater. Or is it circus? Or church? Or ancient gathering place? And if no human being happens by—he'll tell a story to a squirrel. I've seen him do it. Look in the squirrel's eyes and see what she needs. Or just study her. Learn about poise and movement and attention to detail and wonder where her family is.

I am blessed by the trust Blue and Ruth placed in me, this white Jewish guy from New York usually with notepad or tape recorder or camera in hand. Blue had already shared many incredibly moving stories about his family when he came down with something that he feared was a fatal illness. He and Ruth decided it was time to tell me the story, a long held family secret, about his father's desperate attempt to provide for his wife and children during the Depression, by taking out a life insurance policy and shooting himself in the head. They felt it was a story that needed to be in the book, should others find themselves in a similarly desperate situation. Fortunately, Blue was not as sick as he thought, and his father, it turns out (miraculously) survived as well. Despite our differences in age, pigmentation and heritage, Blue confided in me about his dreams, triumphs and disappointments. As if I was a brother, he spoke candidly about being a black man in the white-dominated worlds of the ivy league, the ministry, the military, public broadcasting—the U.S. of A. In addition to musings on a range of topics from comparative religion to the history of the blues, he continued to tell me his own heartbreaking, often hysterical, always inspiring real life stories of war and teaching and encounters with sages, duchesses, great jazzmen, and angels. Much of that is the basis of my book, *Brother Blue: A Narrative Portrait*. But the greatest gift Blue shared with me is his 200 percent engagement with the moment—his ongoing illumination of the story that is forever unfolding before our eyes. He says of his wife Ruth, "She's my teacher. I just translate her stuff." Whatever achievements Brother Blue has made, in his various interconnected fields, his greatest most profound achievement is his reflective soul. To be in his presence, to be in Blue and Ruth's presence, is for me, like being by a waterfall or a great natural wonder. I leave you with a short excerpt from my book that was inspired not by the telling of a story, but by a particular spontaneous moment. Blue and Ruth were staying at our apartment in Sunnyside, Queens. It had been raining for nearly three days straight, when the four of us were

Ahhhh!

sitting around the kitchen table, the rain stopped, and a little bit of sun peeped through the window.

Where the Light Falls

when you first brought me this orange juice
all i wanted to see was coffee
that's all i wanted
but now i see
god's in the orange juice
cause if you tried to line this up
the likelihood of it
i mean
here's this orange juice
and there's the sun shining right through the window
into this glass
look at the way it's aligned
it's unbelievable!
come over here to this side
stand right behind me
not next to me
behind me
you see right there
how the colorless light is hitting the glass
right at that spot right there where it's sparkling
where the rays of light go out in all directions
that
could be the center of cosmos
what if it's true?
what if it's not all a big accident?
what if the great spirit brought all these things in sync
without having to work for it or search for it?
it's so simple
it's right in front of our eyes
i mean the fact that i'm sitting here talking to you
that i happen to be in this seat
(made of wood)
the curtains parted
the fruit that came out of the earth that made this juice
even within the words
Ahhhh!

orange juice
you've got orange
tree
seed
rain
water
earth
sun
it's all in there
then out from behind the clouds
comes the sunlight
preparing us for something
and the kind of guy i am
every once in a while
if i'm trying to be honest
if i'm trying to make a point
in comes an epiphany
it's like there's that thing again
that thing is life
didn't have to go to some mountaintop in the himalayas
or jerusalem or mecca
didn't have to go anyplace in particular
it's just here
it's right here
it found us
listen
hear the robin singing out in the yard?
it's unbelievable
this moment
by the way
god doesn't give you no encores
(s)he should
but if you missed it
you missed it

Warren Lehrer is a writer and artist, known for his books that seek to reunite the pictorial and oral roots of storytelling with the printed page. His four volume suite, *The Portrait Series*, includes *Brother Blue: A Narrative Portrait of Dr. Hugh Morgan Hill.*

Ahhhh!

The World's First Kiss

Susan Lenoe

It is June 1, 1997. I am having breakfast with Brother Blue and Ruth at the Andover Inn, a quite staid and proper establishment on the campus of Phillips Academy. A young couple is with us who were Blue's hosts at the Academy where he had told stories the night before.

The couple are wide-eyed and enthusiastic about stories and about Brother Blue, as we sit chatting. A guitarist is warming up in the corner of the dining room when, as if on cue, Blue begins to tell a story. It goes something like this:

"Once a young lion woke from his sleep. The sun was warm on his golden fur as he stretched and then began to prowl through the forest. He was restless for something, though he knew not what." Blue stood now and his voice carried out across the dining room in concert with the strumming guitar.

"Suddenly he chanced upon a beautiful lioness roaming in the distance. The lion was mesmerized. He approached, and in his eagerness, he pounced and began to fight with the enchanting animal. She responded by smacking him with her claw. He fell back in pain. And then something happened that changed the history of the world. The lion glimpsed a rose growing in the forest. He did not pick the rose and offer it to the lioness. Instead, he opened his mouth around the flower, inhaling its sweetness so that the fragrance entered him. Now, he turned and came close to the lioness, offering her the bouquet of his breath. This time she did not fight. It was the world's first kiss!"

That sudden story sent a whoosh of fresh air surging through the old ark of an inn, and through my head, too. We, the inn and I, will not be the same again.

Susan Lenoe acts historical women of note, including Harriet Beecher Stowe, and works at the Andover Bookstore where she hosts storytelling events and a weekly Story Hour for preschoolers.

Ahhhh!

Blue Thoughts

Barbara Lipke

Brother Blue…

In a crowded, dingy apartment in JP, it was my turn to try and tell a tale. I had only come to a couple of these potluck story swaps. The first one had been attended by three people who contributed carrot sticks, potato chips and two loaves of "bunny bread." At this one, the food was weird (raisin and onion pizza?) but plentiful—and there were lots of people in the room, including this strange, sweet man who smiled at everyone.

I sat on the designated "storyteller's seat," a couch whose inner character was broken springs and whose outer aspect was cat hair. I was nervous. I can't remember now what tale I told—just the gut feeling that I was clinging to a slippery board in a raging sea and I was probably going to drown. And there was this man, probably older than I, sitting on the floor directly in front of me, and smiling. It was a gentle, encouraging smile. I gulped, took a breath and began. All through my story, his eyes never wandered from mine, his attention never flagged. There was understanding, encouragement, faith in those eyes. Faith in me? In my tale? And afterwards, the words he spoke encouraged me further, but it was that look, that utter attention during my telling, that got me through the story and has been there ever since, giving me courage and faith. That look is with me still wherever I tell, whether it is in a classroom in the inner city, or at First Night, it has been with me when I tell a tale to three people or to hundreds. Thank you, Blue.

Brother Blue is a minister, a man of faith, a man of strong beliefs, a man possessed by a true calling. Storytelling is not his calling. It is his vehicle. People are his calling. His belief in people, in their ability to find strength and confidence within themselves, is his calling, his ministry. It has been my privilege to witness Brother Blue practice his calling

Ahhhh!

for many years. May I have that privilege for many years to come.

No tribute to Brother Blue can be complete without Ruth. There is no Blue without Ruth. I think, in those early days, she was not always there in person, though her spirit surely protected him. Now, I know them better. I hear Ruth's kind scolding, see her loving care, watch with awe that radiant smile they both have when they look at one another. They are complete love, a balance, a ministry to each other and to our special and privileged world of storytelling.

Barbara Lipke is a storyteller/educational consultant. She taught in the Brookline, MA Public Schools and learned that storytelling is the world's most powerful teaching method. She wrote *Figures, Facts, & Fables: Telling Tales in Math and Science*, Heinemannn, 1996. Barbara has released two storytelling tapes/CDs.

Ruth & Blue–watercolor by Mike Ahern

Ahhhh!

Jazz Storyteller

Doug Lipman

Blue has done it all, and he's done most of it before the rest of us came along. He has forged his own path, leading the way for others to develop their unique styles of storytelling and their unique interpretations of the role of storyteller. Just by being himself so unreservedly, he has made it a little easier for the rest of us to do the same.

Who is he? Like anyone who lives his creativity, Blue is easy to recognize but hard to define. Here are a few angles from which to view him.

Blue is a jazz storyteller. The veins of his stories flow with the blood of saxophones, drums, and Bix Beiderbecke's cornet. His heart pumps with the rhythm, "dum-ditty-dum," making him dance and sing his words to a jazz beat. Like any great jazz soloist, he establishes his own basic rhythm and then solos over it in implied counterpoint. He plays the standards of his repertory—his own life stories, his original poem-tales, Shakespeare's plays, and folk and religious tales—but he always adds a new riff, an extra chorus, a turn of phrase born in the ecstasy of the improvised moment.

Blue is the spiritual descendant of the African *griot*. He begins his storytelling sessions with his own version of an invocation of the ultimate Creative Force. He tells the story of the universe, from the Big Bang to the Big Wow. He lovingly passes on his passion for the great beauties of our human heritage.

Blue is a poet. He uses stories as water and sunlight for the images he plants in our imagination: the butterfly, the peek-a-boo with our scaredy-selves and our saintly-selves, the rainbow, the trees, the angels, the bard. By the time he is done with us, we have a garden full of images in our minds that seem like they have always belonged there.

Blue is pure flame. Some of us have our feet firmly on the ground but in exceptional moments reach the transcendent. Blue, on the other hand, has to take his shoes off to make even fleeting connection with the

Ahhhh!

ground—but his lightning rod is always conducting the Saint Elmo's fire of the divine. He never loses touch with that which unites us, animates us, frees us. And he never tires of reminding us—for the thousandth time—of what we were born knowing.

Blue is a holy fool. Concern for his own dignity never interferes with his devotion to waking us up. He sees us for who we are, he offers his smile, he tells us secrets we are sure to recognize as our own. In our timid age, of course, some people turn away from him in disgust—but he lives for those who respond as though they are hearing in his stories, far off, the long-forgotten song of creation.

That song sounds to me like a riff from a ribbon-garlanded fool, dancing into eternity, turning back one last time to caress his harmonica across his lips and to kiss from it...a butterfly.

Storyteller Doug Lipman has coached and performed on three continents. He has offered incisive, supportive training to hundreds of organizations and individuals from oil company executives to elementary school teachers to professional performers.

Corporation for Public Broadcasting
1975 LOCAL PROGRAM AWARD
Presented to
DR. HUGH MORGAN HILL - "BROTHER BLUE"
for
OUTSTANDING SOLO PERFORMANCE
"MISS WUNDERLICH STORY"

Ahhhh!

The Blue King

Joan Littlewood

What's all this "tribute" business? Is it to be a speech? A song? A poem? "To his feet thy tribute bring!" Isn't that for some king or other? Or maybe a god? Nowadays, it could even be a dictator—in which case it would have to be a priceless offering—a bag of rubies, an oil well—even the Nobel Prize would not do! And a certain party (mentioning no names) would simply turn round and offer his prize to the nearest beggar!

So you think you'll simply dedicate a song to the Sun? But what about the Moon? They're inseparable! If I were you, I'd forget it. Go on wandering round the world and one day, as sure as eggs is eggs, you'll be caught in the chute of a falling star. When will that be? Unpredictable! It's all very well being told to "Go and catch a falling star!" You can't! Any more than you can catch a shower of rain in your hat.

I often enjoy losing my way, but on this particular day, I didn't. Finding myself in a part of Paris I'd never seen before, I kept turning and returning till I was tired and bored. Somewhere in this noisy maze there is a quiet room where a young man listens to music. He loves all kinds of music, from north, south, east, and west—and you were free to join him if you too loved the music of our planet.

I went over the address he'd given me in my head. I asked this one and that one. Do you know this district? This address? None of them did. Had I got it wrong? I only met the young man once, but I was sure I remembered it correctly. I've a good memory. Well, I hadn't! And I didn't! I was fed up! I stopped by a lamppost and sighed. I was giving up! "Can I help you?" asked a passerby. He was wearing a black floppy hat. "I'm afraid not," I said and summed up the situation. "Well, listen!" said the stranger.

We both listened. Faintly I could hear laughter.

"It's up there!" I said.

AHHHH!

"Third floor back! The door will be open," he said.

And it was! And I knew I was entering the right place. Nobody asked my name, all I got was a half smile.

I sat on the floor and listened, someone was telling a story, but it was accompanied by gales of laughter. No wonder. The storyteller was the most comical clown I have ever heard or seen. As his story unfolded it turned out to be a tale of two sweethearts, a pretty couple—sad, because they weren't allowed to marry! What was the trouble? Race? Religion? No! Rival families! It was—it couldn't be—yes, it was Romeo and Juliet, but with all sorts of portentous characters butting in and giving the young ones ridiculous advice. And the whole thing told in the most colorful, fancy language! Jokes, puns, asides to the audience had us all in fits of laughter!

"Who is he?" I asked.

"Eh?"

"Who is that wild character with his crazy jokes?"

"You mean you don't know Brother Blue?"

"Well, I do now."

"We all do..."

We were interrupted by another burst of laughter. It was a long time since I'd heard such joy!

"Stick around, sister. There's plenty more where that came from."

I was where I love best to be, among people enjoying themselves, people laughing. Brother Blue seemed to be enjoying himself as much as we were as the next story finished, he opened his arms as if to embrace us all. On his right palm I noticed a blue butterfly. No! Not a real one! He'd painted it on.

I've combed the highways and byways all my life. Sometimes alone, sometimes with young "rogues and vagabonds" who wanted no place in the greedy world. Blue had me tapped straight away, a fellow clown! So did the Lady Moon as I called her—Ruth, his beloved wife and partner...

From that time on, we became inseparable. They had only a few more days to spend in Paris but together we roamed the wide, gray streets, with only his stories and his blue butterfly for passport.

Our ways had to part, but my special telescope could focus on that Sun and Moon wherever they were. "Watch out!" I'd tell all of my friends.

Ahhhh!

"They're coming your way." "Brother Blue?" "Yes! Don't miss him! He's Mayday. He's sunshine in winter. He's the heart of the rose, the first primrose. But don't try to hold him!"

Joan Littlewood is world renowned theatre director. She won a Tony Award in 1965.

Watercolor by: Ann Hoban

Ahhhh!

Brother Blue Memories

David Loftus

The strongest lingering image I have of Brother Blue is his inevitable response whenever someone finishes a presentation in his workshops. "That was a great story, a really great story," he gushes, almost tripping over his words as he formulates his thoughts in the process of stating them. "And lemme tell you why..."

If you have witnessed many such episodes, you may mentally roll your eyes. They can't all be great stories, you tell yourself. If it's your story he's addressing, you may still feel that way, but you listen intently, because such approval, such warm praise for one's efforts, is rare enough in this life. And if you listen carefully, a pearl of wisdom will come pouring out in a torrent—a pearl about love, about life, about you, about the great gifts of storytelling: the gift of telling, the gift of being there to listen, the gift of being heard.

I ran into Blue on the Brattle Square island—alone with his ribbons, pins of butterflies and rainbows, drum and voice, with traffic whizzing all around and only an occasional pedestrian stopping to listen and rap. I sat down and drummed for him as he related a version of Othello to no one, to the air.

Sometimes the style or content of another person's story irritates me. One very good teller related even traditional folk tales with self-conscious digressions and post-modern cultural quips which, I felt, betrayed the purity of the narrative. But Blue always found something good—and true—to say about every teller and every tale. He said I had an Apollonian approach to storytelling, while the other man was Dionysian.

Ruth was a silent but powerful fixture at these sessions. It was hard to tell what she thought about anything, because she rarely commented. We could see the absolute respect with which Blue regarded her, though. With a look, she could cut short his wilder flights, bring him back to

Ahhhh!

earth in an instant. She was like a line that safely tethered the wildly bouncing helium balloon of her husband back to the planet.

I had occasion to correspond with the novelist and poet Robert Penn Warren, who had been one of Blue's teachers at the Yale School of Drama in the early 1950s. Of his former student he wrote, "...at Yale he was certainly one of the most intelligent and gifted people in the seminar. He might very well have turned out to be a writer of plays, I was inclined to think. He did write a very interesting play, which, I thought then, had sections showing a real dramatic grasp. I liked him very much indeed and wish we could have met much more often. He is one of the few people of that place that I vividly recall—it was some thirty years ago."

The least I can say is that storytelling with Brother Blue confirmed what I learned in other quarters: that all of human life consists of storytelling. If all human life depends on storytelling—consists of storytelling—then it becomes imperative that we listen carefully to one another, and recognize that the story—our many stories—is how we survive.

I feel lucky that since I have returned to Oregon, Blue and Ruth have come to my home state several times and we have been able to share stories. As I learned on that concrete island in Brattle Square so long ago, Brother Blue is one of those spiritual beings who sweeps you along into doing things you hadn't thought of doing, things you didn't even know you wanted to do. I did not know him then, and he probably never asked my name on that day, yet there I was, performing with him to a preoccupied and only fitfully attentive world. Blue makes you feel that anything is possible and everything is wonderful.

There is something pure and childlike about him that can tempt the rest of us, cynical and wise as we like to think ourselves, to believe that he came from some other planet, that he doesn't know the score. One may be seduced by his typical street stories about butterflies and rainbows into thinking Blue does not acknowledge the presence—let alone the force—of racism, poverty, war, pain, or death in our lives. But in his tales there are flashes of those harsher truths, and Warren Lehrer's wonderful book made manifest Blue's darker personal history and wisdom.

In the spring of 1981, before I became a storyteller, I interviewed Blue for a news piece that never got published. Among the many things he told me was the following: "Most of the stuff I do, I call it prayer. I preach like a minister or a rabbi. What stories can we tell that are like

Ahhhh!

offerings? Stories that'll do some good, that will transform the world, open up our awareness…"

If there are ugly truths out there, well…it's mostly someone else's job to report them. Blue is here to remind us of the joy.

David Loftus lives in Portland, Oregon with his wife Carole Barkley, a dog and two cats. He performs morris dances and reads aloud for friends, live audiences, and radio broadcasts. His book, *Watching Sex: How Men Really Respond to Pornography* has been published by Thunder's Mouth Press (2002).

Painting of Blue by Theresa Shimer

Ahhhh!

Children's Hospital at Christmas

Kevin R. Loughlin, M.D.

To paraphrase Shakespeare; Brother Blue, like Romeo, could be cut up and made into a thousand stars. When Brother Blue comes into a room, he lights it up. When you look into his eyes, they twinkle. Brother Blue has a manner about him that makes everyone feel at ease, from infant to octogenarian. How do you describe Brother Blue? He is part poet, part troubadour, part teacher and part friend. He is all those things and more. Through his career he has traveled the globe and left the world a better place. Each one of us who have been fortunate to know him is better for the experience.

A memory for me that really captures the essence of Brother Blue was seven years ago when he, Ruth, and I went to Children's Hospital at Christmas time. He entertained all of the children with his stories, but it was his gentle manner that was truly remarkable. That incident not only crystallizes the kind of person that Brother Blue is, but it illustrates something else very important. He and Ruth are a matched set. They are inseparable. She is his soul mate. They amplify each other, and I am lucky to have known them both, and I love them both. I think the quote that sums up for me what Brother Blue is all about comes from Henre-Dominique Lacordaire. "It is not genius, nor glory, nor love, that reflects the greatness of the human soul; it is kindness."

Kevin Loughlin is a Boston area physician who takes care of Brother Blue.

Ahhhh!

Lay Down Your Life!

Jack Maguire

As a home-dwelling Buddhist, I occasionally chastise myself, "If I'm really serious about this, I should become a monk!" As a spawned-in-the-60's storyteller, I occasionally chastise myself, "If I'm really serious about this, I should do what Brother Blue does: Hit the streets, preferably barefoot, and sing out my soul!"

Blue has always been a symbol to me of storytelling courage, passion, commitment, and, yes, extremity. But more than a symbol, he's been a kind of personal magician in my storytelling life, popping up mysteriously at times when I've most needed the pop, whether or not he or I have known it.

The most recent instance was during the 1999 Sharing the Fire conference in Boston. I was about to give a workshop called "The Power of Personal Storytelling," based on my book of the same name. As I sat waiting for people to arrive, in walked—no—in danced Brother Blue. I was simultaneously excited and scared. I felt as if I were the White Rabbit hosting an open house on the Queen's behalf and suddenly the Mad Hatter showed up.

Maybe this off-balance sensation led me to be more cautious, more rabbity, than I would otherwise have been. Early in the workshop, the discussion focused on protecting your audience and yourself from the heavier, darker stories in your life, the ones full of unresolved emotions that might be upsetting to tell or to hear. It's a familiar and compellingly controversial issue among personal storytellers. In my book, I address both sides of it. However, in my post-publication workshops prior to this one, I had found myself increasingly reinforcing the need to be careful about what you tell—to make sure that your story doesn't invite telling or listening problems because it's too raw, ragged, distressing, or painful.

Ahhhh!

This perspective is certainly defensible. It's polite, safe, and psycho-therapeutically sound. No doubt I'd been encouraged to express it more and more freely in my previous workshops because it had tended to be the only opinion on the issue voiced by the participants. Perhaps even more to the point, it happens to fit the tenor of my own personal narratives, which are naturally inclined toward humor and the smaller, gentler crises in life. But in this particular workshop, after a chorus of people had once again intoned the wisdom of the careful approach, Brother Blue blew his horn. "Lay down your life in your stories!" he cried. "Never be afraid to tell what you've got to tell! Shake people up! Give them the word!"

Blue's plea was a personal wake-up call. "Yes!" I said to my poker-faced (rabbit-faced?), workshop-leading self, while surreptitiously scribbling his words into my notes. Although it's good to care about the emotional comfort of yourself and your audience, it can also be a transformative experience for you and your listeners if you occasionally rise to the challenge and pour forth your big, dark, hairy stories with full throat and full heart. Blue had caught me drifting along in the current of least resistance and had recalled me to the beauty of the shoals, the rapids, the whitewater.

But the teaching wasn't over yet. After the workshop, Blue alluded to a story I'd told about the Virgin Mary and asked, "You seem like a very spiritual person to me—are you?" I told him I was a Zen student. "I knew it!" he declared. Then, in a characteristic burst of generosity, he said, "You know, I'm going to tell a Jataka tale just for you, tonight, at the swap." Jataka tales recount the lives that the Buddha progressed through—many of them animal and even plant lives—on his way to becoming an enlightened human being.

Of course I showed up at the swap eagerly anticipating Blue's story. The tale he'd chosen was a well-known one about Buddha's life as the Banyan deer, the leader of his tribe. As the story goes (check Rafe Martin's *The Hungry Tigress* for a fuller version), the tribe is driven into a park for the local king's hunting convenience. Grieving over the large number of deer wounded or killed on a daily basis, the Banyan deer proposes that the king kill only one deer each day, selected by lot to come to the palace. The king consents, but he's so impressed by the speaker's magnificence that he insists this deer be excluded from the lottery. Eventually a pregnant doe draws the sacrificial lot. After she begs the Banyan deer to let her first have her child, he shows up at the

Ahhhh!

palace in her place. The king is so moved by the Banyan deer's story of the doe and his selfless response that he spares them both. "But what about the others in my tribe?" asks the Banyan deer. The king realizes that they, too, deserve to live, and as the Banyan deer keeps pressing his argument, the king winds up saving all sentient beings in his kingdom from the danger of being hunted.

I'd become accustomed to hearing Blue deliver deeply impassioned personal stories. As fate would have it, I'd never heard him tell a strictly traditional tale, and yet this one was communicated with a degree of personal fervor and involvement that I'd rarely encountered in listening to any type of tale. He incanted the goodness of every part of the Banyan deer with such love and intensity that he brought the deer to life in himself. He invested the deer's story with such personal wonder, anguish, and joy that it took place right then and there. In Blue's telling of "The Banyan Deer," what I'd known for years as a simple, safely remote tale of idealistic self-sacrifice was transformed into an immediate, startling, awe-filled event that I myself took personally.

And so, at least for now, I join Brother Blue, the Banyan Deer, in crying, "Lay down your life in your stories!" It doesn't matter whether the material is autobiographical or traditional, factual or fantastical, mythical, mysterious, or mathematical: Don't be afraid to shake people up! Blue has also claimed, "Enough fleas can stop an elephant. Storytelling is to change the world." Some of the stories that are most needed to change the world, and most capable of doing so, are the ones that truly buzz, bother, and bite.

Jack Maguire is a storyteller and writer living in Highland, NY. His books include *Creative Storytelling* (Yellow Moon Press) and *The Power of Personal Storytelling* (Putnam).

Ahhhh!

Son of Blue

Bruce Marcus

There's this man who calls me his son, and he's not my father. I once had a father and he's not him.

He doesn't call me this casually, as in, "Nice to see you, son." He usually proclaims it publicly, in front of an audience, when I've just finished engaging in my preoccupation as a performing storyteller. He'll jump up, point at me from across the room and shout, "That's my *son!*"

I generally indulge him in this; you see, he's kind of famous. Fancies himself a storyteller of sorts too, I guess; got his picture in some major national glossies a short while back, lots of articles about him in the papers over the years, does appearances on radio and TV all the time. Stuff like that. And he calls himself—get this—Brother Blue.

He's old enough to be my father, this much is certain, but my skin is a different color than his. (He is, in his words, "the color of earth," while I'm "wrapped in snow.") "Somebody must have hopped the fence somewhere," I would often say.

After a time I found I was able to bear his public proclamations with better grace and simply play along, smile and say something like, "Yes, I'm the white sheep of the family." At one performance my parents—my biological mother and father—were in the audience. Blue was hosting. After he introduced me as his son and took a seat, I asked my parents what they thought of his saying this. "You can have him!" my father shouted. (At the conclusion of the program my mother announced, "We'll take him back," much to my relief.)

On another occasion I had just closed a show with fellow members of the Jewish Storytelling Coalition when Blue jumped up and began loudly singing our praises in superlatives (not because we deserved it, but because this is something that Brother Blue, ten times out of ten, is wont to do.) In this setting he told a crowded theater, once again, that I was his son.

"That's funny," I said, "I don't *look* Blueish."

Ahhhh!

The role of Ersatz Son of a man like Brother Blue, Master Storyteller, mentor, tireless preacher of the Storytelling Word and self-proclaimed fool, carries with it certain obligations and responsibilities. I haven't figured out what these are, but when I do I shall apply myself to them diligently. If pressed, I suppose I could say he might hope that I will always try to be myself, to speak out against injustice wherever I see it, to feel free to experiment with creative expression and, finally, to make a supreme spectacle of myself every now and again. Blue once told a gathering of his storytelling disciples, "You haven't done it until you've *overdone* it." Watching him in action, I must say that he certainly does embody this philosophy.

Generally acknowledged is the notion that one of the few things keeping Brother Blue reasonably in-bounds is his wife, Ruth Edmonds Hill. If he's a helium balloon, she's the string that keeps him from sailing away. Warm, down-to-earth, practical, well-organized and hugely magnani-mous, she not only accomplishes her own work as an oral historian, but serves as a perfect compliment to Blue's head-in-the-clouds approach to life, taking care of the Man himself and the behind-the-scenes details of his storytelling career. She handles all of the bookings, scheduling, travel arrangements and archiving, as well as smaller matters, such as making sure Blue eats and sleeps. Without her, I'm convinced he would try to exist entirely upon air, sunshine, and raw, manic energy.

A self-aware fool, Brother Blue will be the first to tell you how impor-tant Ruth is to his life and work. I too cherish her a great deal, although I don't seem to recall her ever referring to me as *her* son. Consequently, I'm a bit confused as to what exactly my familial relationship is to her.

In the early 1990's, Blue and Ruth began hosting a weekly storytelling gathering in Cambridge, which, at the time of this writing, recently celebrated its tenth anniversary. What they created was a space where storytellers could meet, practice their art, share and grow, stretch bound-aries, cross-pollinate, laugh, cry, rant and rave together. And listen to Blue preach Storytelling, passionately, week after week—to the already con-verted.

For the first few years that this gathering met I retained my eminent, if curious, status as Blue's "only child." But then one week along came Kevin Brooks. Kevin is my height (tall) Blue's color (earth) more massive than Blue and I put together, and infinitely charismatic, both on and off the stage. Blue took an immediate shine to Kevin and right away called him, "My son!"

The disciples gasped.

Aʜʜʜʜ!

A collective entreaty rose from the throats of many of those assembled; Ruth headed the chorus. *"What about Bruce?!"* they cried.

Blue beamed us his radiant fool's smile and said, "I can have more than one kid!" And from that day forward, he did.

Turns out we're *all* his children, us disciples— the whole lot of us, at least as far as Blue is concerned. And like most children we admire and respect our "father"— sometimes— and sometimes we derive amusement from his foibles and peccadillos. Blue loves us all anyway, unconditionally; in fact, he's *determined* to nurture and love us all *to death*. He's got more love in his heart, coloring his words and oozing out through his pores than he knows how to properly channel. Or maybe he does know—he has, after all, built a community around himself, a strong community of darned good storytellers who share and delight, week after week, in the madness of Brother Blue and sensibility of Ruth Edmonds Hill.

But, alas, I fear I begin to wax sentimental.

What more can I possibly convey about what it's like being the quasi-adoptive offspring of a man who compulsively tells stories to all of humanity, regardless of physical appearance, circumstance or cognitive ability? To any and all beasts— two legged or otherwise? To inanimate objects? What can I hope to impart about life as the surrogate son of a storyteller who is as happy doing his thing on street corners, in prisons and in mental institutions as he is headlining at major national storytelling festivals or engaged as a speaker in the hallowed halls of academia?

Maybe that I hope some of the cushier venues that book him will practice nepotism.

Or maybe what I really hope for is to be able to carry forth some of his spirit, some of his inspiration, some of his love for all things living or formerly alive. To recognize the ember that he apparently sees glowing in the dark lump of coal of my being— to feel its heat. And to somehow, some way, manage to live up to the moniker of "Son" of the inimitable, irrepressible, irreplaceable, and utterly irresistible one and only Brother Blue.

Bruce Marcus is a Boston-based storyteller who has been presenting his original contemporary stories and rhyming ballads in settings as diverse as theaters, mountain huts, and large festivals since 1990. He's been a regular at Blue and Ruth's weekly gathering of storytellers in Cambridge since the series first began in 1992.

Ahhhh!

Blue is Always Blue

Lee Ellen Marvin

People ask me about Brother Blue.
    What is his real name and
    what is he like in real life?
    I tell them, his name is Hugh Hill,
    but everyone calls him Blue.
    And, I say, Blue is always Blue.

Blue is always Blue because
    stories are magic loaves, bread for our souls,
    And we're all hungry. On a windy street corner,
    where we tramp by, our steel masks set,
    there's Blue: a burst of balloons and bells
    Finger popping, toe tapping. Frightened,
    we peek at him and then we hear it:
    Your soul is a butterfly, let it fly free!

And Blue is always Blue because
    there are so many souls to feed.
    So many gray lives, famished hearts,
    and tarnished souls to shine.
    Work to be done at any place, any time.
    Street corners, subway cars,
    chance meetings in line at the bank.
    Why stop at the edge of the stage?
    The hours are long, the pay is poor,
    the sidewalks are harsh, but
    Blue is always Blue because
    he can't afford to slack from the job.

Ahhhh!

Blue is always Blue because
   this is not an act.
   Hugh Hill doesn't take off
   "Brother Blue" like a suit
   at the end of the day.
   Blue is always Blue.

All the way through,
   Blue is always Blue.

   Lee Ellen Marvin has explored the art of storytelling as performer, producer, teacher, and organizer since 1976. She was a radio producer for the NPR children's program, *The Spider's Web*, for which Brother Blue recorded more than fifty programs. She was the founding director of the Sharing the Fire Storytelling Conference. She is completing a Ph.D. in Folklore and Folklife from the University of Pennsylvania.

Ahhhh!

Mockingbird Cake for a Blue Monarch

Dorothy Massalski

Ah Blue, Ah Blake, Ah Birthday Cake!

The black cat prowls around the night's corner
And I inhale the fragrance of the season's grapefruits at my table.
The candle lights the page for this inscriber, bibber of a "Blue's" revelry
That has shaken fabled Sleep, unstable.

Earthquake, Blake, Birthday Cake!
Blue, blew, my Brother blue!

"What has four legs and cannot walk?
How can I fall in love with a thing that cannot talk?"*
The revel, it is there forever in the heart,
And his hug holds hard its embrace.
Imprint! Inscribe! entwine the thing forsooth, a bright burning lace!

Blake, Birthday Cake, Earthquake!
Blue, blew, my Brother Blue!

The morning train has beat the dawn
But not the darling mocking bird.
His schedule is his heart-thrust song
His Blue notes in my blue ear bent before the hard dark rail,
Metallic sound—the train arrived and almost gone.

Blue, blew, my Brother Blue
A color, a word, an impress.

Ahhhh!

I am content to entertain mocking
For my songster is resplendent in such refined folly.
Confuse. Confound. Delight. Astonish.
Bluets, butterflies, Blue Monarch of soul's blue notes.

I sense the Brother, and the Destiny.
Both beyond mediocrity
Both before the dawn:
"First there was Once, then there was Upon and then, A Time."*

Ah Blue, Ah Blake, Ah Birthday Cake!
Join the royal mocker of the morning, noon, and eventide
Butterfly, Mocking bird, Ruthed in phoenix fire
Ancient celebrant of songs,
To the Monarch present the Mockingbird cake
Illumined with an echo glow of joyUs magnificence.
Rehearse your silences!

Askwa, Askwali**

*Quotes from Brother Blue
** Hopi word for "thank you" in the feminine form, spoken only by
women in gratitude and appreciation.

Dorothy Claire Massalski works as a modern ballet choreographer and as an educator
integrating the arts into mainstream curriculums with the Boston Latin School Connec-
tions Project. She worked with Brother Blue and Ruth Hill in conjunction with the
Composers in Red Sneakers. Presently she is an educator with the American Indian
tribes of the Southwest, the Greater Chicago Gifted and Talented Program and
international curriculum design projects in Mexico and Africa.

Ahhhh !

Butterfly

Bruna Maybach

I met Brother Blue at Lincoln Plaza (Out of Doors Festival 1994), NYC. He was the second performer of a row of storytellers. I loved and appreciated all of them, but the most enchanting person was Brother Blue. His looks, his costume, the way he moved (sort of hovering across the stage), his voice, his glances—was the man real? Or was he a phantastic appearance, sent into our lives to free us from self-conceit and self-absorption; to connect us with the most faithful moments in our childhood, when life seemed to be promising and the future full of possibilities. Brother Blue's butterfly-myth may not turn a heart desert into an oasis, but it fills the listener with hope and gratitude. The way in which Brother Blue works this ancient image into a simple touching story is masterful.

To me, Brother Blue is the walking symbol of metamorphosis. He achieves more than teaching a moral with his tales, like 'Never give into resignation.' With his butterfly metaphor, he opens numerous windows into the world of art and the history of mankind. And what is more, he makes us feel akin to him, Brother Blue, and all other brothers and sisters.

The butterfly had been my heraldic animal before I encountered Brother Blue. At the university, I had learned that the Sanskrit word for butterfly meant "master of all creatures" and was used as an epithet of Brahma. The Irish name of the butterfly meant "God's creature," "shining insect of God." The Slavs' concept, however, is ambivalent in as they use the word to denote a witch and a will-o'-the-wisp. The Bhagavadgita describes butterflies as birds flying into flames to die. In astrology, the butterfly is assigned to the zodiac sign of Gemini, indicating its flighty character and its preoccupation with "vanitas."

I was lucky to get to know Brother Blue in a moment of my life in

Ahhhh!

which the wings of my soul had almost come to a standstill and everything that was ahead: Crash. (I was recovering from a love-affair with a saxophonist from New Orleans.) Brother Blue picked up the missing link of my heart-chain, that I had not been able to find. He made it whole again.

Brother Blue's magic still works (not only through the letters and picture postcards we exchange). The lesson that this wonderful poet taught me: "when you believe you're a poet, then you are saved."

Bruna Maybach was born in Austria and studied literature, language, and art in Vienna. For many years she taught in elementary schools in Vienna and now enjoys painting, acting and travelling. She lives in Graz, Austria.

Ahhhh!

Never a Discouraging Word

Frank McCabe

Keeping with tradition, this must start with a story—what else? As a child growing up in the Boston area, I attended the local Catholic school. The music teacher was an elderly nun who spoke with a thick Irish brogue.

During my first attempt at singing, she took me aside and gave me an offer that I could not refuse.

"Francis, you are a nice boy, and if you open your mouth and don't let anything come out, I will give you a B in music." Naturally, I accepted the offer.

A few months ago, I attended a concert with the music director for a church in Belmont. When I told her the story of my B in music her comment was simply "How many children have been driven from music by that approach?"

No one has ever been driven from storytelling by Brother Blue. No matter how bad the performance, he sees through the rawness of the performance and provides the needed support. The encouragement to persist is conveyed with a wave of the finger, a hug, or even a nod of the head.

An appearance on Tuesday night is, for a beginner, a beginning. Not simply a one nighter with a get lost glance. From the first performance, the confidence to forge ahead is generated and instilled in the novice storyteller. Success with Brother Blue is evident in the number of Disciples of Storytelling that are in his Congregation.

A resident of Everett, Mass., Francis B. (Frank) McCabe has been active in storytelling since 1996. He is currently working with his son Tom McCabe in developing a storytelling program for people who have lost a loved one.

Ahhhh!

Tell Stories!

Tom McCabe

Every so often a young performer will nervously approach me and ask me a most interesting question, a question so many of us have asked, "How do I become a storyteller?" When asked that question I always tell the same story.

It was 1977, and I had a dream of being a storyteller.

"Why?" my mother asked again and again and again. I couldn't put words to it. I simply felt in my heart that being a spinner of tales had to be the coolest thing you could do with a life.

But how do I become a storyteller? Where does one begin? Is there some test, a guild, a path to follow? I was clueless. The only storyteller I had ever heard of was Brother Blue. *The Real Paper*, a Boston arts weekly, listed Brother Blue as performing weekly in downtown Boston. I believe it was at the Emmanuel Church. I know it was off of Boylston Street near the Common.

I took the Orange Line in town one Sunday evening, not knowing what to expect. The performance space was a small chapel with about half a dozen people sitting in the pews. In the first pew to the right was a man wearing lots of colors. I figured he must be the show. Sitting beside him, saying not a word, was a woman quietly knitting, Ruth.

I don't think Blue looked at his watch. He simply stood as if this single moment was the perfect time to begin. He stood before us festooned with balloons and streamers and began to snap his fingers. The rhythm moved up his arms into his shoulders and down through his body. The painted butterflies on his cheeks and palms seemed to dance. I had seen a lot of theatre up to that point but nothing compared to Blue. He snapped as if in search a cosmic rhythm— aligning himself with some unseen force. As the rhythm built, words flowed, then gestures, and his dance began.

Ahhhh !

220

Blue told us of "peek-a-boo," as, behind his butterfly-etched palms, his face vanished and reappeared. He told us that our very souls hide, only revealing themselves just every so often. As he talked I felt my soul rising to join him. Our trust in him now complete, he transported us through tale after tale.

I had never seen such a performance, yet I felt no urge to copy or mimic. This man was unique. It would be pointless, a folly, to imitate him. However, I was inspired.

But I still had my question. I went to see him three weeks in a row, always sitting in the back, always too nervous to approach him. On the third week I summoned up all of my nerve. I got there early and sat right in the front. Blue and Ruth were there but they said nothing. Blue's head was down and Ruth continued knitting. When Blue stood, Ruth stopped her knitting. She seemed to be Blue's link, the anchor that drew him back to Earth when his dreams were spun. I turned around. There was no one else there. I was the audience, an audience of one. Blue didn't seem to take notice. He stood directly in front of me, looked me in the eyes and he began his finger snapping search for the cosmic pulse. I raised my hand. He stopped, looking a little confused.

I said, "It's okay. I'm the only one here. This is pointless. I'll come back next week."

He smiled and said, "Did you come here to hear a story?"

I nodded.

Blue resumed his snapping, "Then I'm going to tell you a story..." That's how it began. That night he told *Othello*, which he boldly pronounced "O-Tell-Oh." To this day, when I hear someone mention the title of the play I always wanted to correct them using Blue's pronunciation. I remember he also told *The Ugly Duckling*. He apologized to Hans Christian Andersen and then told me that, as a boy, he *was* the Ugly Duckling. I imagined a young Blue as a poor neglected little mallard. He showed me how fairytales can actually be personal stories. That performance was more than 20 years ago and I still remember his telling with vivid clarity.

Then the performance was done. We were back in the chapel. As he packed to leave, I waited, summoning up courage. Finally, I asked my most important question, "Blue, how do I become a storyteller?"

He stepped back and grew large as he resumed his Blue persona. In a gesture that seemed to include all the world he grandly said, "Tell Stories!"

AHHHH !

I smiled and nodded. I felt he was dismissing me with such a pat answer. So, I said, "I know, tell stories. Rehearse a lot! But then what? What do I do to become a storyteller?"

With the exact same gesture and the same grand inflection he repeated, "Tell stories!"

He would say no more. I was frustrated but, having no other advice to draw on, I did what he recommended. I began to tell stories. That was twenty-one years ago and I have been telling ever since.

So when, every once in while, a young performer shyly approaches and asks, "How do I become a storyteller?" I re-tell the tale of my meeting with Brother Blue, ending with a feeble copy of his gesture and his two word bit of advice, "Tell stories!" Most often the young performer looks confused. I see myself then. And when they ask me to embellish my statement, I repeat the gesture and say, "Tell stories!" For those two words represent the best and only advice that a young teller needs.

Tom McCabe took Blue's admonition to "Tell Stories" to heart and, for nearly a quarter century, he has traveled throughout the United States and abroad presenting programs in schools, libraries and festivals, hospitals, mental institutions, and prisons.

Ahhhh!

To Brother Blue and Sister Ruth, How do I love, think of, and remember you too

Patrice McDonough

The first time I met you, Blue, you were barefooted, up on stage, your soul naked, telling a story, "How My Daddy Taught Me to Pray." We became friends. Later I struggled and confided in you, "I want to tell stories with depth and with soul." I remember that you paused and said, "Your stories are silly, they make children laugh. Do you think there is anything deeper, more important, or with more soul than that?" You helped us bless and welcome our son Will into the world. Bread and Puppet and stories of Bucky, like you, I hold dear and near.

Now Ruth, I met you second (there is nothing too surprising about this), but your love was not outshined by our Bro. My love and admiration for you has done nothing but grow. It's a joy that our daughter, Ruth Lupine, shares your fine name. Berry picking with you one early August morning in northern New Hampshire is one of my favorite memories. Whenever you call, it's always "out of the blue," a wonderful surprise that I always welcome, too.

Patrice (Trice) McDonough has been a friend of Blue and Ruth's for twenty years. A storyteller and interpreter, she lives in Vermont and is Director of the New Hampton Child Care Center and After School Program, in New Hampton, NH.

Ahhhh!

Serendipity

Stuart McDonough

I remember seeing Blue and Ruth in so many contexts, on the street in Harvard Square, in churches, in my parent's leafy backyard in Concord, in the hills of Vermont at Bread and Puppet...

I recall being at some sunny little college. I had to pee. Blue did, too, so we set off on a mission together. I was eager to hear Blue talk, so I asked, "What does 'serendipity' mean?" and he told me that serendipity would be finding a bathroom right then. It was poetry at the time, and a lesson for me about the humanity (and at that moment, the priorities) of this man I admired so much. Stories, stories, stories...

I have always loved "Muddy Duddy," hearing Blue riff on Shakespeare, his family stories are deep and moving—trying to hold on to these things is like trying to hold onto live music, great jazz solos, or the motions of dancers. There is something about the rhythms of Blue speech and the presence of the speaker that is not easy to express on paper. After Bread and Puppet one year, Blue and Ruth stayed in our home in New Hampshire, and Blue, in the driveway, with his brilliant drummer from student days, told tales (surprise?) of Bucky Fuller that blew my mind, as Ruth pulled his sleeve, (Time to *go!*)

Stuart McDonough is a resident of Northern New Hampshire, and a friend of Blue and Ruth's. In 1995 he gave up his storytelling and juggling following a serious stroke, which left him with speech and coordination difficulties. Presently he is eagerly awaiting further plot twists in his own labyrinthine story.

Ahhhh!

Toast To Brother Blue

Elizabeth Gordon McKim

He can dance in the dark
Summon the shark
Through salt and through silk
Through honey and milk

He's Blue He's our Brother Blue

He can travel in time
Break into the vault
Of flim/flam deception
And gauzy perception
He cuts through
He's Bro Blue

He can travel
Without his galoshes
He can wander the foreign places
With his tear streaked face
And his butterfly grace

He can meander
He can wonder

Turn around twice ask for advice

He's Blue He's Brother Blue

He can wing it he can take it he can bring it
And I've seen him do it
He's Blue he's our Brother Blue

Every City has its heart
And we have Brother Blue

Ahhhh!

He pours it out and gives it up
For me and you
(You see he's generous.)

The more he gives it out
The more he gets it on
And me too and you he's ours
Till Miss Ruth Blue calls him home
And then he goes he's done for now
But he'll be back oh yeah you wait and see
He'll be back he does it for you and me

Have you seen him barefoot in the snow
Rappin' on what he knows
Standin' under his tellin art'
Till we understand something
We did not know before he names it
Hey people That's his art!

That's Blue that's Brother Blue

Have you seen him in the open air
Of a summer night in Harvard Square

Or on the riverbanks conversing with a child
Or walking the streets of Cambridge with his wild sure footed Beatrice
Ruth Blue
Have you seen him talking truth on a ride in the uni/verse
Taking us out for a spin and inviting us in
In and in
You see he is the heart of our city
And you know every city has its heart
He's Blue
He brings us the syncopated news
Yeah he's the one
Jumpin'
On the beat
Stringin' out the pearls
Sortin' through the syllables tunin' up the heat
Lassoing the truth with freedom seeking
Hoping and hopping on the story
Oh yeah he's a butterfly of hope and glory

Ahhhh!

Have you seen him
Giving us Othello and Juliet and that Romeo too
And his brother we love back to life till the tears pour through
And his grade school teacher Miss Wonderlich
Who believes yes who believes
In this butterfly being named Blue
Have you seen him
Out on the avenue in the park in the square in the open air
In the patch of sunlight coming through something bright and Blue
He's takin' a turn for you
He's puttin' his hands together for you
He's Blue
Have you seen him dancing on the cutting edge
Yeah he's the tall black wonder dressed in blue butterflies
Yeah he's the one he's our griot
He's bringin' us a sonnet a ballad or the blues he brings us the
syncopated news
Might be a jazz riff or an epic or a croonin' all around town
You know he's Blue
He's getting down with the people
Yeah he loves the people
With a click of his fingers
And a swing/ he's back in the ring
You can hear his stories sting and sing
Until the tears come
He's back again with a stomp
Ladies and gents ahmen and women
This is Brother Blue
He does it for you
And as you know every city has its heart
And that's why we love Brother
We love Brother Blue

Elizabeth Gordon McKim is a poet whose roots are in the Oral Tradition of song, story, and chant. She reads, performs and teaches throughout the United States and internationally. Her book, *Body India*, was published by Yellow Moon Press in 1976, and her latest book of poetry is *The Red Thread* published by Leapfrog Press (Wellfleet Ma.) 2003.

Ahhhh!

In His Heart, Like Butterflies

Patricia McMahon

Brother Blue
    holds us in his heart,
    like butterflies.

Then lets us go,
    soaring upward
    on his gently whispered "Aaahhh."

Patricia McMahon is a storyteller, writer and software consultant from Boston, Massachusetts.

Ahhhh!

The Storyteller

Manitonquat (Medicine Story)

The sun is darkening as it moves quickly down behind the trees of the opposite hill. And now the red flame is gone, leaving only a stain across the western sky. The women hasten to put away the last remnants of the evening meal while there is still plenty of light. The firekeeper stirs the coals and places new wood on them. This is a signal for the small band to come together around the fire, and soon they are all seated, children in front on the ground or on the laps of the old ones, women behind on one side and men on the other. They are all tired from the journey they made this day, the men running ahead to scout the way and search for danger or for game, the women gathering berries, nuts, and edible plants, and then setting up this new camp.

But now the storyteller rises and begins to speak, and all weariness is banished in the magic of the pictures he draws with his words in every mind. He has used flowers and berries to stain his face and mark his body blue, the color of the sky full of dreams he opens for his people. He tells them who they are, this little wandering band, what was their beginning and where they have been. He tells of the morning of the world, after the first darkness, and of the coming of the lights in the sky, the rising of the waters and the mountains, of the monsters and giant creatures that were larger and more dangerous than those of today, and of the great heroes and their fantastic adventures, of magic, of sorcerers and witches good and bad, and of strange lands and creatures beyond the hills.

The fire dances in the faces and in the eyes of all the listeners, and even as the eyelids of the little ones begin to droop and their heads to sink they murmur, "Tell us another story, Uncle Blue."

Now the world rolls on through the centuries. The people learn to plant seeds and to tame the wild goats and oxen and horses. And so they

Ahhhh!

no longer wander but settle and make a village, and the villages spread. Because there is now more than enough food there are ever more and more babies. The villages grow to towns, the towns to cities, walled and strong, the cities become nations, and nations reach out to become empires, which in their greed and violence, rise and fall, rise and fall through the ages.

Through all of this the people suffer. Their young men are taken to die in battle. Many become slaves. The avarice of their governments impoverishes them, and famine and pestilence stalk the world. But in this suffering new storytellers continue to rise to nurture and guide the people.

In China a gentle scholar in robes lined in blue tells stories of the Way of Creation, of the beauty of the natural world, of the dreaming of butterflies. In India blue Krishna plays his flute and tells of love and gentleness and the purity of spirit, and later Prince Gautama sees the sickness and the suffering and teaches how to rise beyond in compassion and wisdom.

Love, too, is the doctrine of Rabbi Hillel in Palestine, and it becomes the central teaching of a certain storyteller from Galilee, whose stories capture the hearts and minds of those who gather to listen, and then are spread throughout the world known to them.

History tumbles on, and in every era storytellers everywhere continue to try to open the minds and hearts of their people, to bring to life the mysteries of the past, the myths, the legends, the epics, the sagas, the eddas, the tales, the ballads, and to light the fires of imagination and wonder.

As the cities grew and the inventions of people multiplied, there came devices that could bring the sounds and pictures of stories into every home. It was a great wonder, but the cost was too great. Not in money, but in two ways more important than money.

First, the people now sat apart in their rooms, no longer coming together to feel the marvels of the living storyteller speaking to their hearts. And second, the wealth it took to make these pictures and the wealth that was made from them was so great that the stories no longer belonged to the people and their storytellers, but to the bankers and the businessmen who owned them.

But look now, here in this city of Cambridge, Massachusetts, the people hurrying along the sidewalks to get to their rooms and watch the

Ahhhh!

pictures are pausing. Something is happening. A crowd begins to gather. For this moment curiosity stills the pace and the people wait to find out what is going on here.

A lean man in blue clothes and a blue beret on his head steps forth into the little space made by the onlookers. His eyes are afire with a merry sparkle, and his smile shines with gleaming teeth against his brown face. He begins to speak, and as he does his body, arms, and hands, seem to rise and flow in the pictures painted by his speech. The story begins quietly, with many little pauses and expressions that make the people giggle and laugh aloud, and then builds and moves more swiftly, carrying excitement, danger, desire, possibility, and hope wrapped in suspense, racing on a wave carrying the hearts and minds of all the listeners, rolling and pitching and breaking finally in a burst of shining spray on the shores of its destination.

The people applaud and cheer and whistle and congratulate the story-teller, and then go on their ways, back to their separate lives. But for a while they have lived the larger history of humankind. They have traveled into wonder and shared an ancient dream. They have extended their lives and they go home larger, taller and deeper than before. Because they have been touched by the magic, the imagination, the healing love, and the blossoming hope that are the gifts of Brother Blue, storyteller of the ages.

Manitonquat (Medicine Story), Wampanoag storyteller and author of four books, *Return to Creation, Children of the Morning Light, Ending Violent Crime*, and *The Circle Way*, is at work on a new book, *The Original Instructions*.

Ahhhh!

Seeds of the Universe

Peggy Melanson

While driving alone, just before the rain, down a dark and winding road in Arlington, Massachusetts, a falling star caught my attention. Shooting across the heavens, it seemed to come straight at me. A little bit frightened and filled with awe, I drove faster to get out of its path. When I turned to look back, I saw a jagged burst of lightning pierce the night sky. The brilliant flash of light streaked low over the tall trees behind me. It was then that I remembered who Brother Blue was and how we were connected.

Pulling my car over to the side of the road, I wrote this story on odd bits of paper found in the car, while the rain pummeled the roof and the thunder and lightning crashed around me.

It was a millennium ago while slumbering in my ancient soul that I was awakened by a golden comet streaking through the heavens. The splendid brilliance raced through earth's atmosphere, weaved and danced amidst a stand of trees. As if searching, it moved and then suddenly struck a colossal tree, setting it ablaze. Glowing and split in half, though still attached at the roots, the tree thundered to the ground. Sparks from one half of the burning wood flew like fireflies, imbedding themselves within the tall timber of the surrounding forest. Deep, deep, deep they burrowed, to slumber within the wood, waiting to be awakened when the time was right. Thus Brother Blue was born to seed the world with stories.

Spiraling shafts of light from the other half of the felled tree sprang up and raced to spin protectively and embrace the trees that the sparks had entered.

It was then that Ruth was released to preserve and shield Blue's brilliant seeds. Born together out of the unity of the universe and brought to

Ahhhh!

earth from the light of life, Brother Blue and Ruth prepared the world for their children—stories!

Many years passed before fire was discovered and wood was used as its fuel. As people came to sit around the fires, Blue's sparkling stories awoke from within the pieces of burning timber. They began to snap and touch the cave dwellers who sat for warmth. Slowly at first, with hesitancy and care, the act of sharing stories gave birth to other sparks that entered other people and stories spread throughout the centuries.

My ancient soul came to life again, one day when a storyteller walked me into a cave of books where Ruth and Blue's children lived. I saw my ancient Father and Mother and my brothers and sisters in all the pages made from the wood of those spark-filled trees.

Many people were there, drawn to Brother Blue's light and Ruth's glowing kindness, because fireflies of memory danced in their minds.

Blue stood before them, dressed in a rainbow of butterflies, arms raised, eyes cast towards the heavens, perhaps seeing his own comet's light and pronouncing wonders. When he took my hand and proclaimed that my first told story was perfect and wonderful. . . I believed him.

When I saw the smile and flash of agreement in Ruth's eyes, I felt the rolling of the old thunder.

On that day, the world hesitated in its turning to allow my ancient soul to be awakened once more by the power of Brother Blue's ageless, universal spirit. My own spark was set free to fly around the campfires of the world, telling, telling, telling. And I'm home again!

In a menu of nostalgic stories about growing up in Boston, Peggy Melanson delivers profound and sometimes "Merry Tales of Mirth." As newspaper and magazine columnist, "Chef Nostalgia," she is well known for her storytelling food columns.

Brother Blue & Peggy Melanson

Ahhhh!

The Best Lovers I Know
Nancy Mellon

I adore Brother Blue and Ruth. They are the best lovers I know. One day not long ago, they created so much Love on a walk to the grocery store, six blocks from their home, that it took them all day to get to the store and back home again with a bit of bread. That walk was Light to even the little bugs on their path: everything and everyone came into the Love story.

I first met the Blue&Ruth phenomenon in the back seat of a station wagon going across the Charles River for an evening out with friends in 1981. On that journey Blue told me his *King Lear* in Jazz from start to finish. By the time we arrived at our destination there was truly nothing more to say. Ruth held the tether for us both. I always without fail get that feeling of ultimate communique with the great Lover whenever I meet Blue&Ruth. They are transcendent deLight in my cathedral of Life—forever.

Nancy Mellon has been a pioneer in therapeutic storytelling as an adult educator for over twenty years. Her work has reached healing arts specialists world-wide, as well as parents and grandparents, teachers, librarians, writers, broadcasters, storytellers, and artists. A former K-12 teacher and author of the well-known *Storytelling with Children*, she is a psychotherapist who specializes in healing through the arts.

Ahhhh!

Dedication

Ifeanyi Menkiti

For the man in blue crowned with butterflies
The man crowned with many crowns;
He is the blue man among us
Who is brother to many clans.
His world is a world of stories told
Under one tent; a tent of many colors,
A tent without dent or limitation;
No rain falls on the children under it,
Nor is any child excluded from it;
He is our brother in blue,
His crown a crown of butterflies.

Ifeanyi Menkiti teaches philosophy at Wellesley College. His wife Carol is active in community affairs. The Menkiti family have been long-time residents of the Cambridge/Somerville area. Enuma Menkiti is a 2001 graduate of Williams College, and is one of the Menkiti's four children.

Ahhhh!

Foolnanigans

Carol Menkiti

Over the years my children and I watched and listened to the butter-flies. He is, in the words of Harvey Cox, "*homo festivus, homo fantasia* …The cause for jubilation and the visionary dreamer—mythmaker."

Whenever we met Brother Blue on the mundane streets of Cambridge the "holy fool" would tell a story inviting us to take a gentle butterfly flight. In baffled wonderment and joy we would all become airborne.

Later, much later, my daughter in her college art class drew this picture of breathing out her independence, depicted in the circuitous route of a blue butterfly.

Self Portrait, Enuma Menkiti

Ahhhh!

The Dalai Lama of Cambridge

Thomas Mikelson

Who could imagine Harvard Square, Harvard University, and Cambridge without Brother Blue and his wife, Ruth? I have known Cambridge for 19 years and through that entire period they have been central to its life and culture.

"Blue," as I call him, is a quintessential social artist, a public person, a contributor to the corporate life, a landmark, a familiar signpost, a must-see-must-meet kind of person, a scholar, thinker, performer, warrior, actor, muse, gypsy, entertainer, sprite, wizard, poet, slam-champion, jester (W. C. Handy would have loved him), preacher, moral teacher (Martin Luther King, Jr. would have loved him, too), pied piper, healer, dancer, acrobat, magician, prophet, priest, musician, an unforgettable voice, the biggest smile in town.

Blue has the generous, twinkling heart of a child and the uninhibited mind of a sage. He is a monk in clown's dress, the Dalai Lama of Cambridge—unforgettable, unflappable, unpredictable, and un-categorizeable. He makes you laugh, cry, think, forget, wake up and feel all at the same time. Like all truly creative folk, he steps "outside the frame," he stretches us. For everyone who has met him, he is a blessing, a gadfly, a new friend, a mentor, a trail-blazer.

And, oh yes, he is a storyteller without peer and the partner of a great woman whose love and devotion are at the heart of his creativity.

Eternal thanks to Blue and Ruth.

Thomas Mikelson is the Parish Minister at the First Parish in Cambridge, and a lecturer at Harvard Divinity School.

Ahhhh!

How Brother Blue Changed My Life

David A. Moon

The train of my life started out rumbling down a narrow track that led in a straight line as far as the eye could see.

There were no surprises in view. Brother Blue, however, was waiting like Jesse James just over the horizon. Around the end of the 1970s, I was in the habit of working very late hours. Some nights, I might not leave work until the sun came up. On nights when I left work at a "reasonable" hour, like 1:00AM, when I got home I would put on the radio to wind down before sleeping. I always listened to Tony Cennamo's jazz program on WBUR. When the program ended at 2:45, Cennamo finished up with Frank Sinatra singing "It's a quarter to three, there's no one in the place, but you and me." Then before they shut the station off, some guy would come on for a few minutes with the strangest spoken-word stuff I'd ever heard till then, or indeed, ever since. He said his name was Brother Blue, but that name meant nothing to me then. He would do things like jive-talk retellings of stories from Shakespeare or present-day reinterpretations of the Bible, full of rhythm and improvisation. This fit in rather well with the jazz program; it truly was Word Jazz. I was enthralled. Soon I made a point of being near a radio at 2:45AM every night, so I could hear what Brother Blue would tell next.

I didn't realize it at that time, but Brother Blue had thrown the switch that shunted my life train onto another track. It was a track that seemed parallel to the original, but it began to deviate, ever so slowly at first, and then faster and faster. Brother Blue's stories were like nothing I had ever heard before. To a suburban white-boy computer nerd, they were a bolt out of the, well, out of the blue. They opened some windows in my mind that, until then, had been painted over. They let in some fresh air

Ahhhh!

from an outside I had not even known existed.

A few years later, I saw Brother Blue in the street, or perhaps on the subway. Until he spoke, I didn't make the connection between this teller in the flesh and the voice on the radio. But I should have, because his clothes looked exactly the way his stories sounded.

Ten years pass.

Thinking I ought to get out more, I started going to music and poetry open mikes. I didn't go to perform, since I have no musical or poetic talent; I went just to listen. Hiding among the poets there were a handful of storytellers, among them a very talented teller, Raelinda Woad, who had her own unique style, one completely different from that of Brother Blue.

After a couple of years of listening, to my surprise, I started telling stories at open mikes. I was nervous as hell and afraid that no one would really want to hear any story I might tell. But, surprisingly, the poets and musicians really liked a few of my stories. Someone told me, in fact, about Tuesday night storytelling sessions being held at the Bookcellar Cafe in Porter Square, Cambridge. These were hosted, it turned out, by Brother Blue and his wife, Ruth Edmonds Hill. (They were the butterfly and the flower: one flits, the other supports. Both are beautiful.) There, I got to hear a lot more of Brother Blue's repertoire, and he became a person to me, instead of a media personality.

Joining that community of tellers, listening to their so-varied stories, and getting their reaction to my own stories changed me. Now the train of my life started to shoot around some wild curves, the original track almost out of sight.

I went to Ireland for the first time and used the storytelling skills I had developed in the encouraging atmosphere of the Bookcellar. One night on that trip, in a public room in Lisdoonvarna, I told a version of a Selkie tale, tailored to my particular ancestry. This tale captured the attention of one very special listener. Two years and three months later, she became my wife. It was fitting this tale should take place in Lisdoonvarna. It is historically known as the match-making capital of Ireland.

So while I'm not saying Brother Blue is solely responsible for the birth of our daughter, I will say that he did play a part in her arrival.

David Moon loves to listen to stories, and sometimes returns the favor by telling personal and traditional stories. He makes his living as a computer software developer.

Ahhhh!

Following Blue

Glenn Morrow

By the luck of the open mic draw, I have been several times in the odd position of following Brother Blue. Following Blue is, of course, impossible. What can you say after Blue has shown us God creating the world out of spittle and snot ("this stuff is real, you've gotta deal with it") or tells us of Saint Francis – no, *becomes* Saint Francis – and the Wolf of Gubbio? Who could have as huge a presence, as total a conviction to his story as Blue? My strictly amateur status as a teller tells me I'm in way over my head. But following Blue is, of course, simple. All you have to do is tell to Blue. For when Blue leaves the stage, he becomes the world's most appreciative audience. He wants your story, all you need to do is let it out.

Following Brother Blue has changed my storytelling. All my cleverly contrived story ideas seem much beside the point after experiencing Blue opening his heart to the spirit and having the tale come through. In the echoes of Blue I've been inspired to truly seek the story that I already thought I had, getting past the ingenious plot twist and the clever use of words. Gradually, those tales that I had in mind to tell have been working their way down, from the mind to the heart.

It seems that in so many things I've been following Brother Blue, struggling to come to understand what is unambiguously clear to him. It is not that Brother Blue is obscure, or changeable. He says what he believes clearly and yes, repetitively. His ideas and beliefs are straightforward, and his words and actions are consistent. And yet…

Blue can be frustrating because he doesn't behave like most people. He isn't like most folks, because he has turned his life into a work of art. I don't just mean that he's made artful stories from the events of his past. Blue has, of course, done that, but he has done more.

Ahhhh!

He lives as story, making of his life a tale of the power of story itself, and being story as love made manifest. A few examples:

One Tuesday night storytelling was in progress at the Bookcellar, tales rebounding off the shelves of used fiction that lined that bookstore basement back room. Into our midst burst a street person, a man who had seen Brother Blue's name on the sign outside. He was deeply agitated, interrupted the story in progress to petition Blue and Ruth. His family was in crisis, someone was dying, he needed to be with them on the other side of the country, but he had no bus fare. The real world had crashed in upon our little world of storytelling. What would you do? What would Blue do? After soothingly welcoming the man into our circle, Blue invited him to tell us a story. Like many of us, the man didn't quite understand. He was in crisis, he needed money; Blue wanted a fairy tale? Sheepishly, he got up before us and told what amounted to a two-minute barroom joke. And he sat down amid polite applause. But while he had been telling, the people in the room, unprompted, had been passing the hat, and he got his bus fare. More importantly, as I only later realized, Blue had shifted the dynamic from intruder and beggar to participant and paid performer. The intruder had been integrated into the story of the Bookcellar, and the story had a happy ending for all involved.

The Bookcellar series was forced to move from The Bookcellar to another bookstore named Foozles also in Porter Square, then to the library of the Episcopal Divinity School (EDS) just outside Harvard Square where it continues today. Due to Ruth's incredible dedication and organizational skills, Brother Blue's has met through relocations and business closings, during snowstorms and on national holidays. Eleven years without missing a Tuesday night. Always there every Tuesday as a place to go.

And so it was that on Tuesday, September 11th, 2001 Brother Blue's storytelling group met at EDS. The library itself was closed, like most every other public building, in the wake of that terrible day. So Blue and Ruth held the storytelling on the stairs in front of the library. Not many came, and those who did talked out their grief and anger and numb incomprehension. Blue was as shaken as the rest of us, and I wondered what he would say. Some rallying cry? Some profound speech that would make sense of it all? No, Blue spoke only for himself, and what he said was "I have to continue doing what I've been doing." At the time, I didn't understand. With time I have seen the wisdom in Blue's sad

Ahhhh!

and courageous rededication. Perhaps the hardest and wisest thing to do in times of panic and dislocation is to not become a reactive echo of the crisis, but to continue the work already begun, to persevere. Especially if your work, like Brother Blue's, is to create peace in the world by sharing our stories and thus making it impossible to hate.

Blue lives his principles. He makes of his principles a didactic and healing work of art that is indistinguishable from his life. He inspires creativity and self-esteem, he offers praise and love to all, he listens, and thus defeats despair, gives solace to grief, and gives the suicide a reason to continue and to heal. This is not rhetoric. These are literal, witnessed events, happening every Tuesday night.

Glenn Morrow is a storyteller and storytelling advocate. He edits *The Museletter*, published by LANES, and is chair of *Storytelling Magazine*, published by the National Storytelling Network. He also serves on the boards of directors of these two organizations. He got his storytelling start at Brother Blue's weekly series, and continues to tell there regularly.

Ahhhh!

For Brother Blue

Motoko

The first time I met you
I saw an instant love light in your eyes
I felt shy yet elevated
And I hid behind your wife

Another time I saw you
I was with a partner of my own
"What do you see in him?" you asked
"Everything," I said and you smiled

In my dream I saw you standing
Leaning against a rainbow
No, it was a little boy with heartache eyes
Clutching to Miss Ruth's scarf

Now every time I see the two of you
I sit and listen, full of joy
Drinking in your words of life
And bask in Miss Ruth's quiet dignity

Ahhhh!

Three Poems in Japanese
Motoko

つないだ手
はなすまい　ふと
目が覚める
この手には青い
ふうせんひとつ

I held your hand
Never to let go. Then
I woke up
All that was left in my hand was
A single blue balloon

暮れなずむ
街角ロミオ
ゆきずりの
少女の笑みに
ジュリエットを見る

At dusk
Romeo on the street corner
Sees Juliet
In the smile of a little girl
Passing by

玉手箱
こっそり開けて
不老不死
そよ風に舞う
双つ蝶々

You secretly opened
The Magic Box of Souls
And became immortal
Like two butterflies
Dancing in the breeze

Motoko first met Brother Blue and Miss Ruth in 1996 and has loved them ever since. A native of Japan, Motoko has told Asian folktales and original stories in schools, libraries, and festivals up and down the East Coast.

AHHHH!

From Black and White to Color

Noel Murphy

I was ten years old when I first met Brother Blue in a Unitarian church in Bedford, Massachusetts. I attended church there in my quest for spirituality. I'd explored both the Catholic and Baptist churches. I liked the Unitarian church because the pastor read *The Little Prince* to the congregation and no one stopped me when I played the piano after the service. My playing was like chopping wood, yet no one seemed to care. I was a ten-year-old explorer, an adventurer, a seeker. I was a child in search of purpose. My quest for the Holy Grail, yet I'd never even heard of the Holy Grail.

One particular Sunday morning I walked into the 200-year-old sanctuary just as the fire alarm went off. I saw a group of people standing around a tall black man wearing all blue. He was covered with butterflies and ribbons and wore bells tied to his legs. To see him for the first time was like being inside a kaleidoscope with the smell of fresh baked chocolate chip cookies in the air. He was happiness, wonder, and dreams coming true all at once. Bedford was *white* white. Brother Blue was the moment in *The Wizard of Oz* when it turns from black and white to color. I don't really remember color before that moment.

As the alarm pierced through the church, I, of course, knew what to do. I broke through the crowd, grabbed this man's hand and led him to safety. A mere failed fire alarm was how I met Brother Blue. It was that day he asked me to join him in front of the congregation in a tribute to a jazz trumpeter who had died. I read from the book of Corinthians. Having saved his life, it was only fitting that I be asked to contribute. Thus begins a 28 year mentorship.

He later took me to Harvard to perform for the faculty with him. We rode the subway all the way to the end of the line. He danced and told stories and I played the flute. We went to churches together, to the

Ahhhh!

streets, to radio stations. Anywhere I was allowed to go, I went. While I was away at private school, I listened to Blue on "The Spider's Web" on National Public Radio. Brother Blue was my pride, my hope, my confirmation, and my spiritual communion.

When I was 15, Blue and his incredible wife, Ruth, went to a lawyer to see about making me his manager. They couldn't because my signature wasn't legal. Imagine! I guess I was part Don King back then. I had so many ideas for Blue. I was so inspired by him.

As I got older I started to drift away from my former self. The young bright kid gave way to an angry young man who, in turn, gave way to a budding drug addict. I had lost my way. I was alone, hurt, and addicted. In New Hampshire I ran out of heating oil in my house. I was being evicted. I had only two things, electricity and illegal HBO. I sat in the cold one night watching a movie called *Knightriders* and suddenly there he was—Brother Blue! I felt warm, alive, like I came from somewhere. I remembered, for a moment, that young happy kid I had once been. But I wasn't out of the woods yet.

Not long after that night I moved back to Boston. One night I needed drugs and walked out of my rooming house and, as strung out as I was, I ran straight into Ruth and Blue. I felt humiliated. Here was my hero with his angel and this was what I had done with the gifts I'd been given!

Well, more time passed and my brother Todd was in Seattle at a university. Brother Blue was speaking before a packed house in the lecture hall. Blue apparently was telling a story when he spotted my brother Todd in the audience. He stopped the story he was telling and stared. "You're his brother!" Blue exclaimed. He proceeded to tell the standing-room-only audience the story of Noel and Blue. He told of how this little white child was the son he never had. And he told of my life's purpose and told our story. Well, I wish the children who watched him on television, saw him in films or heard him on the radio could know him the way I did— know the blessing, the exhilaration and the grace of being made personally important by Dr. Hugh Morgan Hill, the genius, the spiritual man, the visionary and the friend. That they could know the love that I received from Brother Blue, live, appearing in my life for the last 28 years.

I've been clean and sober for almost 14 years now. When you get sober, they suggest that you pick a concept of a higher power, something you love. It could be anything, as long as it is all loving. Back then I was sick and needed to get well. I chose Brother Blue as my concept, my higher power. The only one, it seemed, who hadn't hurt me or betrayed

Ahhhh!

me in some way. Today I call my concept God. Today, Brother Blue is my God's wise sage, visionary, shaman, jester and messenger.

Today I speak all over the country at Salvation Army Centers, companies, and college campuses. I do radio, I have a television show, I'm writing my first book, I am making a big difference in the world. There is nowhere I go that I don't hear Brother Blue's voice prodding me, coaching me, reminding me that I am who I am today because of the brand of value Brother Blue burnt onto my heart.

A few years ago I went to Boston and attended his storyteller's night. I told our story. He told our story. This is what he says: "If you don't have a story to tell from your heart, don't tell it." This story comes from the middle of my heart, where all things come from with Brother Blue. The ten-year-old saving the man in one moment who would save the boy forever. So, today when I speak, sing, perform music, do comedy, tell stories and move audiences, I am grateful to this man who changed my life and planted the seed that has grown into an oak. Today I am a leader, a storyteller like him. Proving simply that the acorn never falls far from the tree.

Noel Murphy leads transformational weekend seminars using storytelling, humor, and music, and attributes it all to knowing Blue. His favorite story to tell is the one about knowing Brother Blue.

Ahhhh!

Sixteen Seconds

Jesse Myers

In the years I've known Blue, I've come to learn that his finest story is the silent one heard only by his wife Ruth as he looks in her eyes. I've long looked at this lovely couple as grandparents and mentors, and in their love I see all my deepest dreams. Any tribute to the man is incomplete without mention of the love that defines his life, and there is no finer example of this than the glances he and Ruth share.

I wrote this with a dream in my heart after spending a night talking with Blue and Ruth, and seeing the love in their eyes. To these two I say thank you. As I chase the dream this was written for, I look to you and know that it can be reached.

Late one chill October night the moon was full, the air was clear, and there was a silence despite the noises that filled the air. It was still. Mothers had long since tucked their children into bed and kissed them goodnight. Lovers, exhausted and content, now lay sleeping in each other's arms, and the only color outside fell from the bulbs of streetlamps, casting dramatic yellow cones of light to the ground.

Under one of those carefully placed streetlamps on the street—in the city, the country, the middle of nowhere—stood a man. With deep breaths he drew in both the icy air and the hot smoke from his cigarette. He was a thoroughly average man, nothing striking about him. He was neither handsome nor ugly, but he was real. As he stood under the streetlamp he watched the smoke spill from his nose into the light and disappear into the darkness. The world stood still around him.

No light escaped the darkened windows of the mothers and the children and the lovers. Outside those fragile panes of glass the world was bleached of all color by the brilliant moonlight from above. Seconds passed like hours as the world slept peacefully, all but the man standing under the streetlamp and the woman walking towards him.

Ahhhh!

She was beautiful. Stunning. Silent. The only sound she made was the scuffing of her heels against the ground, but as she walked under each streetlamp she seemed to fill the entire night with color before blending back into the sea of muted white as she left the yellow light.

He could hear her coming. As she drew near, he simply exhaled a plume of smoke which twisted and danced its way up through the light, passed into the night, and in his mind curled all the way up to the moon. Feeling the cold air fill his lungs, the man turned his head towards the footsteps approaching him just in time to see her ankle fall into the light and fill his world with color.

She was radiant. Time simply stood still and waited for her to fully emerge from the darkness and break through into the light. The man watched as first her ankle fully appeared, then her leg, and what seemed like an eternity later he saw a hand, followed by her chest, and finally she was complete. They felt their hearts beating together as his eyes met hers.

More was said in that silent moment than in all of history before it.

Alone now in their sanctuary of color, the two newfound lovers continued to gaze into each other's eyes, both exploring the depth and fullness of the other's soul. Reaching out her arm, she slowly laid her hand on his chest and felt his heart beating, now and always for her, no longer simply for his own life. His hand rested on her cheek, and simply feeling her skin he knew that all her emotions were open to him. Together they were whole.

In this timeless pose the world revolved around these two, and without uttering mere words that would be inadequate, they showed the night how to love. And under the moon that night, as the mothers, children, and lovers slept in their beds, these two may have gone their separate ways or their separate ways may have become one.

The night always has to end, but not even that can change that I will always love you.

Blue and Ruth watched Jesse Myers grow up and now he runs his own business designing websites.

Ahhhh!

Balloons for Sam

Mike Myers

Brother Blue is pictured in my dictionary under "storyteller" and he is holding Ruth's hand. I can't think of anyone who listens better and is more nurturing. Blue always sees the good in people, and helps to make them believe in their own potential. He is the teacher of so many.

If storytellers were launched like ships, just think about how many Blue and Ruth have launched.

Years ago Blue and Ruth asked Bonnie and me if they could see Sam's grave. We drove over to the cemetery. We all got out of the car. Blue fell to his knees and told a story for Sam at the cemetery. When he finished, we all held hands, hugged and cried together. The pinwheels spun amid the daffodils and lilies of the valley and Brother Blue tied some jingle bells to the tree and left balloons for Sam. That was when I realized that we were family.

Mike Myers is the OUAT (Once Upon A Time) Storyteller, the world's oldest 5 year old, former president/administrator of LANES, past director of "A Day for Sam" storytelling festival, recipient of NSN's Northeast Service Award for 1997, and a builder of instruments for use in performance. Mike and Bonnie are the parents of Sam and Jesse Myers.

Blue with Mike Myers at *A Day for Sam*

Ahhhh!

Copies and Originals in Plato's *Parmenides*

Greg Nagy

[In the tradition of the academic festschrift, what follows is original research on a subject dear to Brother Blue: the improvisational nature of oral story, as originally described by his Harvard mentor, the late Albert Bates Lord.]

In another project, I have explored allusions made by Plato to the performances of Homeric poetry by *rhapsôidoi* 'rhapsodes' at the Athenian festival of the Panathenaia.[1]

Here I focus on another such rhapsodic allusion, in the *Parmenides* of Plato. The dramatic setting for this work is the quadrennial or Great Panathenaia in Athens. This premier city festival, as we learn at the start of the *Parmenides*, has just attracted a visit from the luminous Parmenides himself, accompanied by his charismatic friend Zeno (127a). The whole dialogue of the *Parmenides*, featuring the "quoted words" of Parmenides and Zeno and a youthful Socrates (126b-c), is represented as spoken by the character of Kephalos, who says that he heard these quoted words from Antiphon (126b and following), who in turn heard them from Pythodoros, a friend of Zeno's who was present at the occasion of the dialogue.[2] The elusiveness of establishing the "original words" of this dialogue is relevant, I suggest, to the dramatic setting of the Panathenaia, which also serves as the historical setting for the performance of Homeric poetry by rhapsodes.

This dramatized occasion of the dialogue that is the *Parmenides* coincides with a public reading by Zeno of a written text (*grammata*) that he is introducing for the first time in Athens and that the youthful Socrates has been eager to hear (127c). Socrates now hears the whole reading by Zeno. Not so Parmenides and Pythodoros, who are late in arriving and

Aʜʜʜʜ!

miss most of the reading (128c-d). A detail is ostentatiously added at this point: Pythodoros had already heard Zeno perform a public reading on a previous unspecified occasion (128d). When Zeno finishes reading, Socrates asks him to read again the first hypothesis of the first argument (*logos*), and this re-reading becomes the point of entry for the dialogue to begin, with a direct "quotation" of a question by Socrates (128d-e) in response to the re-reading.

By the time this Platonic dialogue gets underway, we have already been given the impression that its words may well be just as textualized as the words of the written text from which Zeno had performed his public reading. Kephalos says that Pythodoros told the dialogue to Antiphon over and over again (126c) and that Antiphon then practiced 'remembering' (*apomnêmoneuei*) the dialogue, word for word, over and over again (126c).

As Socrates and Zeno pursue their dialogue extending from Socrates' question, it becomes clear that Zeno's argument, extending from his written text (*gramma*: 128a, 128b, 128c), is meant as a reinforcement (*boêtheia*) of Parmenides' unwritten poetry (*poiêmata*: 128a).[3] A detail is ostentatiously added at this point: Zeno, who is represented as nearing the age of 40, claims that he originally produced his written text when he was still a young man, and that this original written text was then surreptitiously copied and has been circulating as a copy ever since (128d-e). Socrates, Zeno tells him, should insist on the uniqueness of the "original," shunning the multiplicity of the copies (128e).

The elusiveness of this "original" text of Zeno, as parodied here by Plato, is analogous to the elusiveness of an "original" text of Homer. Each time the poetry of Homer is performed, it is recomposed in the act of performance.[4] Plato's meditation on the unattainability of the "original" invites further meditation on the immediacy of bringing the word to life in dialogue, in performance.

See page 378 for footnotes.

Greg Nagy is the Francis Jones Professor of Classical Greek Literature and Professor of Comparative Literature at Harvard University. His book, *The Best of the Achaeans: Concepts of the Hero in Archaic Greek Poetry*, won the Goodwin Award of Merit, American Philological Association, in 1982. Mr. Nagy is furthering and extending the work of the late Albert Bates Lord on the improvisationl nature of traditional oral narrative. Lord was a seminal colleague of Brother Blue.

Ahhhh!

Hugh Hill and Brother Blue
Nancy Niebuhr

I first met Ruth and Hugh many years ago on a day that has a special place in my memory. The day was an Easter Sunday in the early 60's—a happy time before our country became so involved in the Vietnam war. The place was the home of Dorothy and Gordon Kaufman in Lexington, and the occasion was Easter dinner. Anyone who was fortunate to have been invited to a dinner planned and cooked by Dorothy will understand that that in itself makes an occasion to remember. The guest list was long. This was before our children had left home for college, so there were fourteen around the table. There were the four Kaufman children, David, Gretchen, Ann and Edmond, our two children, Gustav and Sarah, and Gregor Goethals was there with her son, Rob. Karen Lindsley, a graduate student, was there—and Ruth and Hugh Hill.

Dorothy had made her stuffed leg of lamb. I had brought a lamb cake, using my grandmother's recipe for coconut cake.

The conversation that day was lively and gradually progressed from food to other things. In time, it became clear to all that we were in the presence of a master storyteller, as Hugh told us stories of his past, his relatives, and his days at Yale. As the dinner came to an end, it would have been only natural for the adults to go into the living room and continue the easy-going conversation. However, Hugh, with his sense of inclusiveness and loving generosity, realized that by doing that we would be leaving the young people out. So he gathered them all around and organized a basketball game in the Kaufman's driveway, where Gordon had installed a basket for goal shooting. This was wildly successful, and it wasn't long before the adults were outside also, trying to make a goal.

After that day, we didn't see Ruth and Hugh regularly, but from time to time our paths would cross. We might see them at Memorial Church, or the phone might ring, and it would be Hugh with a bit of news or

Ahhhh!

story he wanted to pass on. Sometimes at Christmas time Ruth would appear at the door with one of her truly wonderful fruit cakes. I complimented her so many times that she finally gave me the recipe!

Sometime later, we began to see a familiar figure in Harvard Square dressed in the now famous blue costume and surrounded by a crowd of people, young and old. We learned it was our friend—now "Brother Blue the storyteller"—a most fitting name for a person of his special talent and ability.

Nancy Niebuhr, native of North Carolina, studied music and singing. She married Richard Niebuhr in 1950. In 1956 they moved to Cambridge and have since been members of the Harvard Divinity School community. She is the mother of two children, Gustav and Sarah, and three grandchildren.

THE LANES MUSELETTER

A Project of The League for The Advancement of New England Storytelling

Volume 4, No. 5 - February 1992   Price $2.00

BULLETIN BOARD

• There's a new storytelling coffeehouse, hosted by Brother Blue, on Tuesday evenings at the Bookcellar Bookstore in Cambridge, MA. Open mike at 7pm; feature at 8pm. If you'd like to feature, call the bookstore at (617) 864-9625 or Ruth Hill (617) 495-8399.

Bookcellar Storytelling Series, every Tuesday, hosted by Brother Blue, 7pm open mike, 8pm feature. Bookstore/cafe in Cambridge, MA. **Feb. 4,** Jay O'Callahan, **Feb. 11,** Brother Blue, **Feb. 18,** Patricia McMahon, **Feb. 25,** Stacie Marinelli. (617) 864-9625

Ahhhh!

The William Blake of Storytelling

Jay O'Callahan

In addition to being the William Blake of the storytelling movement and an earth treasure, my wife, children, and I feel as if Brother Blue is a member of our family. He is always present to us. I want to mention two particular moments which were important to our family.

When our son Ted was nine, he wanted more than anything to be the center fielder for the Boston Red Sox. Our whole family went to a Storytellers In Concert performance in Cambridge, Massachusetts one night, and Ted told Blue of his baseball hopes. Brother Blue immediately launched into a story for Ted: "Ted is in center field, and the hitter swings and drives the ball far over Ted's head." Blue was rocking and pointing toward the imaginary ball as it was headed out of the imaginary park. Blue went on, "The crowd was on its feet, the announcer was shouting '*home run!*' to the radio audience, but Ted, the center fielder, didn't give up. Ted watched the ball so hard that the ball stopped in mid air and zoomed down into Ted's glove." My son Ted glowed with delight. Brother Blue gave Ted a hero's hug. It was a wonderful moment, and typical of Brother Blue's generosity. Blue is a giver of gifts; he saves nothing.

On another occasion, Blue gave a similar gift to our daughter, Laura, who was ten at the time. Blue was performing at the old town hall during the Three Apples Festival in Harvard, Massachusetts. Brother Blue had begun a story and suddenly pointed to Laura who was sitting in the front row. Blue said, "I need an angel to help me with this story." Then Blue laughed and turned away saying, "That blinding light in the front row is my angel. Come up here, Laura, and bring me some sun glasses." Laura came up on stage and Blue took Laura's hand and they began to perform together. He made it easy for Laura. He would give her some lines and made her the star, since she was the angel. That was

Ahhhh!

Laura's debut; she entered the greater world with Blue as her mentor. What more could a youngster ask? What more could a parent ask?

It would have been fascinating to live in Elizabethan times; all that drama. But I wouldn't trade Shakespeare for Brother Blue. What a difference he has made in my life. In all our lives. He is one of the wonders of our times.

Jay O'Callahan is a writer and storyteller. He has performed at Lincoln Center, The Abbey Theater as part of the Yeats International Drama Festival, the National Fine Arts Complex in London, and with the Boston Symphony Orchestra. *Time* Magazine called him "a man of wit, poetry, and elegance." Jay O'Callahan's stories are heard on National Public Radio. In 1996, he was inducted into the National Storytelling Network's Circle of Excellence. He was awarded a National Endowment of the Arts Fellowship for Solo Performance Excellence in 2001.

Photo: Margo Kempinshi

Blue and Ruth at *The Bliss Festival,* Cross Village, MI - July 1998

AHHHH!

The Timely Messenger
Charles J. Ogletree

Brother Blue: The timely messenger with the timeless message. There are so many things that are influenced by the arrival of the New Millennium. Technology seems to offer cutting-edge advantages in the volume and speed of information. The economy has gained from new discoveries. Some who were powerless have become powerful. And yet, there are some things that, despite the change of time, remain as true now as ever. The true source of our energy and commitment here in Cambridge, often viewed as the citadel of higher learning, is Brother Blue. His message of love, struggle, unity, and peace, is never weakened. His message is always timely and timeless. His insights are extraordinary. His appreciation of our capacity for greatness offers all within the sound of his voice the desire to strive to do more. His caution to all—to do for others as we would want them to do for us—is a sign of his prayer for our own need to express humility. His self-sacrificial philosophy allows us all to see that in God's eyes we are but children, yearning to learn and grow.

To Brother Blue, we praise him not by our constant references to his greatness. We can only truly praise him by using our talents and abilities to lift up others who are in need. Our dear Brother Blue, you are truly timely, and timeless. We are yours in the struggle.

Charles J. Ogletree, Jr is the Jesse Climenko Professor of Law at Harvard Law School, and a prominent legal theorist. He is the co-author of the award-winning book, *Beyond the Rodney King Story: An Examination of Police Conduct in Minority Communities (1994)* and was selected by the National Law Journal as one of the 100 most influential lawyers in America in the 2000 survey. He is the founder and Director of the Harvard Law School Saturday School Program, and the Criminal Justice Institute. He is also a fan of Brother Blue!

Ahhhh!

The Importance of Entrances

Laura Packer

I could tell you all about how I met them (it was a dark and stormy night). I could tell you about the many ways that they have changed my life (not only giving me the gift of storytelling, but by believing in me). I could tell you about the wonderful people I have met through them and come to consider family. But I will not tell you about any of those things. Instead, I would like to tell you about the first time they came into my home. It was a sacred event and one I will treasure forever.

Brother Blue, Ruth, and I had known each other for several years. We had had many adventures together, both through story and through time shared outside of storytelling, but we had never met in my home, in spite of many good intentions. We had repeatedly talked about them coming over for dinner, but each time we made plans, something else came up; we never got around to it. In retrospect, I think it was the hand of God that kept them from coming into my home until I truly needed them.

I had decided it was time to change my life; lost, as one may be when in the midst of redefinition. Among other things, I had moved and was still struggling to get my feet under me. Brother Blue and Ruth held out their hands and pulled me up, letting me lean on them until I found a way to make my house a home.

We were at Tuesday night storytelling. I was describing my new apartment to a group of friends, including Ruth. As I told them about the new spaces around me, and my feelings of both excitement and loss, Ruth declared, "We'll come over and Blue can bless your home for you!" I had never had a home blessed before and liked the sound of it, so we set a date.

When the day came I was still barely unpacked. I had invited friends and family to join us. I cooked. The house was full of good smells and better people. When Brother Blue and Ruth arrived they became the focal point of the living room. The conversation and laughter became a whirlwind that filled my apartment, and swept it clean of any darkness that might have lingered in the corners or closets. We ate together, and then we Began.

Ahhhh!

Brother Blue led us into the foyer outside my front door. We held hands in a circle. Blue began to talk about how important entrances are, how each step taken into a home is sacred, about how the doorway to the house blesses everyone who passes through it. We exhaled together, and then passed into the apartment. As we went from room to room, Blue told us stories about how each part of a home is holy, blessed. In the living room, we faced the east and welcomed sunrise into my life. In the work room, we welcomed the honesty of hard work and labors of love. In the bedroom, he offered me good sleep, good dreams, and then delicately touched upon companionship, sexuality, and passion. In the back room, still full of boxes and crates, Brother Blue laughed and told me how much he liked that room, soothing away my embarrassment over such a mess. He told me, "God has a room like this, where He puts everything He hasn't had time to get to yet." And we blessed the need for time and patience too.

In the back hall he looked at my books, and asked if anyone had anything they wanted to add. Ruth spoke up. "All we need to tell you is that we love you." I filled with tears. As we went around the circle, each person told me they loved me, as I told them I loved them. In that moment I knew for the first time that I would survive the chaos I had made of my life, and that the love Brother Blue, Ruth, and all the others were giving me was a deep river that I could drink from freely. I knew for the first time that I could truly be safe in my new home. I cried. From the back room we went, lastly, to the kitchen, the heart of the home. And there Blue blessed each and every one of us surrounding us with light and the force of his compassion. We were done.

I was exhausted, yet happier than I had been in months. We all talked and ate and laughed a bit longer, then everyone went home. I finally was able to sleep. Brother Blue and Ruth made it possible for me to continue in that new space through the coming months and difficult times.

Through Blue's stories, Ruth's infinite patience and good humor, as well as their support and faith in me and many, many others, they have helped us all grow and live our lives well. The world is a far better place for their presence. The seeds of love, compassion, and storytelling that they have planted have grown deep roots and sent up many shoots.

Brother Blue, Ruth, I will always be grateful for your love and friendship. Thank you. I love you, too.

Laura Packer is a storyteller who now works for the company I ROBOT designing computer games. She's very involved in LANES, and co-chaired two recent Sharing the Fire storytelling conferences.

Ahhhh!

The Blue Preacher

Peter Panagore

I.
Preacher, teacher, story dreamer,
Blue in bells, in blue, in butterflies
twinkling, tinkling buoyed by balloons
pranced down the aisle at our church
of the frozen chosen
(as we chilly Christians call ourselves).
The only black and Blue man in a gathering of white faces.
300 drop jawed, wide eye, surprised expressions.
The only black man maybe ever to preach
at the Orange Congregational Church
United Church of Christ, Connecticut,
for my ordination to the clergy service,
on the Ides of March in 1987.

The Reverend Doctor Hugh Morgan Hill
from Cambridge, Massachusetts,
was what it said in the bulletin.

What they saw,
what they heard,
the oral word,
what they felt,
through and through,
was Blue.

Preacher, my teacher, story dreamer,
told to me my life's work that day,

Ahhhh!

and rose me up on winged words
and lifted all of us to angel's glory
come from poetry, from his soul
in dance from his toes,
in the waggle of his front pew finger,
not hidden behind a pulpit's artifice,
jangling on the floor among the folks,
the influential man
spoke.

They came by train to New Haven.
Ruth holding his toes to ground,
that he might function
remember to eat falafel, dear,
have a drink of tamarind juice, Blue
to dampen his telling throat.

Ruth steadying him that he might
become the street level stories
instead of moralizing
or plain preaching
from high above us.

Telling tales of truths, of life
let the story tell it.

Let the story tell itself.
Get out of the way.
Let the words roll
and the soul speak
and the tongue talk
and the body jazz.

II.

The Very Good Reverend Doctor Ibeah Fool,
a fictional character, a pontificating
big voiced preacher,
being truly, partly, me,

Ahhhh!

another of God's chosen fools,
inspired by Reverend Blue,
flabbergasted Boothbay Congregationalists,
when a white faced child of Blue
wearing a cleric's black robes
and a sponge red nose with
half a log fixed over one eye
by duct tape,
started shouting funny judgments,
at the people
while half blindly trying to remove a speck
that no one else could see
from a scared and trusting and utterly unwarned
        volunteer's eye,
by way of a smallish chain saw,
that would not start,
pull as the Fool might,
and laughter
filled the meeting house,
and laughter and outrageous behavior
of a comical nature
birthed from Blue
and serious truth
by Christ, was spoken,
in a whimsical way,
clear your damn perception
before you try to clear another's
see yourself's soul first, fool.

III.

Blue is a hero in the corner of my mouth
who speaks in rhyme,
for me,
who prays aloud in poetry,
he's a sparkle in my heart
the waggle in my bare toes
exposed
behind the Sunday morning's pulpit

Ahhhh!

262

and he, the Brave Brother,
has balloons to lift me
and my loves to heaven,
and is, nearly always,
with me
in memory
and motivation.

Reverend Peter Panagore's home, on Linekin Neck, on the coast of Maine, was built from the wreckage of the salvaged schooner *Aberdeen*. Michelle Miclette, his wife, is a 5th grade science teacher. Alexa (age 12) studies violin with the Daponte Quartette. Andy (age 9) is a "goofy" on a snowboard. The family sails, skis, skates, and in August swims in the cold sea. Peter is a graduate of Yale Divinity School, Yale University, and a staff writer for *Homiletics Journal*, *(Communication Resources, Inc.)*

Blue at *The Bliss Festival*, Cross Village, MI - July 1998

Ahhhh!

Hey Mister Parent, Who Is That Dude?
Michael Parent

Brother Blue has been a teacher and mentor to many a storyteller. For me, at a very crucial time, he was a "mentor by example." One day in 1975 when I was teaching at Cathedral High School in the very ethnic South End of Boston, my friend Shawn Smith called and told me to meet him at the Arlington Street Church that night for a unique experience. Shawn was an old, trusted friend with very eclectic tastes, a brilliant mind, and strong opinions. If something was interesting to Shawn, I felt no need to ask any further questions.

I arrived and he led me into the church. There were a half-dozen people sitting in the front pews, listening to a strikingly dressed man who told stories unlike anyone I'd ever heard. His costume was a revelation of blue colors, butterflies, and bells, and his style was a mixture of actor, mystic, and whirling dervish. I was transfixed by his stories of "Muddy Duddy" and "Miss Wunderlich". He was totally unself-conscious, totally himself, and totally *in* the story. And I had not listened as closely and intensely to anyone for a long, long time.

I approached him at the end of the session, told him how much I'd enjoyed his stories, and asked how I could arrange a visit to my school. I told him we had a huge variety of students, that many of them lived in tough housing projects near the school, that they'd been responsive to the stories I'd been telling them (to illustrate class material and expand their attention span), and that I was convinced they were ready for and hungry for *his* stories. He thanked me and pointed to an elegant lady in the front row. "Talk to Ruth. She arranges all that." Ruth (Blue's wife and ever-present partner) and I talked, made arrangements, and the two of them arrived at the school a few weeks later.

As he walked down the hall in his storytelling regalia, curious, slightly amazed eyes followed his every move. The kids who were in my English classes gave me a look that said, "Is this guy the *king* of all weird people you bring in to English class or what?"

Ahhhh!

264

One particularly skeptical student sidled up to me as we walked along and said, "Hey, Mister Parent, who is that dude?"

"You show up for English class today for a change, Pete, and you'll find out," I replied.

I gathered two English classes into one room. There were stares, whispers, and not a few snickers as the students took their seats. Ruth sat near the front and Blue began. He took off his shoes, then his socks, and started dancing. The kids turned to each other with "Is this guy for real?" looks on their faces. Some of them glanced over at me, obviously puzzled about the point of all this. Then Blue launched into his story of "Little Blue Riding Hood" who lived in the projects, and that was the end of any whispers and snickers. He danced, played his harmonica, and, if memory serves correctly, moved right in to "Muddy Duddy" and "Miss Wunderlich."

When he finished, I watched the students very closely. They did not make their usual dashing exits. They looked like they could have stayed another class period or two. Then, after a few seconds of silence, their hearty applause seemed to say, "You're amazing, Man. You ain't afraid of us. You know who we are. Thank you!"

Later, the same student who had approached me in the hallway to ask who "that dude" was, said to me, as coolly as a city kid from the projects can, "Hey, Mister Parent, that dude with the stories, he was somethin', wasn't he?"

"You got that right, Pete. You got that right."

The transformation of my English students from tough city kids to wide-eyed children as Blue spun his magic is an image that still brings tears and goosebumps. Seeing Brother Blue tell stories on that occasion, in the church before that, and on subsequent occasions, has had a very deep impact on me. I realized that what I tried to do with the kids through stories was much like—though only a shadow of—what Blue did every day of his life—like a priest offering a sacrament.

In 1977, I started pursuing my own path as a full-time storyteller. I have since had the privilege of being encouraged and supported by Blue and Ruth on many occasions. Their love and shining example have been a spirit-anchor for me and many others who undertake the storytelling journey. Thank you, Brother Blue and Ruth.

Michael Parent, a Mainer of French-Canadian descent, has told stories in both English and French and has presented workshops in the U.S. and beyond since 1977. He is a 1999 recipient of the National Storytelling Network's Circle of Excellence award.

Ahhhh!

Picture of a Father
Sydelle Pearl

My father died on April 1st, 1995. One month and one day later I found myself at the Bookcellar Cafe hoping to have my name pulled from the cookie tin, so that I could tell my father's story. My name was called and I rose, filled with a tremendous sense of mission. I was by my father's side when he died, I eulogized him at his funeral, and I carried the profundity of all that I had experienced in the past month as I turned to face Brother Blue and Ruth's audience. In eight minutes' time I told the story I had told when I eulogized him and somehow, the act of sharing it with this community of tellers and listeners was extremely moving to me. After the stories were all over on that long-ago May night, I was getting ready to leave when Blue called me over to him. "Do you have a picture of your father?" he asked. I nodded and fiddled in my purse for the photo of David Pearl as a young man on the streets of Brooklyn. Blue reached out his hand to look at the picture more closely. It was as if he wished to glean more of my father's story from the photograph of his face. I am most grateful to him for this moment.

Sydelle Pearl is a storyteller, author, and songwriter. She often incorporates original songs that spring from the multicultural folktales and original stories that she tells to preschool, elementary, and family audiences. Her book, *Elijah's Tears*, published by Henry Holt and Company, has gone into a second printing.

Ahhhh!

A Butterfly Tribute

Elisa Pearmain

Butterflies are said to represent the spirit. I think this butterfly tale represents the spirit in which Blue and Ruth live.

The Butterfly Sisters

A German folktale, adapted by Elisa Pearmain

Long ago in a far away place,
lived three butterfly sisters,
full of love and grace.
One was yellow, another was red,
and the third was as white as these hairs on my head.

Now they lived near a garden,
and that's where they hung,
all day long just flitting in the sun.
They loved the flowers;
each color so unique,
and the smell, so heavenly,
they could barely speak.

One day they were so caught in their ecstasy
that up in the sky they failed to see
clouds so dark were covering the sun.
By the time they looked up,
it was too late to run.
The rain was coming down in big fat drops,
making dents in their wings with each plip plip plop.

Ahhhh!

"Help," they called.
"Help," they said.
"If we don't get under cover, we're as good as dead!"
"I've an idea," the red one cried.
"Inside the flowers
we can safely hide."
So the butterfly sisters began to flit about,
from flower to flower they began to shout:

"Save us, save us,
from the rain.
Till the sun comes out again."

Well it wasn't long before a red tulip sighed.
She opened up her petals and they started inside.
She saw that red butterfly fluttering in,
and her face broke into a gigantic grin.

"Oh, you are gorgeous," the red tulip cried,
"You're just like me, come on inside."
But then she saw the butterflies yellow and white,
and she snapped her petals closed, she shut them up tight.
"Butterfly red is like me, so she can stay,
but you guys are different, go away, go away!"

Well, butterfly red wasn't buying that spam.
She said, "If you don't want my friends, I'd rather scram!
Let's scram."

But now the rain was coming down in steady sheets,
hitting their wings like sharp birdie beaks.
So the butterfly sisters sang out again:

"Save us, save us,
from the rain.
Till the sun comes out again."

Well, it wasn't long before a yellow tulip sighed.
She opened her petals and they started inside.
She saw the yellow butterfly fluttering in,
and her face broke into a gigantic grin.

Ahhhh!

"Oh, you are gorgeous," the yellow tulip cried,
"You're just like me, come on inside."
But then she saw the butterflies red and white,
and she snapped her petals closed, she shut them up tight.
"Butterfly yellow is like me, so she can stay.
But you guys are different, go away, go away!"

Well, butterfly yellow wasn't buying that spam.
She said, "If you don't want my friends, I'd rather scram.
Let's scram."

Well, the same thing happened with a lily so white,
she saw the others and shut her petals up tight.

And now the rain was coming down so hard and fast,
the sisters could not fly, and they fell at last.

That could have been it for the butterflies three.
But it wasn't the end of this story.

You see, the sun was watching from a crack in the sky,
and she was moved to action, action on high.
When she saw the love that the three friends showed,
it made her so happy, it made her glow.
She pushed back the clouds with a hot burst of fire,
and shone on those sisters before they could expire.

Soon the butterflies had dried their wings in the sun,
and they skedaddled home, just as the day was done.

Now those three sisters,
they always stayed true.
And that is my wish for me and for you:

No matter what others look like,
or what they like to do,
take care of one another,
like Ruth and Blue do.

I first heard this story as "The Butterfly Brothers," from Annette Harrison, who
included it in her book *Stories for Young Children* (National Storytelling Press.) She gave
me permission to include my version in Blue's tribute book. When I contacted her, she

Ahhhh!

wrote that, "I have never met Blue, but I LOVE his work!! The Rainbow child is one of my favorite stories. It is such an extraordinary story…he must be an incredible person." Indeed he is. I am investigating a source that claims there is a Japanese version very similar to this one, but I haven't found it yet.

Elisa Pearmain is the award-winning author of *Doorways to the Soul: Fifty-two Wisdom Tales from Around the World* (Pilgrim Press, l998.) She tells stories professionally, teaches storytelling through Lesley University, and listens to the stories of others as a mental health counselor.

Blue at *The Bliss Festival* Cross Village, MI - July 1998

Photo: Margo Kempinshi

Ahhhh!

Colorful Kaleidoscope

Guy Peartree

I met brother Blue in 1969 or so at the Tufts campus in Medford. He gave an intimately Blue performance dressed in his inimitably Blue regalia and butterflies. This was a time of deep soul searching for me as has been every subsequent year of my life since then. Blue's message and performance was one of love and an unexpurgated heart opening. I would see Blue over the years, on streets and on buses, and he always created a loving scene wherever I'd see him.

It was in 1973 when he asked me to participate in a group performance for his storytelling project at a prison. And so I played the violin while he rhapsodized about beauty and the soul—the soul being the music of the violin moving ever higher into harmonious love and benediction.

It wasn't until fourteen years later that I first got an inkling of being a storyteller. Once I embarked on storytelling I quickly became reacquainted with Blue. My openness to dreams had become richer in this time of my life, and I had a dream about Brother Blue which goes something like this: I am telling stories to a group of children and I wish to tell them a legend. Suddenly I started saying, "There was a man who saw a glass of water...he took the glass of water and—" As I was miming reaching for the glass of water, I saw tall, lanky Brother Blue come into the room. He was wearing orange instead of blue and I said, "This is the first time in twenty-five years I've seen you with anything other than blue." Brother Blue looked pensive and swaggering. As he came closer, his clothes became blue. When he went away, the colors in his clothes changed from blue to blue and orange, then red and starkly iridescent in different parts, until at a certain distance they were all blue again. These changes had the effect of a visual kaleidoscope.

Of course this dream is my unconscious tribute to Brother Blue. For throughout the years he has been the most supremely colorful kaleido-

Ahhhh!

scopic storytelling, praise giving, appreciating, all-embracing soul presence I, and all of us, have ever known.

Guy Peartree has been telling stories and performing historical portrayals of notable African American men for over ten years. He owes much of his love for storytelling to southern African American oral culture, as well as to poetry. Mr. Peartree is completing a degree in Religious Education, with which he hopes to incorporate the magic and ministry of storytelling.

Photo: Margo Kempinshi

Blue at *The Bliss Festival,* Cross Village, MI - July 1998

Ahhhh!

The Man Above and Below
Butterflies
Maggi Kerr Peirce

Who is he? What does he do?
I can't understand him. Why do they ask him?
Who is she? She walks in his wake?

They are the poet, the dreamer, the performer
They walk together like two dickey birds
They care together, eat together, sit together.

She is quiet, determined. All stillness.
He is smiling, all rhyming, all movement.
Listen to him sing. She her watchfulness.

They are as sun is to moonbeam
They are as pool is to thundering waterfall
They are as plot is to story.

Brother Blue is he who embellishes the small
    quiet space within a story
And a riot of colours, ribbons, and glistening
    starfall surrounds the listener…so that
    we stand enchanted…

But in his doorway of enchantment stands Ruth
the Ready, and we bow to her too.

A traditional Northern Irish storyteller, singer, and reciter since 1980, Maggi Peirce is also known as a writer and poet. The National Storytelling Network conferred its Lifetime Achievement Award on Maggi Peirce in 2001.

Ahhhh !

The Blue Man

Lee Pennington

The Blue Man sun dances
warm laughter, colors the fog
his color, chases fleecy clouds away
with his looking, and the early
spider webs of dawn reflect his doing.

The Blue Man bathes in butterflies
stirs songs from shadows
splashes away the night
dripping with love
where water wings slip by.

The Blue Man wakes the silence
melts the dark waiting
trembles spring into flowers
makes mirrors beyond glass;
love waits its turn
whispering the Blue Man yes.

Lee Pennington is the author of 19 books, two nominated for the Pulitzer Prize. Along with his wife, Joy, he produces the annual Corn Island Storytelling Festival. Held in Louisville, KY, the festival is now in its 26th year. In 1996, Lee Pennington, along with Brother Blue, was inducted into the National Storytelling Network's Circle of Excellence.

Ahhhh!

Ruth and Hugh and Brother Blue

Jeanne Marie Penvenne

Way back in the 1960s in Pittsfield, Massachusetts, Berkshire Community College's wonderful librarian, Ruth Hill, hired me for my first
library job. Mrs. Hill was the picture of dignity, efficiency, and kindness.
Eventually I also met Hugh Hill. From the outset he was a mystery,
quite a contrast to Ruth. He shifted effortlessly and quickly from unexpected spurts of movement, laughter, and performance to sudden re-
treats into a calm quiet, with hands clasped, while still maintaining direct
eye contact. Hugh could surprise, disconcert, and distract me, mostly
because I had never known anyone like him. I was not brave enough to
respond to play with play—the fact that I usually only saw him while I
was at work may have had something to do with that! After that year in
Pittsfield, our travels separated us for many years.

Returning to Cambridge from a Peace Corps assignment in Brazil in
the early 70s, my first job interview was for a position at the Harvard
Museum of Comparative Zoology Library. When I knocked on the
Librarian's door, it was opened by Ruth Hill. I do not know who was
more surprised. I was just delighted. In many ways, Ruth and Blue had
not changed a bit. They were still committed to the sane, simple diet
and lifestyle that would salvage this planet for posterity if more than a
half dozen people actually followed their example.

While we all loved our homes in the Berkshires, I could see that the
greatly enhanced artistic and intellectual life in Cambridge brought out
the very best in both Ruth and Blue. I particularly recall Ruth beginning
to wear dresses made from beautiful fabrics woven all over the world.
She had always been beautiful and carefully dressed, but in Cambridge
she added color and drama. And in Cambridge, Hugh Hill increasingly
became Brother Blue. It was a lovely and logical transformation.

Ahhhh!

After more travels, I settled on Nantucket Island in the early 80's. There, I was writing my doctoral dissertation and tending my two baby boys. Seeing in the paper one day that Brother Blue was performing on the island, I left my infant son, Louis, with his father, and took my two year-old, John, with me to the performance. He responded to Brother Blue the same way I did in the mid 60s. He was startled and disconcerted! The quick movements and flashes of color initially frightened him. Slowly, as he saw the delight on my face and began to focus more on the warmth of Hugh's voice and the gaiety of his laughter, John became a bit more confident and was eventually drawn, still somewhat tentatively, into Brother Blue's performance.

After thirty years of friendship, marked by separations lasting up to a decade, I still always feel wonderful when I see or think of them. I treasure several of Ruth's marvelous recipes, and think of her whenever I make them, or even just pass by the recipe card written in her marvelous clear writing. They've sustained their values, the simplicity, the warmth and depth of their work, and their mutual commitment. I sometimes glimpse the same slightly amused look on Ruth's face as she watches Brother Blue move into his own! They know each other so well, yet they still delight in each other. That is so fine and rare. They are a precious team and a treasured love story.

Jeanne Marie Penvenne is a native of Lenox, Massachusetts. She met Ruth and Hugh Hill while studying at Berkshire Community College. She is Professor of History at Tufts University, and writes about the labor history of Maputo, Mozambique. She lives with her husband and sons in Duxbury, Massachusetts.

Ahhhh!

The Butterfly and the Bee

Wolfgang Pentzek

Once there was a butterfly whose wings were colored with the blue of the sky, and his wish was to visit every flower in the world. As he flew from one flower to another, he met a beautiful bee who was sweeter than honey. They fell in love and, hand in hand, they flew away together, never to let go of one another.

No flower was so high that their wings could not touch. No flower was so low that their eyes could not behold. Every flower welcomed the butterfly and the bee because they would brighten the colors of its petals and sweeten its fragrance. The butterfly did this by telling colorful stories, and the bee by being the sweetest one of all.

This I know, because I was one of the lucky flowers who was visited by the butterfly and the bee. Since their visit, I bloom bright colors and give sweet fragrance. And so does all the world around me. With all my heart, I wish to thank the butterfly for all his stories, and the bee for all her sweetness. They are flying still, and continue to brighten and sweeten the world. One day soon they may come to brighten and sweeten yours.

Wolfgang Pentzek, a visual artist and storyteller, was born in Germany and grew up in Canada. He attended Emily Carr School of Art and Design, and graduated from the Tooba Physical Theatre Centre in Vancouver, British Columbia, Canada.

AHHHH!

Me and Brother Blue

U. Utah Phillips

One of the earliest festivals I played was a little college called Osinas. I was there to be part of an evening concert and workshops during the day. After I finished a workshop on labor songs and stories of the people's history of work and class, I went for a walk. The weather was threatening. It appeared as though it was going to rain, and I worried that this would damage the outdoor events of the festival. I was walking through the campus and there he was, Brother Blue. Big as life. His hat covered with butterflies. Dressed in blue with ribbons streaming off his body. I could see him at a distance with his head moving, with his back arched. He was bobbing up and down. His arms were enflaming, they were sculpting the air. I walked up and listened. There were a whole bunch of kids gathered around him. He was telling a story—God, it was a long time ago—a story about Muddy Duddy, that had to do with rain and had to do with mud. And those kids were absolutely enraptured. He had reached them. He was leaning into them, and they embraced what he was saying and what he was doing. His face was a mask of the story. His gestures matched everything that he was saying. He didn't throw anything away. It was like watching somebody dance and speak at the same time.

That was my first real adventure with the art of storytelling, watching Brother Blue do that. And it made me happy. At the same time the story made me deeply sad. In fact, I wept at the beauty of what I was seeing. I saw also that way of the storyteller that can be funny and at the same time deeply moving. Now, I don't think Brother Blue had been invited to this festival; I think he was just there. I think he just showed up. And he wasn't on the stage; he was on the sidewalk. He was reaching toward people. He was not waiting for them to come to him, alright? That was a powerful, powerful lesson to learn. He became, as I say, my first storyteller.

AHHHH!

There were three others who influenced me greatly: Gamble Rogers, Marshall Dodge, and Seamus Heaney. Gamble showed me the sculpture of a great phrase beautifully intoned. He used a great deal of language. Marshall taught me the value of humor, but humor to frame what it was you really wanted to get at. And Seamus Heaney, the great Irish storyteller and singer in Gaelic, taught me that deep, deep mythic sense.

And so, between the four—Brother Blue, reaching toward others and using your body, using your whole self and reaching into yourself, and handing what gift you have to others; Gamble Rogers, the use of words, Marshall Dodge, the use of humor; and Seamus Heaney, the mythic sense, I was instructed on how to build, how to make my stories, how to make the stories that I tell. They're not mine. I inherit. I'm an inheritor of Brother Blue. I'm an inheritor of Gamble Rogers, Marshall Dodge, and Seamus Heaney. And I'm an inheritor of the people I rode on freight trains with; of the people on picket lines who told me stories of their lives. I think one of the marks of growing up, of approaching old age, is to finally acknowledge what you authentically inherit and then put back into the world.

Well, now they say I'm a storyteller, and I've been invited to some storytelling festivals. I regret it in a way. I was at the National Storytelling Festival in Jonesborough. Brother Blue was there. I always appreciated his support for what it is that I try to do and often get away with. I do, however, feel that storytelling is becoming too formal, too stage-bound, and is probably the most over-examined art in the United States today. Over-examined to the point that the magic is being hammered right out of it. When I feel the temptation to be sucked into the vortex and consumed by it, I cast my mind back to Osinas, to that lowering cloudy sky and to Brother Blue. Blue, happy, and the children in front of him, happy…reaching toward each other and sharing a magic that, hopefully, will continue to defy all explanation.

That's about all I have to say. Brother Blue, I send you my highest regards and want you to know that what small ability I possess as a storyteller began with you. Thank you.

Described by himself as the Golden Voice of the Great Southwest, U. Utah Phillips is described by others as a true eclectic: archivist, historian, activist, philosopher, hobo, tramp, member of the IWW, and just about everything in between. Utah's memory contains a wide-ranging wealth of lore, which he lets us romp through by way of his shows and recordings. U. Utah Phillips is a nationally known folk artist, singer/story teller, Grammy Award Nominee for his work with Ani Difranco, and hosts his own weekly radio show—*Loafer's Glory: The Hobo Jungle of the Mind*.

Ahhhh!

Wedding Anniversary
Franklin & Claire Picard

Dear Brother Blue,

What were you doing at the Oral History Congress in New Orleans in September 1996? Several times we surprised you in the hotel lobby, free smiling, flitting from one group of persons to another.

For us, who had arrived from another continent, you also seemed to have landed from another, mysterious world, from an unknown planet—which appealed to us more and more. Your wings, your smile, your inspiration gave an unexpected grace and fantasy to that gathering of intellectuals. At the same time, you inhabited your body so fully that, when beside you, each person felt your closeness to their humanity.

Where did you obtain that poetic audacity of which Jean Cocteau used to say that it is "an exhibitionism which is brought to bear on the blind"?

We discovered Ruth—discreet but ever-so-present—whose loving gaze was the tightrope along which you walked as an artist among mankind.

At that moment, Claire and I understood that it was together with you that we wished to celebrate our wedding anniversary. Had you sensed this barely-conceived-of desire? Ruth and you were already making yourselves available for the evening, and all four of us found ourselves seated on the terrace of a small restaurant in the sticky heat of New Orleans. In the instant communion which was established between us, we related how Providence had caused our destinies to meet in a botanic garden in Normandy, and then united us for fifteen years in profound choices of liberty—from the passionate love of plants to the search for the historic voice of peoples…And to so many other things, which you guessed at even before we recalled them.

No doubt you are the only one to remember the place where you led us to give us, as a wedding present, an extraordinary moment of grace and love shared together.

Ahhhh !

280

That room, although quite impersonal, suddenly filled with a strange mixture of suspense, beauty, and fervor when you began your improvisation, revealing to us the story of our lives: the encounter between two almost ethereal beings destined for eternity and discovering one another in mutual wonderment, he exclaiming "Oh," and her "Ah,"

With your almost palpable inspiration, your subtle changes in tone, your supple and always unexpected gestures, you opened up to us the unformulated secrets of our intimacy and your gazes—both Ruth's and yours—met ours, and assured us that all this was true.

Through the magic of this fleeting encounter we grasped that you had come to New Orleans merely for that moment of eternity, traversing our lives with the grace of a dainty and shimmering butterfly which vanishes in the light. And the moon's honey still flows in our hearts.

Franklin Picard is the chair of the French Institute for Sound Archives (Paris). He is also involved in oral history. Claire Picard, his wife, graduated from Geneva Interpreters' School (English and Russian). They have three children: Colombe (19), Remi (17), and Louis-Marie (14).

AHHHH!

The Brick

John Pirolli

A FLASH OF COLORS
IN SHADES OF BLUE
A BUTTERFLY DANCING
WITH WORDS THAT ARE TRUE
THE STORY AND THE GLORY
OF MY BROTHER BLUE.

Like, I'm an old *Harvard Square Hippie* from Way Back.
    I'm talking *SIXTIES* here.
I'm talking "TRUC IN THE ALLEY" and
"CRACKER JACK'S" for a Hip threads feast.
I'm talking High School Fantasies and "HEAD QUARTERS EAST."
I'm talking the "GREAT WHITE" blasting on outside amps
and street weary wanderers making camps.

I'm talking my Harvard Square
Before the Yuppie Scum wannabes
Were even welcome there.
    As I was saying:
I'm an old hippie who, while still in
youth, split the Bay State for the south
by way of *WOODSTOCK* which just happened a
few months after my high school gradua-
tions. Yesseree Bob, this Harvard Square
Hippie became a Blue Grass smokin' moon-
shine drinkin' Country College Boy at the
University of Kentucky.

AHHHH!

But after a few years I became homesick
for my *HARVARD SQUARE*
So I came home to find it wasn't there.
The head shops were not allowed
and neither was my old crowd.
TALK ABOUT A BUM TRIP
One day I was just sitting listening
to the beat, you know, the music of the
street. The Brattle Street Folk music
"Please come to Boston" in the Summer,
two bits in the hat Mean Scene beat, when
to my surprise I saw a BLUE MAN

WITH A BUTTERFLY IN HIS HAND
WHO FLICKED HIS WRIST
AND MADE THAT BUTTERFLY FLY
AND I KNEW FOR SURE
I HAD TO CHECK OUT THIS GUY.

So I sat there and I listened as he told
people the story of "The Buddha and the
Golden Impalas." (Being my name is Buddah
you know I just had to remember this
story.)

To say I was blown away would be an un-
derstatement, HELL; I almost cried. The
scene I missed had now been found. I now
had a reason to hang around and I did.
I formed the Stone Buddah Folk Col-
lective, which played the Boston and area
Folk scenes for two years. And during
those two years I made SURE I HIT THE
SQUARE for my weekly visit with Dr. Hugh.
You know of whom I am talking, BROTHER
BLUE. WITH MY WEEKLY INGESTION OF HIS
GOOD CHEER

AHHHH!

I REALLY DIDN'T NEED DRUGS OR BEER.

Well, after those two wonderful years my collective went
bust and I split back to Kentucky.

I returned to the Boston area in 1980. Broke beaten and
almost married. I had no hope

no car

not even bus fare

but I still dragged my butt

to Harvard Square

for my weekly dose of the words that were true

the wonderful lines of BROTHER BLUE.

By the mid eighties I was established on the scene

As a poet and editor of *STREET MAGAZINE*.

NOW LET US FAST FORWARD
THIS STORY BY A DOZEN OR SO YEARS

On June Fifth 1996, my dear friend and unofficially adopted sister,
JAN KEROUC died (actually she was murdered, but that's another
story.) Eight months later, a week after my Birthday, my father died.
Four months after that my wife threw me out of our house. And to make
things worse, I couldn't find Blue in the Square.

I WAS AT THE LOW TIDE

TALKING SUICIDE

SLEEPING IN THE CELLAR OF MY MOTHER'S PLACE

HIDING FROM THE HUMAN RACE

**I'm talking the I-don't-give-a-rats-ass-on-a-chinese-rolling-
donut-low-down-mutherfuckin'-mind-meltin'-blues.**

Well one day I was running an errand for my older brother who
became my boss after dad died, when I saw copies of the Brother Blue
Book for sale. Well of course I began to cry.

That night, while reading **THE BOOK,** I BEGAN TO CRY.

All the pent up pain and grief of two years of death, with love's relief,
came bubbling up like a volcanic eruption. **BROTHER BLUE KNEW
MY PAIN AND HE DIDN'T GO INSANE.** So I knew there might
be help for me. I also came to the realization why I felt such a closeness
to Dr. Hugh and why I felt he was

Ahhhh!

My BROTHER BLUE

Both our Dads were *"BRICKIES."* That is, they were men who supported a wife and family with a trowel in one hand and

BRICK

IN THE OTHER
THE MEN WHO BUILT THIS COUNTRY UP FROM THE WILDERNESS

LAYING GOOD CLAY BRICK

My dad started as a laborer, then as a deliverer, and finally with money from the GI loan, to purchase his first truck, the owner of his own business. He built his kingdom with brick. And Blue said the words that connected us together. To quote the master about his special brick.

"My father was a brick layer and this is one of his bricks.

All red brick is precious to me and inside every brick is a story.

Now what I want to do folks is I want to build a cathedral around this one brick..."

Well, praise the lord, I was back to normal again. (well at least as normal as this old mind fried beat hide hippie reprobate, whatever you think normal is can be.) And I had a goal, I had to find a way to thank Brother Blue for helping me keep it together all these years.

AHHHH!

At the time, I was one of the Regular Poets at Jeff Robinson's Gig at the Lizard Lounge, and Jeff announced that Brother Blue was going to be a featured guest on a Sunday night in the future. Well, now I had a place and time to honor him, but

with what????????????????????????????

Well I went back to Harvard Square for some inspiration. I sat on the concrete bench where I usually listen to **BLUE** WHICH HAPPENS TO BE AT THE SAME SPOT THAT I FIRST HEARD BLUE, SO MANY YEARS AGO, AND I DROPPED MY HEAD IN SILENT PRAYER AND, LO AND BEHOLD, THE ANSWER TO MY PRAYER WAS THERE. THE SIGN FROM GOD THAT CONNECTED US

BRICK

NOT just any brick, mind you, but the official brick of Harvard Square, *"The Stile and Heart Boston City Hall Paver."* I knew he knew the brick because it was my father's company that supplied the brick to the CITY OF CAMBRIDGE. My decision was made. I called the brick plant the next day and had them bake a special brick, a brick I would personally design, with BROTHER BLUE'S NAME INSCRIBED RIGHT IN THE CENTER. I HAD THEM MAKE A LINK THAT LINKED OUR FATHERS AND OUR LIVES. BROTHER BLUE WANTS TO BUILD A CATHEDRAL TO HIS DAD, AND I WANTED TO SUPPLY THE SECOND BRICK AND DEDICATED IT TO HIM.

On the night of the feature my quest to give thanks was complete, for after my presentation the room was filled with applause. Applause for him. And way in the back I felt the spirits of our fathers applauding too.

John Pirolli, a.k.a The Buddah., a.k.a Reverend Colonial, is the president of the board of The Stone Soup Poets. He is also a founding member of the Barnum and Buddah Poetry Circus, which performs across the east coast, from New Jersey to Maine. In 2001, John won the Cambridge award for: Poet That Makes You Think, Best Short Poem, Best Poetry Radio Show, and The Multimedia Award. In 2002 he won the Poet of Merit Award. He is the author of *Madman on the Merrimack* and *Humbug to Hallelujah*

Ahhhh!

Brother Blue
Fred Richards, Ph.D.

The first time I met Brother Blue was in the mid-70's in Carrollton, Georgia, a small town in rural Georgia an hour's drive from Atlanta. My wife, Anne, and I had come to Georgia from Colorado to share a teaching position in the Psychology Department at the State University of West Georgia (then West Georgia College). I was a 35-year-old psychology professor and a drunk with a great, though often misdirected passion for life.

Brother Blue was a featured presenter at a conference sponsored by the Association for Humanistic Education. I was both fascinated and frightened by Brother Blue. His passion and energy exceeded my own, but his dance was more the Dance of Life and the communal dance of humankind. Mine, I came to see, was too much frantic footwork.

Brother Blue was a whirling dervish, an ebony Rumi, inviting me and others with his soulful poems, songs, and stories to discover and embody our own stories and the stories that connect us to one another and to God. He was (and I'm sure still is!) a prophet, a singer of sacred stories, a natural born lover from cover to cover calling upon the Lazarus in each of us to step out and live.

When Ruth shared the story of going in search of Brother Blue to feed him strawberries and cream on the streets of some big city because he wouldn't stop his storytelling long enough to eat, I knew he had found a calling, a freedom and joy I had not yet found. Oh, how outrageous he was as he roamed the streets of our little town, covered in blue ribbons, streamers, stars, balloons, and bangles, unnerving, disarming, and intriguing conference participants and local citizens he encountered everywhere he went. He was the voice of the Big Story of Life, a man whose Presence transformed stage and street into sacred space for celebrating love that makes us all brothers and sisters and children of

Ahhhh!

God. And those of us who shared his presence years ago, feel his presence still.

Not long after Anne and I met Dr. Hugh Hill and his devoted wife, Ruth, I drank some wine (I quit December 23, 1982) and wrote the following poem. Greg Smith, mentioned in the poem, was a gentle clown and graduate student who shared some of those wonderful times back in the 70's. illilli was the name of a singer and storyteller who participated in the conference and shared in all the late night festivities.

To Brother Blue (Dr. Hugh Hill)

Brother Blue, storyteller,
streetstruttin' soul brother.
Well, you saw I had some madness,
some natural baby grace, coo coo
(but I've considered growin' up
to survive in this world.)
You knew I was still alive.
So you played peek-a-boo
to the middle of me
from the middle of you.

When Ruth told me
you went seventy-two hours
living stories on the street
without eating, I went out
and bought a freezer. Right now
I got five-thousand pounds
of strawberries and cream
waitin' for Jesus. I hear he's
been hidin' out, gone underground.
So y'all come back now
and we'll share.

Talk about natural baby grace—

Ahhhh!

no unnecessary moves!—bring along
Greg Smith and illilli. They're
dancers too. Only last night
I caught the spark of a star.
Let's dance until we apprehend Jesus.
I hear there's a reward!

Fred Richards appears around Carrollton, GA as an Easter rabbit, Santa Claus, and a clown. He's also a psychotherapist in private practice. Anne C. Richards is a retired as a Professor in the Department of Psychology, State University of West Georgia, Carrollton, GA and serves full-time as trustee of the Field Psych Trust, honoring the professional legacy of Arthur W. Combs.

Ahhhh!

Caro "Fratello Azzuro"

Alfred Romano

I know no better way to pay tribute to you than to write this personal note of thanks. For your unequivocal life-giving spirit, I thank you. For your stories and the greatest story, which is you, I thank you. For your courage, especially to live your convictions so fully, I not only thank you, I remain awed by your complete state of grace.

You are, in my heart, the heaviest of heavy. You occupy the same heavenly space as 'Trane, King, and Mandela. You are a giant among men. You humble me.

I only regret that we have not been in touch more often, although you have indelibly etched your person on my soul. I carry you with me (or should I say that you have carried me?) in my quest to be better, to live up to the gift of my life. And what is more important is that I know you have done this for countless others. You have carried the cross for me and them, and for this I love you.

One small, but not insignificant, note about your craft: in my humble opinion, I consider "Muddy Duddy" (and other Blue creations) to stand among the greatest of all stories. It is distilled Homer and Jesus.

Peek-a-boo, I love you.

Alfred Romano earned a degree from Harvard Divinity School. He is an entrepreneur, and is involved in all sorts of poetry, music, and storytelling.

Ahhhh!

290

Merlin

George Romero

Every once in a great while, you run across a human being with a pure soul. You know it right away, on first contact. There's none of the usual (he or she) "seems nice, but we've only just met, so I'll have to wait and see." In this world of dashed expectations, we've all been sorely disappointed by our authorities, advisers, neighbors we thought of as friends, even, many of us, by relatives. Unfortunately, but understandably, this has conditioned us to mistrust our first impressions of the people we meet. But even the most cynical of us, on encountering the rarest of our kind, a genuinely pure soul, an essential innocent, immediately feels what is almost a religious sort of comfort, a confirmation of mankind's worth within the whole of what is.

Big words? Oh yes, because we're talking about big stuff. How many truly virtuous people have you ever known? I'm privileged to number four; six if I were to include my children, but they are too young to be tallied. I include my wife, Christine, my dad, Jorge, and my collaborator, Dr. D. The fourth is the man to whom this is dedicated.

I'm a filmmaker. When we were inches away from the 80's, I was planning a film called *Knightriders*, a study, an argument really. I meant to illustrate, in part, what I've been discussing above: the difficulties faced by a virtuous individual in disrespectful times.

The story was loosely draped over Arthurian bones. There was a character named Merlin, a medical doctor in the world he rejected, now a troubadour in a traveling Renaissance Fair. Merlin was to be a man of wisdom, of measured response to reality, but also a man of faith, of spirituality, of faith in spirituality; a man so in harmony with the universe that his judgments and observations seemed, and possibly were, divinely inspired.

Somebody said, "We need a really good actor."

Ahhhh!

I said, "No. We need the guy! The real guy!"

"Fat chance. There is no such guy!"

I knew one such guy: Dr. D. (Donald Rubenstein, poet, composer, friend.) But he wasn't African American, nor pure African, which would have been fine. It's been a habit of mine (a conceit, I suppose, as a Caucasian) to portray "minorities" (I hate that word) as the most accurate "observers."

Actually, it was Donald who suggested some guy he knew who was "A gas. Totally out there. He's got degrees, man, he's like an academic, teaching at Harvard, but he still gets down, down in the street, and he tells, like stories, man!"

"Stories?"

"Storytelling is, like, the oldest art in the world, man. Before the printed word, there were storytellers. Storytellers invented most of the words that later got printed! Storytellers told us everything that happened, man—told us who we were, what we were, where we came from." Much of this was probably unspoken, but I credit Dr. D. with inspiring the thoughts.

"He's this guy," said D., "goes around with, like, a bongo-drum, ribbons hangin' all over him, butterflies painted on his hands, his face."

"Wait," I said, "I know this guy!"

I hadn't actually 'known' him, I'd known of him. I'd seen a children's television program on which "this guy" had been a regular. My memory had been of him sitting on the floor, telling stories which had then been discussed by both children and adults as part of the "learning experience." That might not have been exactly the way it was, but I had thought, certainly, at the time, as I still do now that "this guy" had been one of the most interesting, compelling, delightfully entertaining and yes, magical presences I'd ever seen.

"Magique, musique," I quoted to Donald. "He used to say Magique, musique."

"That's him, man."

"What's his name?"

"Dr. Hugh Hill."

"Wait…this cat is a Doctor? Named Hugh?"

"Yeah, man, but he calls himself Brother Blue."

Not long after, it was arranged for Blue to come in for a meeting. He

Ahhhh!

came with his wife, Ruth, who I feel remiss in not tallying as the fifth "pure one" I've known. As I said, when you meet a genuinely pure soul, you know it right away. I knew it the moment I met Blue. When we first shook hands, his "magique" passed warmly into my heart. We visited, rapped, ate a meal together, listened to some Dylan. And much to my gratitude, Blue agreed to play Merlin.

Handshakes soon evolved into daily embraces. I remember his slight frame feeling fragile in my arms. But Blue is anything but a fragile man. His body is a strong servant. His heart and soul are mighty. His energy exceeds the hurricane. When Blue is around, everything becomes art. I was going to write, 'everything becomes beautiful,' but that wouldn't have been quite right. Dr. Hill knows, very well, that all is not beautiful. For his most important work is on America's ugly streets. He's seen the tragedy of disenfranchisement, the wasteful spending of morality and humanity in exchange for false national prosperity that benefits only a few.

He stands not on art's ivory tower, but on the anvil, in the center of our spiritual desert, and he uses the ugliness, spinning it, like gold from straw, into an essential component of his particular talent, which is to express beautifully, even when what is being expressed is not beautiful. He is today's minstrel, having replaced lute with drum, harmonica, be-bop and jive, telling a tragic tale to tragically deprived listeners so that its very telling inspires, invigorates, elevates.

He brought dimension to Merlin, and a reality which I, as author, could do no more than vaguely imagine while I was writing the screen-play before I met Blue. The character of Merlin, the film, and I, for whatever credit I've received, owe a great debt to Hugh Hill. I can only hope that, by way of working off a portion of that debt, the film will serve as some small, very incomplete record of the contribution he has made to humanity. Twenty years after it was made, the film is still being seen on video, and I delight in the thought of new young viewers experiencing the gift of Blue's work.

The production of *Knightriders* was fraught with challenges. Largely an outdoor film, the weather was against us. In the end, our ninety-six days of shooting brought seventy-eight of rain and worse: a small twister destroyed our set, our warehouse flooded. Relationships, even marriages were broken and made. There were serious injuries due to dangerous stunts. There was an Actor's Guild strike. Money and patience wore

Ahhhh!

thinner and thinner. But we made it through. We became that troupe of Renaissance souls, united in our determination, and determined to stay united.

Blue was one of the "forces" that made this miracle happen. D. was there, never losing faith. Ed, Tom, and "The Rev" helped, spiritually, to turn us from despair, But Blue…

…Blue, man…

…he'd come walking across the field with his drum, his ribbons, and his aura of butterflies, with Ruth always at his side, and no one…no one on the set, from producer to "gopher," had any heart to discourage, disparage, or dissemble. Blue would not allow it. He made no complaint, no criticism, he wasn't a "Star," except in several of our minds. He would not allow, by his sheer presence, any sort of despondency.

So used to disappointment, none of us wanted to disappoint Blue.

Weary, my wife Chris and I would drag into our motel room at the end of the day to find that an audio tape had been slipped under the door. Each was a tribute to the film and, often, to myself. Has any director ever had such support? I doubt it. Those tapes, most of them with D sitting in, gave me the "magique, musique" to keep on keepin' on.

Blue became Merlin. The film wouldn't be the same without him. The film's concept wouldn't have existed without him and those rare few like him. In the final sequence, shot in the rain, with D singing, when Blue opens his hand over the king's grave, the butterfly painted on his palm, inhabits me and unfailingly makes me weep.

Brother Blue is a unique personage. The things I've written above have as much to do with me as they have to do with him. But they are inspired by him. They are thoughts, with me forever, that he has given me. This is a man who believes in mankind…not as a breed, but an ideal.

I've never met anyone like him. You've never met anyone like him.

Blue…if I don't make it to Heaven, sing some stories about me to the saints up there, will ya?

Filmmaker George A. Romero is a pivotal figure in the development of the contemporary horror film. His first feature, *Night of the Living Dead*, redefined the genre. He has made 14 films, most shot in his beloved hometown of Pittsburgh, Pennsylvania. *Knightriders*, shot in 1980, features Brother Blue as a mystical physician.

AHHHH!

Blue Priest

Dale Rosenkrantz

The jive priest of story calls the muses down,
heartens us with sweaty inspiration
to believe in the assured transformation
of this funky world
through our pulsing, wet, blue-black words.
Hearken to his rap, goddesses of memory, story, and desire!
Rise and strut your stuff,
shades of nether regions!
Let the cat bend your ears,
dwellers of this middle earth!
Chill now,
sainted ancestors,
those who have descended to the depths of shadow,
those of gossamer flesh who roam still our living scene!
This is no place for humans,
but for all creatures of this sorry-ass, exalted planet.
We make love with beasts, ghosts, and angels,
caress the night,
wrap our raggedy, old selves around
stones, starlight, and streams
till straggling souls surface slithering
from devil's depth into open air.
Now in the presence of whatever was, is, and shall be,
we witness this thrumming, eternal, earth moment,
sweat this breaking spirit dance
under the howling, rocking, hopping sun and moon.

Dale Rosenkrantz is a movement improviser, storyteller, reader of (particularly
Jewish) traditional sources, and sometime poet. He currently lives in a loft in
Somerville, Massachusetts with his packmate, Rusty.

Ahhhh!

An Instant Occasion

Martha Ross

I first met Brother Blue and "Sister Ruth" near the Dallas/Fort Worth Airport in 1985, as we were all assembling to honor an anniversary of the Baylor University Oral History Program. Several participants had not yet arrived, and the group was being assembled at a nearby motel dining room for lunch while we awaited the last arrivals, before being taken by van to Waco.

When Blue and Ruth appeared, it became an instant occasion. Within minutes, he was performing his street-language version of "Hamlet" or "Macbeth" for us right there in the restaurant! I must say to my amazement, admiration, applause, and encouragement! The waiters paused in their duties to watch; patrons finished with their meals paused on their way to the cashier's counter, and diners entering the room paused on their way to their tables, to watch and enjoy.

What an introduction to the remarkable and unique Brother Blue, and his equally gifted (if considerably quieter) wife, Ruth! Delighting in his originality and his creativity, I urged him on; the performance went on and on, expanded to other works. I don't remember when any of us ate lunch!

On that day was born a friendship that persists to this day. Wherever we find ourselves sharing a hotel corridor, a room, a sidewalk, even an elevator, we manage an instant reunion! At a national conference of the Society of American Archivists in Chicago a few years back, I got into the hotel elevator on the sixth floor, enroute to the airport to come home, when I found Brother Blue and Ruth among my fellow passengers! Between the sixth and lobby floors, we had a grand, warm, boisterous reunion that must have left other passengers wondering what in the world was happening. Hey! A convergence of Blue, Ruth, and Martha!

Ahhhh!

My husband and I have been honored to serve more than once as their Washington area hosts when they visited our nation's capital on various missions. The most recent occasion was his appearance on the Black Entertainment Television Network, which sent a limo to take him and Ruth to the studios. The white limousine stretched all the way across the front of our Bethesda property, no doubt giving us new status among our neighbors, especially when he emerged from the house in full costume, complete with ribbons and balloons!

Perhaps our greatest honor and pleasure came when Blue and Ruth accepted our invitation to attend the 1988 wedding of our youngest daughter. They not only attended the wedding, but became part of the extended family for the entire wedding weekend, getting to know the whole family and particularly blessing the rehearsal dinner with an original story by Blue to the assembled beloveds, assisted by the presiding priest (improvising rhythm accompaniment using restaurant spoons) and the bride's brother, a professional whistler! What an evening! And all captured for posterity on videotape!

When I learned of the death of the priest, who I always thought would preside at my last services, the first thing I thought of was to ask Brother Blue to offer a few remarks over my bier, when that time comes. I'm not sure he thinks my invitation is serious, but I have so advised all my family members who are likely to be involved in making my final arrangements. Since I hope the occasion will be a celebration of my life rather than a mourning of my departure, who better to liven up the proceedings than Brother Blue? And who among all my acquaintance really knows me better than this man, whom I have known, enjoyed, admired, and respected for all these happy years?

Martha and Donald Ross were married in 1946 and both worked for Clinton Engineer Works until their retirement in 1988. They have six children and thirteen grandchildren. Martha has been an oral historian since 1969 and was a founding member of Oral History in the Mid-Atlantic Region.

Ahhhh!

Without Any Rehearsal

Donald Rubinstein

I first saw Brother Blue in 1978, covered in butterflies at a health food restaurant in Cambridge, Massachusetts. We struck up a conversation. He was waiting for Peter Gordon, a french horn player from the Boston Symphony, who happened to be a friend of mine.

Peter called to say someone had thrown sand down his gas tank, and he couldn't make the gig (a duet with Blue on public radio, WGBH, Boston). We decided I should do it instead, and off we went to record (without any rehearsal) *The Greatest Blues Singer that Ever Lived.* That is how I met Brother Blue.

We have since performed publicly on many occasions, and appeared together in George Romero's feature film, *Knightriders.*

Blue is more than I can say. He is a poet—an 'understander' of life, and a great appreciator of the arts. His work speaks for itself. There have been many times that a postcard from Blue and Ruth (his wife and support—her warmth is indefatigable) has kept me going.

Lots of love to a great one who chooses to call himself 'God's fool'— for by any name, love tied to such a spirit is rarely seen.

Donald Rubinstein has written five film scores, including George A. Romero's *Knightrider*s, featuring Brother Blue. He wrote the music for Brother Blue's *The Greatest Blues Singer that Ever Lived* (National Public Radio). Donald's music has been commissioned or performed by members of The Boston Symphony and New York Philharmonic Orchestras. He received the *ASCAP Special Award for Theater Arts* and has recorded and released 10 CDs on various labels. He has written and performed his own concert theatre works to large critical acclaim, including ones with Brother Blue. Five of his CDs are dedicated to his lyric-oriented folk/blues songs, and a new CD of songs was produced by Terry Allen in 2002.

Ahhhh!

My Turn
Stanley Sagov

Brother Blue can it be true?
I get a chance to write a tribute to you!
The first thing that comes to mind is
Your passion to always try to be kind.
You also of course want to entertain.
Instruct, inspire and stretch our brain.
I have known you now for about thirty years
and want you to know
you still have both of my ears.
While I listen to you and catch your story,
I feel you striving to show us your glory.
So, my brother, black and Blue
today it's my turn to send love
back to you.

Dr. Stanley Sagov is a physician who takes care of Brother Blue. Born in Capetown, South Africa, he is a keyboard player and has performed with Bill Evans, and Elvin Jones. He now composes and records his own music at home in his studio.

Ahhhh!

The Honest Current of Life

Vikram A. Savkar

It is very difficult to write a tribute to a man who is, himself, a tribute to so many things: beauty, humanity, language. What street corner can he not transform to a celestial forest? What word can he not make the vessel of divinity? What man or woman can he not unmask as an angel? Where has he been where beauty has not been? Where, love? Where, poetry? Yet all these transformations are not empty magic, fantastic dreams: as he reveals them they are the honest current of life, everywhere present, always hidden.

So what can I say to praise a man who is himself the incarnation of praise? I prefer to listen: to Lear and Romeo, to the Creation of the World, and the King of the Golden Deer, to the countless conversations on street corners and park benches, to the television programs and audio tapes—to every word I can manage hearing by a man, that merely to listen to whom is an exultation. And the more I listen, the more I learn to see with his eyes: with his gentle, forgiving, and mystical eyes, with his eyes that—not at all unknown to sadness—see in all things beauty, goodness, and grace.

These insufficient and limited words I offer in gratitude to Brother Blue who, for over ten years, has made the streets of Cambridge the holiest place in the world.

Vikram A. Savkar enjoys reciting poetry to Blue whenever they meet. He currently works as an assistant to Benjamin Zander of the Boston Philharmonic Orchestra.

Ahhhh!

Sheetmusic: "Brother Blue"

Tillman Schafer

SWING

Ahhhh!

Brother Blue Joins The Circus!

Peter Schumann

Thanks to brother Blue and to Ruth who brought him here! Thanks for many years of enthusiastic performing on our field! Your spirit lives in this field!

Peter Elka and all at Bread & puppet

AHHHH!

Peter Schumann is the founder and artistic director of Bread and Puppet Theatre. Since the mid 60's, Bread and Puppet's innovative use of large scale puppets and archetypal imagery have had enormous influence on puppetry and theater, and has inspired leftist polit-ical movements. The troupe tours with performance pieces such as "Insurrection Mass with Funeral Marches for Rotten Ideas," and frequently participates in progressive political events. Schumann's work as a visual artist has fostered a "cheap art" movement challenging the artistic/commercial mainstream.

In 1970, Bread and Puppet began Our Domestic Resurrection Circus and Pageant, an annual summer performance event in Glover, Vermont, (pictured in the postcards above.) Brother Blue was a frequent invited solo performer at this weekend-long event. Baking and giving away bread has always been an important part of Bread and Puppet events.

Ahhhh!

Blue and Lady Blue

Shelley Selkovits

We stood in the hall, Blue, Lady Blue, and I, inspiring the air.

Blue was invoking his Granddaddy, a spirit enslaved in the past century. Now others seemed pretentious. He himself is a street poet whose fortunes have taken him far from Harvard Square. He wears blue, as does his lady.

Blue and Lady Blue were my guests, courtly, as they acknowledged my home a nameless flower, a wordless beauty our communion.

I'll show you the house after lunch. Just now, two rooms.

Their spirits were alive; they were not pale or anemic.

I had two rooms ready for the day.

The dining room table was set ahead, for Valentine's Day, with a cloth of red and lace; white vessels. A heart-shaped chocolate cake, butterless and sugarless, adorned the table. The Blues ever sweethearts.

They preferred the Sun Room, heated by the sun, set in blue. Sky blue cloths covered the table, under a large vase of flowers; a blue pattern. The light we shared passed through goblets of blue glass like gems.

We settled in like the leaves of a ficus tree, once moved.

Careful not to interrupt. To give full reign to my guests, that their mood flower. Blue was reigning, ascendant, poetic. No apologies, being a masterpiece.

The mood, the ambience, drew Blue into an oral poem. His attentive wife and I were suspended. There was happiness in the Sun Room.

His romance in life is with Lady Blue, ever a librarian. I told her that libraries were sanctuaries, that I wrote about this in my story "Sanctuary."

Ahhhh!

What a thing to be able to say. Yes, his Granddaddy was a spirit enslaved in the past century. Blue's father proto-literate. Books are treasures, libraries the architecture of God.

He, himself, is an ordained minister.

He hardly ate, a tall, thin man. Our food was a Spanish soup of chick peas and spinach. The vegetable croquettes were festive as roses, their rosy dispositions.

If they had been an hour late, I would have made a sauce for the croquettes. Two hours, who knows?

This is a great meal, said Lady Blue.

All vegetarians, we savored the meal of shared values.

They left in time for an evening performance.

Lady Blue kissed my cheek and I hers, a Cambridge custom.

Blue performed a long good-bye.

I was not used to people of color.

Shelley Selkovits was born in Pittsburgh to Jewish parents in 1940. She began her college education at a girls school but changed to a university. She married early. A writer of narrative poems and poetic stories, she lives in Cambridge.

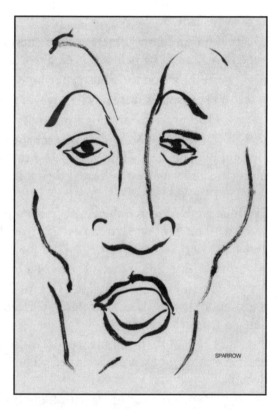

Brother Blue—Story Singer by Deb Sparrow

Ahhhh!

A Dance of Kalimbas, Blue, and Buckminster Fuller

Warren Senders

Twenty-some years ago, when all my time was free, I festooned myself with kalimbas, and wherever I went I'd play. My thumbs, tender, grew tougher—I could pluck the metal tongues for hours, keeping up a running percussive commentary on the events around me. And, of course, practically all of those events happened in Harvard Square. Eighteen, long of hair and wild of eye, I'd sit for hours on Cambridge Common's grass, Brattle Triangle's concrete, or on the stone floor of the beautiful echoing entrance to The Harvard Coop, and play, play. One acquaintance sat with me for a while and said "You know, whenever a pretty girl walks by you play better."

Well, maybe so, but my very best playing wasn't sparked by any of them. None of us can remember when it first happened, but looking back, I'm pretty sure it was a weekend afternoon sometime in the late 70's that I turned the corner towards Brattle Triangle, and saw him for the first time. All blue but for bright ribbons and bows fluttering in self-generated breeze, polychromatically parasolled, talking a rainbow streak, leaping up, landing lightly…approaching, I saw he was shoeless, and his bare feet were taking a beating, but it didn't seem to slow him down a bit. Children and adults watched in astonishment and delight.

I didn't need prompting. The minute I heard his rap I was along for the ride. Perhaps he was telling Muddy Duddy, about a little boy in love with the earth that gives us life, and my thumbs knew they'd found a friend. I started—and damn, he was fast on the uptake. It took him about half a second to widen his sphere to include my music, and he danced with a life-force that made the air crackle and hum.

From then on it may not have been regular, but it was frequent. Brother Blue and I would encounter each other, and I couldn't resist his madness.

Ahhhh!

Feeding off my kalimba rhythms, he taught me what it meant to listen widely. For all his unconscious, joyful jammingness, he was an astute performer who, telling tales, turned into a giant antenna picking up vibrations from everywhere.

I'd never had anyone respond to my music like that; it was flattering. It would have been frightening, too, except that as I came to know Blue better (and met Ruth Hill, his life-partner and perfect compliment) I found in them an ingenuousness, an innocence that seemed to gain strength with the dues they'd paid and were still paying. They never seemed depressed; Blue was always on, and I marvelled at Ruth's wry good humor. They personified a circumstance-transcending grace, and when I played and Blue spun his umbrella round and round, a few molecules of that grace fell on me. When I was around Blue, magic was pretty close to the surface; the world was full of surprises.

"Psssst! Hey brother!"

There he was, sitting, Ruth at his side, in an aisle seat at the Harvard Science Center. Covered as usual with kalimbas, I was on my way to my seat; in a few minutes we were going to hear Bucky Fuller speak. "Hey, Blue!"

"Brother, I've got an idea. You know when Bucky was here last year, I told a story for him, and he liked it a lot, and he remembered me. Now the people who organized this event, they asked me to come up at the beginning, and tell a little story about Bucky so that the children in the audience would know who he was. So I want you to play for me."

Fuller came out, and there were some introductory remarks: somebody presented him with a t-shirt honoring his great-aunt, the pioneering feminist Margaret Fuller, and he put it on over the vest of his three-piece suit. Then the emcee announced Blue, who made his way down to the central stage. I followed, and lifted my large gourd kalimba, which had a beautifully deep tone. After that, I can't remember a thing, except that I followed Blue as best I could while he made his usual magnificently digressive magic, spinning a web of images and sounds that somehow embodied Fuller's principle of synergy, riffing loopily on the attributes and character of the man. Then it was over and there was a lot of cheering and clapping, and I dashed back to my seat; this was, after all, Blue's moment. I was the backup band, and damn happy to be there.

The clapping died down and Bucky took the mike.

"Blue," he said (I'm remembering now over two decades), "I can't thank you in words. There are no words that will do the job. The only way I

AHHHH!

can thank you is by dancing."

He turned and looked through his thick spectacles at me, twenty rows back.

"Come back here, young man, and play some more of that wonderful music!"

I was onstage in a hot New York minute, my thumbs going happily.

"Thank you, Blue!" cried Buckminster Fuller, and he started a free-wheeling tapdance ballet, spinning across the stage with the joyous energy of a child.

Blue jumped up; the two began a kinetic conversation, Blue leaping, Bucky tapping, both full of light and power and humor and grace, and the strength that comes from knowing the world's own secret languages. And there I was, nineteen, watching two of the world's great imaginations pull music from my hands with the force of their dance.

Thank you, Blue!

I've known Blue and Ruth for over twenty years. Over that time I've had a chance to see them, fearless and joyful, giving their entire selves to sustaining stories for all of us. What I see on their faces is something you don't see too often. I saw it on the face of the 98-year-old Russian émigré musicologist Nicolas Slonimsky, and on the face of the avant-garde composer John Cage. I saw it on the face of the great Hindustani singer Mallikarjan Mansur; I saw it on the face of the South African pianist and composer Abdullah Ibrahim; I saw it photographed, on the faces of Ornette Coleman and Dizzy Gillespie and Allen Ginsberg, and on the face of an elderly pacifist tax resister who'd made the IRS back down with the simple power of his pure goodness. And I certainly saw it on the face of Bucky Fuller. It's a radiance and clarity that come from a life lived in adherence to inner dictates, and from inner dictates charged with love.

Blue and Ruth embody this courage; they live peacefully upon the earth, never violating their principles, always doing not only the right thing, but that which is most right. In a world of compromised visions, commercial-ized versions, they are real and unadulterated, steeped in mythic and historical understandings, charged with wit from wry to zany, full of *levitas* as a dragonfly's zigging and zagging, rich in *gravitas* as a grove of sequoias.

I am lucky to know them, to have learned from them, to love them.

Warren Senders is a musician, composer, teacher and writer who has lived in the Boston/Cambridge area for many years. A specialist in the musical traditions of India, he is a faculty member at the New England Conservatory of Music and the director of the acclaimed and innovative "world music" ensemble Antigravity.

Ahhhh!

Praise That Wakes the Heart

Laura Simms

I first met Brother Blue in the late nineteen-seventies. I had heard about a barefooted storyteller incanting hip hop Shakespeare on the streets of Cambridge, Mass. Most storytelling that I had experienced in the US at that time was closer to the American style of recitation, where memorized texts wore the title "Oral Interpretation." It was passive, often engaging and interesting, but nothing similar to what I had learned about oral traditions in cultures. I was at the time infatuated with traditional styles of storytelling, ritual performance, and praise singers as part of my own journey to create a contemporary artform that had the potency of myth-based drama and serious storytelling.

I found Brother Blue outrageous, passionate, unique and somewhat disturbing. He behaved out of a deep inner calling with little regard for the conventional forms of performance, or the reticent and polite retelling of tales that I had seen around town. He was moving Jazz. He was raw and vulnerable. He was brassy and glitzy. He paid no attention to audiences that were ready to leave or were uncomfortable.

When I found myself hesitating to get up and speak, or at a loss for words, he had already jumped up at festivals, concerts, and workshops. He was moving to the front of the room, bells jangling, covered in jeweled butterflies and ribbons, singing what he felt. I was still contemplating if it was the right time or place to speak up. He took the audience by surprise. He dared to combine the street world of African Americans with the oldest and most potent oral tradition of the praise singer. He mediated between the audience and authority, their hearts and heads. As the years passed I recognized the artfulness of this language, mixing high literature, myth, and street rhymed words into a personal expression that struck chords for compassion and directness without ego.

My most unforgettable memory occurred during a festival in New York City. Blue and I were scheduled to tell stories together on the steps of

Ahhhh!

Borough Hall in downtown Manhattan. There were thousands of businessmen and women in suits coming out into the sun to have their lunch. Blue told the story of his first grade teacher, Miss Wunderlich, as the distracted audience left their sandwiches on benches and moved forward to listen.

He was uncanny and wholly human. I was astonished by the energy and his kindness, and loved the response. I was lucky. I now had an interested audience. He had set the mood.

I began to retell a West African folktale called Magooli. Steve Gorn was accompanying me on bamboo flute. Without a blink, Blue began as well. He accompanied me with words and with whistles, he played the harmonica and he danced the boy who was rejected, the Queen who had magic, and the terrible mother. At the end, his face mirrored the face of the boy who lost everything. His presentation was a force of nature, resonating levels of meaning, like repeated waves on the ocean carrying us beat out into space. The entire place was alive. People were crying and leaning on one another.

I tasted the full power of traditional storytelling in a modern setting because of Blue's unrelenting sense of what had to happen—and his fearless desire to break open the rigid binding structures which keep people from enjoying the fullness of their feelings or the dynamism of their imagination.

And through all this—the years of praise singing, the outlandish presentations that dared everyone to see the world differently and themselves as fools and royalty, the music, the foot stamping dance of ecstasy, the wild and careful constructions of language and meaning—Ruth sat in the front of each venue on a chair, watching as a lightning bolt of stillness. Only recently did I understand the profound connection, the active force of her presence, to support him, the hunter of hearts. She was like the Inuit women whose presence at home during a hunt was the essential force that made it possible for the hunter to actually entice a whale to give up its soul for food and clothing. The woman's dreaming in the house appears to us as a passive non-essential act. But it was she who protected the hunter and the village by her presence. She dreamed the hunt while it happened.

Ruth holds Blue with invisible strings of faith and love, and with her own absolute display of compassionate intelligence, allows him to ride the waves of his vision and passion with stability of mind. She protected us by furthering the silence in the story and held it there in space so we could all go further than we expected.

AHHHH!

In the end, both Blue and Ruth have been for us traditional singers of tales. Those that serve as heart, eyes, and ears of the community. And they have been unconventional and daring. Who else could actually break the lethargy of our fear of full and spontaneous language!

Many storytellers have striven to bridge the world of traditional village African storytelling with costume and music. But Blue and Ruth did it naturally, because they captured the essence of the performance and its relation to community and listeners without adopting a costume not their own. They performed a magic act.

I watched a documentary film on the life of Nelson Mandela. A Zulu Praise Singer, wearing western shirt and jeans adorned with the skin of a tiger, leapt up in Congress before his speeches and sang his praises with the poetic language of mythic dignity. He called him a Lion of a Man, a Great Leader, a Hunter of Hearts. This singer softened the formality of the western system and dignified it with the elegance of the past. He managed to bind the present with tradition, and expanded the judicial system to include the inspired wisdom of elders. It was stunning.

Watching that performance, I was reminded of Blue and understood that he carried that role within him. He was mediating between our limited notion of story and a greater realm of communal activity. It rose up from him like fire. He is now an elder and he blazes for us.

I feel privileged to have experienced Ruth and Blue so often in the last thirty years. I want to sing praises for what he has given us. He is a Lion of a Man. She is a Lion of a Woman.

Also, on a more personal level, I want to thank them. There were times in the last thirty years when I felt the pang of becoming a storyteller in a world where it is definitely acultural, or where I felt awkward because I had spent years out of the community of storytelling because of cancer and felt distant or afraid. They always had time for me. Blue always came to me and held my hand and sang me to confidence and happiness with words and meaning. His memory is expansive. He has room for us all. Ruth greeted me like family. Never tired of offering memory and friendship.

Laura Simms has been on the forefront of storytelling as a reciprocal-performing art for the past thirty years. She is a spokesperson and teacher on the meaning and significance of storytelling in the modern world as a bridge to the knowledge and wisdom of the past. She is an author and recording artist. Laura Simms, along with Brother Blue, was inducted into the National Storytelling Network's Circle of Excellence in 1996.

Ahhhh!

That's Only Stories...

Theodore Sizer

Four of us in a university seminar were reporting on "successful" schools. I was to speak last.

Data, meaning numbers, cascaded forth. This school had these test scores, that school some others. This school had this percentage of "free-or-reduced-lunch" kids, that school another. Another set of schools had these dropout rates. And more. Success was a matter of the numbers.

When my turn came, I told stories about three schools that I knew well and which struck me as being "successful" in the eyes of their parents and teachers. Our audience listened respectfully; the children in my narrative lived in beleaguered communities, places usually filled with fear and dashed hopes. I showed the seminar members pictures of the schools and examples of the students' work. At the end, I tried to frame some lessons about why these schools might be called "successful" and what that might mean.

"But," I was abruptly told, "That was only stories...What was the data?"

The "data," I replied, were buried in the complexity of each child's portfolio of work, in each child's journal, in each child's visible sense of him- or herself as a consequential person.

That's too fuzzy.

But growing up is fuzzy. If you simply jerk a few bits of evidence out of a child's life and use them to categorize her, you distort that child. You have to see her whole, against the background of her community and school.

Fuzzy, fuzzy, fuzzy. By blaming complexity you avoid blunt judgment. You chicken out...

Blunt judgment leads all too easily to selective, narrow judgment. The numerical data compiled from items on single tests, for example, are but

Ahhhh!

one source of information, and challengeable even then. Taken alone, they distort.

You have to start somewhere.

So, start with understanding the single child, in all his complexity, his enthusiasms, his flaws, his dreams, his impatience...

We can't afford that.

You and I expect our physicians to treat us as individuals, and not to depend on one or two tests which happened to lend themselves to precision.

That's different.

How different? Are a child's mind and heart less complex than the causes of my eczema?

We need defensible data, objective data to drive policy.

I agree. But the data has to be true to the character of the person or institution being observed. If kids are complex little characters—and they are—then their schools are sure to be complex places. There is no short cut to unearthing reliable evidence that one or a number of kids are being significantly served.

So what would you do?

Tell stories, careful, rich stories, replete with every sort of evidence of a child's or a group of children's work and play. And then work hard to make whatever sense can be made of this varied mass of artifacts and impressions.

Oh, you mean Case Studies!

No, I mean stories...just stories...rich stories, full of stuff...

But that's not science!

Right you are. It's art.

Theodore Sizer met Brother Blue in the 1960s while he was serving as Dean of the Harvard Graduate School of Education. Since leaving Harvard in the early seventies, he has taught at Brown and twice served as a high school principal. He has also written several books, all built around stories. The most recent is *The Students Are Watching: Schools and the Moral Contract*, cowritten with his wife, Nancy.

AHHHH!

Before You Were "Brother Blue"

Arreta Smith

Ruth Hill is my sister. This event took place years ago. Hugh was a student at Yale University. He wasn't known as Brother Blue at the time. Women lived in women's dorms. Men lived in men's dorms. There was a waiting room or lounge area were the two could meet. Ruth was "visiting" with Hugh in the waiting area. Hugh was working on a paper. Ruth mentioned she would like to go to the restroom. It was in another part of the dorm. She would not be permitted to go there alone; it was off limits. She would have to be escorted by Hugh. But Hugh was busy, really concentrating, putting himself fully into what he was doing. Ruth spoke up several times. Hugh just kept on working.

When Hugh finally stopped and said, "OK, let's go," it was too late. Ruth had wet the floor.

While living in Pittsfield, Massachusetts, I went to a day care center with Ruth and Hugh. Hugh took off his shoes. He liked contact with the floor. He could perform better. When the children saw Hugh take off his shoes and throw them aside, they began doing the same. Shoes were coming off and going in all directions. The teacher had to stop them; she wouldn't know which shoes belong to whom. Some of the children didn't either. They stopped a few minutes to gather shoes, then Hugh continued, barefoot.

Hugh ministered to the prisoners in Boston City Prison many times. Most of the prisoners were black. The chaplain was white. On one occasion they had told the chaplain that they wouldn't go to the Christmas eve service unless Hugh could do it. The chaplain agreed. Ruth had made breads and brought them as gifts. Hugh was instrumental in one of the prisoners being allowed to leave the prison during the day and attend music school in the Boston area.

AHHHH!

314

He returned to the prison at night. Many of the prisoners had been in jail for over a year waiting for their case to come to trial; some, for a very minor offense. They had no money for bail. One of the very first times Hugh had performed for the prisoners, he told a story about people being in chains. He had a real pair of chains from a slave market. As he danced before them, he chanted "We all must break free from the chains that bind us." Some of them took Hugh literally. They broke out of prison that night.

The late Arreta Smith is Ruth Hill's sister. She was a physical therapist and longtime head of the Physical Therapy Department at North Adams Regional Hospital in the Berkshires. After retirement, she moved to Cheney, Washington, to live with her brother, James Edmonds.

Watercolor by: Ann Hoban

Ahhhh!

Old Friends

Hale Smith

Dr. Hugh Morgan Hill was introduced to me by his sister sometime between 1952 and 1954. He was then, I believe, a graduate student at the Yale School of Drama. From that day to this, he has been a dear friend whom I admire for his humanity, intelligence, and creative imagination.

Since he (with Ruth) and I (with Juanita) have grown old(er) together—though in different geographical areas—I can hardly speak of such things as influence, except in the hope that they may have been as beneficial to him as they have been to me.

Some thirty years ago, a friend passed greetings to me from a "mutual friend," someone who lived in Cambridge with a name I didn't recognize. After denying any knowledge of such a person, Hugh Morgan Hill was entered, and remains in, my consciousness in his truly iridescent personage: Brother Blue.

Hale Smith began composing at age eight, and was playing in night clubs by the time he was fourteen years old. He worked as an arranger and music collaborator with various artists including Eric Dolphy, Dizzy Gillespie, Ahmad Jamal, and Randy Weston. He was awarded the New Orleans keys to the city in 1991, and was recognized as a United Negro College Fund Distinguished Professor. His seventieth birthday was honored by the Long Island Composers Alliance with a concert of his music. Hale lives with his wife Juanita in Freeport, New York.

AHHHH!

Brother Blue

Jimmy Neil Smith

> *Ever' time I tell a story, I risk all on*
> *that deep feelin'—tryin' to do somethin' real, from the*
> *middle of me, movin' in the spirit, trustin'*
> *completely with my life. For my work is like that of an old*
> *jazz musician: blowin' an old song*
> *but blowin' it ever new.*

For more than forty years, Brother Blue—barefoot and adorned in a colorful disarray of ribbons, bows, balloons, and butterflies—has told stories. Enhanced by the music and rhythm of his voice, he chants a concoction of poetry, story, and song to those who gather, gawk-eyed, to witness the spectacle. His body swirls and stomps, his fingers snap in a poetic cadence, his toes brush the cold asphalt. And while some scoff, there are others, often those standing in the miserable cold of a New England winter, who hang on every word and become immersed in Brother Blue's messages built on image and mood.

Brother Blue is actually Dr. Hugh Morgan Hill, a man who has dedicated his life to telling stories for social change, for world peace with justice, and for love, in settings as diverse as the stories themselves— from prisons to nurseries, hospitals to libraries, seminars to Sunday schools, and often in the streets. And while Blue feels that he must sometimes appear like a "living Christmas tree," the carnival, the birthday party—both flamboyant and colorful—to get and hold the attention of people in the streets and subways, he wants his listeners to see beyond the mask, the costume, and soak in the stories, their words and meaning.

Brother Blue was born in poverty in Ohio to parents who each had

Ahhhh!

only a third-grade education. *"I was the only black kid in a white school, you know, and I kinda had the feelin' that ever'body was different from me. The only black button in a field of snow, you know. The Ugly Ducklin'. And I could hardly talk. I stammered terribly.*

"But somebody said if I could recite poetry or sing, my stammerin' would stop. So one of my teachers gave me a poem to recite. And, you see, I was a small guy. A kinda rough-lookin' kid. A tough little boy. But they had me recitin' poetry for the whole school. I would do that stuff, and the other kids would love it—and mother loved it too. And sure enough, I overcame my stammerin'. And whenever they had storytellin' time, I just loved to recite poetry or tell stories."

Though his parents could barely read or write, Blue's world was filled with tales—of his mother picking cotton in Mississippi, or of his father, son of a slave. Blue remembers how his father, a huge man, the first and most powerful storyteller in his life, stood over his bed at night, casting a long shadow against the wall, pacing back and forth, reading aloud from the Bible. For Blue, it was as if he was singing.

"My father was a bricklayer, a man whose heart and soul were in the church. And I came out of that trustin' tradition, out of the wide-open, rockin' black church, out of the rhythm and blues, out of the shouts and hollers. We'd walk five miles to church every Sunday to hear that preacher man rock, and he'd get up there and show you God scoopin' out the valleys and puttin' up the mountains."

Despite his obstacles as a child, Brother Blue attended Harvard University and Yale Drama School, earning degrees from both. One day, in a class on American church history, Blue told his professor, "You've taught through 1890 and you haven't discussed slavery at all." But the next morning, the professor came into the class and dropped a paper bag on the table. Inside were chains.

"'Yes, Blue, they're slave chains from a slave market in Richmond, Virginia. My great-grandfather got them when he was going through Virginia with the Union army.'

"I grabbed the chains, and I tried to break them, and I found I couldn't. And then I knew...the chains have not been broken...the visible chains, the invisible chains...chains of suffering, chains of hunger, chains of disease...and I decided at that moment that I wanted to spend my life breaking them. I thought about people like my daddy who could barely read and write but was so noble, and I wondered how I could bring to him the beauty I was finding. What I wanted to do was take what I knew and break it down for those who didn't have the

AHHHH!

literary teeth to chew it, so at least they could gum it. The poor, the sick, the lonely."

Blue studied drama, theology, and the oral tradition, and in 1968, he performed "O Martin, O King"—a play, a requiem, a happening—a homage to the recently slain civil rights leader, and a spontaneous theater form of storytelling was born. Blue became a singer and a poet, a dancer and a chanter, an actor and a storyteller. Friends urged him to pursue and develop his newly discovered storytelling style, and in 1972, the ideas and acts crystallized into Brother Blue's Soul Theater. Through this self-made forum, storytelling has become for Blue the perfect vehicle for speaking to people of all ages, backgrounds, and levels of understanding—seeking to effect a transformation in their hearts and souls.

"I've given my life to storytelling; it's sacred to me. We can touch human hearts forever. It's my whole life and being. I want to change the world—to ease the burden of those who suffer, to feed the hungry, to lighten the struggle.

"My kind of theater can be presented anywhere, in any setting, with nothin' but a place to stand—and imagination. I can take it to the poorest people. I can take it to one person or many. I can take it anyplace. It's in my body, in my soul. I've told my stories by candlelight, at high noon beside the sea, in convents, in hospitals, in college classrooms and graduate seminars, in Sunday schools, in public schools, in nursery schools, in theaters, in halls, in prisons—I like to work in prisons.

"I tell stories wherever people are—even in the streets. And when you're there in the streets, you meet the street people. The people who are suffering, dying, lost, some going mad, some drunk. 'Tell the drunk a story, Blue.' You know, you can sober up a man with a story. Stories are healing. But people are in a hurry in the streets. You've got to make things concise. Boom! You can talk all you want, but how does the recipe taste in your mouth and your belly? Did you give them somethin' they can use?"

And wherever there are those who gather to listen, there is always that incessant question: "Why, Blue? Why do you do it, Blue?"

"Once I was invited by a friend to a home of a millionaire. The millionaire watched me all evening, and about two o'clock in the mornin' when ever'body had gone, the man said, 'Blue, tell me your story. Are you jivin' me or somethin'? Why do you tell stories?'

"As I talked with the man and saw his skepticism, I thought of the death of my brother, Tommy, who was mentally retarded. I looked the millionaire straight in the eye, and for the first time since Tommy's death, I told the story of

AHHHH!

my brother.

I had a brother once. He died on me. He could have been you, peekin' through your eyes of blue. He couldn't read or write, but he could read and write music in the air. He lived for love.

I taught him how to say my name, and that became our game. And one night, he said, "Brother Blue." I jumped over the moon with the cow and the spoon. And that's when I began to wear rainbow colors on my clothes.

I tried to teach him how to write his name. He tried, he tried. He couldn't. He didn't want to hurt the pencil. I tried to teach him how to read. He tried. He couldn't. He was scared of the fire in the dragon's eye.

One night when I was far away, they put Tommy someplace. They locked him behind one door, then two, three, and four. He cried. He upped and died on me so fast. If I had been there, would he have flew? It's a true story, true inside of true.

And now, if I see someone on the street—or if you do— who's confused and unhappy, that's my brother. And I'm goin' to love 'im. How about you?

"When I had finished tellin' my story, the millionaire didn't ask me any more questions. He just looked at me. He understood.

"Several years later, I was asked to tell stories at a school in Canada for the so-called mentally retarded. I stood in the middle of a large gymnasium, and I was surrounded by a group of young children. I saw a boy who looked like my brother. I went over to him and began to tell 'im a story. He couldn't talk. He began to cry.

"I said, 'Child, you're so beautiful. I love you.'

"And he cried all the more.

"'I had a little brother like you. He was my best friend. And you know something? He could fly like a butterfly, up into the sky. And so can you. As I turned to leave the gymnasium, the little boy ran up to me, put his head on my chest, and then backed off and spread his arms as if he were flyin'.

"You want to know why I tell stories? If I never get another response from anyone—no one ever again tells me that they like my stories—I've got that memory. And whenever I see someone tryin' to get out of the cocoon of loneli-

Ahhhh!

ness, sadness, trouble, I always think of my brother. There is always a beautiful soul, a butterfly, within.

"For, you see, storytellin' has become a sacred mission. Ever' time I tell a story, I risk all on that deep feelin'—tryin' to do somethin' real, from the middle of me, movin' the spirit, trustin' completely with me life. For my work is like that of an old jazz musician: blowin' an old song but blowin' it ever new."

When Brother Blue was attending graduate school, he was offered an internship at Harvard Graduate School of Education to teach an alternative school for children with special problems. The professors asked him, "What do you think about teaching? What's your philosophy about education? Your theories? Just tell us." And Blue told them a story. "I'm goin' to tell ya about a teacher. Miss Wunderlich. She had blue eyes and skin like snow. But next to my mama and my wife, she is the love of my life. I want to be like her."

Miss Wunderlich

Hey, ever'body. I'm Brother Blue, a street cat callin' you. Come close. Let me touch your pretty nose. Can I tickle your toes? This story is about rainbows. I wear them on my clothes and a butterfly in my hand—for a teacher. Did you ever fall in love with your teacher? It happened to Blue.

It was like this, you see. I was eight years old, and I hated school. The kids were cruel to Blue. I was one black button in a field of snow. You know how it goes. They called me ever'thing but Blue. And I cried. I liked to died. My name was D in everything. D in readin'. D in writin'. D in 'rithmetic. D incarnate, you might say. All I'd do is cry 'cause I wanted somebody to look past my eyes and see somethin' in me pretty.

Hey, people. You wanna hear a secret? In the middle of you and in the middle of Blue, there's some kind of magic. It's there for love. If someone don't love you, you can cry. You could even die. I almost did, but she come along. Like a rainbow song. Her skin was like snow, you know, but inside was her bright soul. She had magic eyes. She could look through muddy water when children cry and see the beautiful butterfly. Well, in school I was cryin' all the time.

I come home cryin' and Mama say, "What's the matter, Blue?"

And I say, "Mama, let's play peek-a-boo."

She say, "Come on. You're no baby."

Aнннн!

I say, "Mama, kiss me once, kiss me twice. It'd be nice." You know how mamas do. When they kiss ya, they mostly miss ya. Talkin' 'bout "blow your nose" and "don't tear your clothes."

Daddy seemed seven feet tall. Like a brick wall. A bricklayer when he could get work. Didn't wear no gloves on his hands, you understand. He had a trick, squarin' off my face. Gonna turn it into a brick and put it in a wall someplace. And I cried, and that's when she come along. When I was dyin'.

Miss Wunderlich. Like an angel. A magical angel. On my first test in arithmetic, I got D minus. I cried. I almost died. She said, "Come on, Blue, give me that paper. Let's play peek-a-boo like children do."

She's lookin' inside of me. She's sayin', "Blue, I love you. In you, I see a butterfly. Come on. Don't die. Don't cry." She took my paper, and she put somethin' on there like a kiss.

Oh! Something happened in my heart. I heard music. I fell in love with the woman. I did numbers in my sleep. One plus one is two. I love you. Two times two is four. I won't be late no more.

Next test, guess what I got, folks? A plus. That's what happened to Blue. If they only knew what love can do. It can change you. I fell in love with school— with the ceiling, the floor, the window, and the door—'cause she was in there. I fell in love with the sky 'cause it was blue like her eye. It can happen to you. All you have to do is fall in love with someone who can look through your eye and see the butterfly in you, in your soul, and you become what that person sees in you.

Well, I went through all the schools, and I went to war. I traveled across the sea. I saw so much dyin'. I heard cryin'. One night a man came to me and said, "Blue, I can't read or write."

I say, "That's all right. Let's play peek-a-boo. I know a lady with eyes of blue. She taught me a trick. Come on, I'll give it to you. I believe in you. I see a butterfly in you. Don't cry. Just try. And I love you, brother, to my soul."

I taught that man to read and write, and when I came home again, I thought I was cool. I went to the school to say, "Thank you, Miss Wunderlich." But guess what. There were tears in my eye. I didn't want that woman to see me cry, and I walked away without tellin' her I loved her. What a fool was I. She died in the snow, you know. I loved her, but I never told her so.

Miss Wunderlich, I'm Brother Blue. I love you. I'm playin' peek-a-boo in the streets, in the jail houses, in the hospitals, in the subways as I travel around the world in my bare feet—and look in the eyes of the people I meet. I pray someday before I die, before I blow away, that I'll save one life, maybe two, like you saved Blue.

Ahhhh!

Good night, Miss Wunderlich. Good mornin' too. I'm Brother Blue. I love you in this life, in the next one, too. I'm a storyteller travelin' through the world. All I do is play peek-a-boo, lookin' for the butterfly in all people. I believe in love. And that's you.

This essay was originally published in Homespun: Tales from America's Favorite Storytellers (1988, Crown Pub.), edited by Jimmy Neil Smith and used with his blessing.

In 1972, Jimmy Neil Smith founded the National Storytelling Festival in Jonesborough Tennessee. Now in its 32nd year, it is the first and largest storytelling festival in the nation. He was instrumental in founding NAPPS, a national storytelling association with several thousand members, and served as its executive director for many years. His efforts to build a National Storytelling Center bore fruit with its opening in 2002 in Jonesborough TN. The National Storytelling Network conferred its Lifetime Achievement Award on Jimmy Neil Smith in 1999, sharing the honor that year with Brother Blue.

Ahhhh!

Blue, Brother Blue
Mary Carter Smith

It was at Artpark, New York
I first laid eyes on you
Gracing the air with your beautiful words
Delighting the eye with your appearance
You stood and created stories on the spot
Shakespeare to the hippest slang
Were equally at home with you
They called you Blue, Brother Blue
Unique from any other
Articulate of tongue
Brilliant of mind
Compassionate, kind
Always encouraging us
You march to a different drummer
I love, respect and admire you
You are a teller without a peer
You are Blue, the Beloved

Mary Carter Smith is a modern griot, whose career was inspired by the emergence of the Black cultural expression of the 1960s and by her concern over misunderstandings among groups. Her extensive repertoire of stories, poems, and dramatic sketches developed from recollections of experiences in her native Birmingham, Alabama and other places where she has lived. Mary is a founding member of Big Sisters International, and co-founder of the National Association of Black Storytellers. She is the author of several books, has had poetry included in anthologies, and has produced several audiocassettes. In 1996, Mary Carter Smith became the second recipient of the National Storytelling Network's Lifetime Achievement Award.

Ahhhh!

Every Colored Girl Needs

Patricia Smith

Every little colored girl needs a colored man who loves her unconditionally, who treasures her frailties, her sins, the mistakes she makes just
pulling in one breath and pushing out the next. She needs someone who
knows how her heart bends almost to the point of breaking. What she
needs is a lanky, loquacious griot swathed in all the colors the sky has
been, a man whose feet never bother to reach the ground, and couldn't if
they wanted to, because of all the glittering butterflies lifting him up.
What every little colored girl needs is a man who spots her in a crushing
crowd, pushes and pummels to reach her side, and then says in response
to everything she has ever done and ever will do "You leave me breathless."

And that moment, like so many others, becomes a story. It sprouts a
spirit and he tells it to her, arching over her awe, showering her with
spittle and spirit. She thinks of turning away because she is awkward
under this, this being the fuel for each sputtered syllable. "You are
wondrous, the things that you are," he says. "You are a phoenix. You
rise and rise, and never stop rising." She becomes, in turn, a tigress, an
angel, a ship on turbulent waters, a goddess, a relentless flame, a star, a
scared little colored girl, a blue bird with wings that can circle the world.
He makes her all of these things, because in this moment, in this place,
he is crafting a gospel, a religion. Butterflies are lifting her up. His
loving her knows no questions, is pure madness. He says, "the sun
shines because you are in the world," and she does not laugh. No one
else could say that and make it so true.

She notices her skin straining toward indigo.

What happens because he is in the world? Because he is here, all
spinning verb and flame, stories beg to be told. From creaking Delta
porches to the city's insistent stone, we are what has happened to us. We

Ahhhh!

are what is around us, we are our histories and what we see when we stare through the stars. He is the way to give voice to this. His lap is where we sit as he tells us who we are.

"I wish I had known your father," he says. This is often not connected to anything else he has said or anything he will say. He knows that her father died long ago, and that this is what drives her to rhymes, that constant bending of her heart. He knows that he can be a million fathers to her, just not the one she wants. He even stands with her as a father would, grasping both of her hands tightly, his lanky body wedged between her and the world.

She loves him for this.

For of course, she has written a poem for him. She wanted more, but words were all she could find to use.

> *Did you speak out the stars? Is that your song?*
> *The twist of twilight from its glory orange heat*
> *to whisper colors was that your work?*
> *It must have been your fingers that coaxed*
> *the stubborn skin of morning to this softness.*

The words were huge in her heart, but they were simply angles and curves and pauses on a too-white page, each word woefully unable to hold what she owed him.

> *Were you the father of this midnight, did you*
> *pull me into this cradle of bunched starlight*
> *and hold me there, weaving the sleepy color brown*
> *the color of my face, my knees, my hair*
> *into the patchwork of passage, into the jumbled quilt*
> *of days that can no longer be reached for, or touched?*

She keeps writing the damned thing over and over. She is angry because the poem will not pull him into the circle of its arms.

> *When my body stutters and I cry hallelujah*
> *into the moon's many mouths, is that you crafting*
> *those syllables of steam? Beneath your gentle mercies*
> *I am convinced that Jesus breathes his shaking*
> *into simple things: wood, candles, a toddling child.*

She is angry because it is not colored blue.

> *And I know now that the stars mystified by their*
> *own unbridled fire, already drunk with blazing*
> *sprang from your throat. You knew how often*
> *I would gaze upon their shifting light, how my eyes*

AHHHH!

would choke on their bright singing, how they would
pulse with glowing even after the both of us are gone.

She wonders if she will ever write anything that's huge enough for him.

Because she steps down from the stage and he is there. In the room full of so many people, they are alone, and his blaring light won't stop rushing over her. She tries to speak, to answer in some way, but any word she manages is only half of what it should be. This is a story that will not end until she does, and that is unthinkable to him, so he blesses her with a voice that can strike down injustice, hair that is twisted from threads of silk, claws strong enough to clutch the sleek sides of mountains. He clasps both her hands, as if their skins touching were essential to the story, and on the back of his she sees ragged butterflies bleeding blue ink. She imagines him every dawn, crouching at a window that seeps newborn sun, filling in the wings with a ballpoint that is soon drained. He ritually stains his skin, laughs aloud as his hands take flight.

I can teach you to fly, he says. She thinks only daddies can do that.

Spindly arms jut out at his sides; he flaps once, throws back his head and laughs. The blue beret doesn't teeter, never teeters. I can teach you because you have taught me.

Now she is his teacher. His words come faster now. There is a message he has for her, something he senses she needs to know, and he will hold her hands until it comes. Never mind that the world insists on moving on around them, without them.

"You are beautiful!" he says now, and they stand there, their souls fused, curious, but not impossible. After all, inked wings flutter on the back of a blueman's hand. Stories move the world forward. Every colored girl needs. And the next days are still warm within the circle of him and she sits down, picks up a pen that flows blue, and writes this.

Patricia Smith, award-winning poet, journalist and performer, is author of the poetry volumes *Close to Death*, *Big Towns, Big Talk* and *Life According to Motown*, as well as a four-time individual champion of the notorious "poetry slam." She also authored the critically acclaimed *Africans in America*, the companion book to the groundbreaking PBS documentary. Smith, who has performed her work in Stockholm, Paris, Brazil and on tour in Germany, Austria and Amsterdam, has also appeared in a number of U.S. venues, including the Nuyorican Poets Cafe, Bumbershoot, St. Mark's Poetry Project and on tour with Lollapalooza. Her one-woman show, *Life According to Motown*, was produced by Nobel Prize-winner Derek Walcott. During the summer of 2001 she was writer-in-residence at the Eugene O'Neill Playwrights Conference, where she developed *What Unravels*, a memoir slated for both literary and theatrical release.

AHHHH!

The Sound of Bells

Rebecca Ruben Smith

August 1979—A world away from my current life, I woke up in the boarding house to the faint sound of bells. Drowsily making my way to the bathroom in the hall, I came across a vision. Dressed in blue from head to foot, covered with layers of ribbons, bows and bells, he smiled at me and greeted me warmly. My brain did not know how to compute this experience. I had met many interesting people in my life, but no one before had gracefully extended their open palm featuring a butterfly. At 7:30 in the morning after a long 12-hour drive the day before, it was almost more than I could bear. I instinctively grasped the extended hand and mumbled some response that could never have matched his enthusiasm at that moment. The vision of this man with magical face and twinkling eyes was forever tucked away in my memory bank.

As I stood in the hallway working through this introduction, my bewildered state was interrupted by the sound of a soothing voice. "Blue, let that poor woman into the bathroom and come for breakfast." The voice of order and reason turned out to be Ruth, the caretaker, promoter, and translator. I would learn that her soul was firmly planted on earth while her partner, Blue, was tethered to her—floating at various heights above, depending on the tale he was telling. They were the personification of yin and yang. A few days later my husband arrived and became totally enthralled with this couple. We all adopted each other because of an intense and immediate connection.

That morning was the dawn of a long and treasured friendship. Blue and Ruth have graced our lives with stories and shared memories of Artpark, festivals, train stations at two in the morning, and backyard picnics. Postcards have arrived at our house from all over North America and many foreign countries bearing travel notes and messages of love from Ruth, and signature icons from Blue. We have followed

Ahhhh!

their travels with pride and admiration, knowing that these two people are always true to each other and inspirational in their dealing with other people.

Blue understood us thoroughly. He began to tell our story, and with each subsequent visit, he elaborated on our lives. Just before the birth of our son, Blue and Ruth visited. Blue regaled us with stories about babies, princes and jesters. Knowing both parents, he predicted the character of the child not yet born. Perhaps that voice was implanted in the child before birth. We know that the magic lives with our son. Like surrogate parents, they nurture and support his dreams.

Years after the rooming house meeting, Blue and our son provided customers at a restaurant with impromptu scenes from Shakespeare's plays. Another wonderful image tucked away in that memory bank.

Bravo Brother Blue! Brava dear Ruth! We celebrate you and the wonderful contribution you have made to our lives. Please accept our love and deepest thanks.

Becca Ruben Smith is a musician, composer, educator, businesswoman, mother and wife, and long time admirer of Brother Blue and Ruth Hill.

Brother Blue—Storyteller by Deb Sparrow

AHHHH!

Praise for This Life

Robert B. Smyth

Like so many, I heard about Blue before I met him. And I'm sure that I saw him and Ruth long before my first clear memory or, better to say, experience of Blue in the late seventies under the streets of Boston on the Green Line between Park Street and Copley Square on New Year's Eve. If memory serves I got on the subway with my date, whose name I don't remember, at Park Street and was working hard at making an impression! On our heels and seemingly out of nowhere, Blue got on, and my efforts to impress came to a screeching halt! In hind sight, I was outdone by a black man with balloons, a harmonica, and a rap that I, a white boy from fruit farm country in upstate New York, fresh out of college and boarding school, didn't appreciate, didn't want to hear, and just plain pissed me off. Who was this guy? I was on a hot date and he had just embarrassed the hell out of me—or so I thought! I tried to keep up a conversation with my date, but Blue would have none of it. He could tell I was trying to impress and he let the whole car know it, that he loved seeing us checkin' each other out! I tried to politely ignore him—didn't work. I tried to tell him I was carrying on a conversation with my date—didn't work. Ruth must have been standing there quietly, the balance that she is, but I don't remember. And so completely un-aware that Blue saw me for who I was. I felt overshadowed; inwardly I shrank, I could think of nothing to say or do that would shut this guy up. I don't remember the rest of the date. Blue succeeded in impressing my date more than I did, and a new year dawned.

A number of years later, I was working with Doug Lipman, Judith Black, Lee Ellen Marvin and the rest of the folks that made up "Storytellers in Concert." Blue was scheduled to do an evening of Shakespeare. I was not looking forward to the evening. I had kept my distance all those years. And then Blue started to do "Willy the Shake"

Ahhhh!

and I was totally taken by his finger poppin' rap of Romeo and Juliet. I saw things in the play that had gone right by me before. I was hearing the story in a new way and it got in! I was impressed. I still didn't get the rest of Blue's persona off stage. Didn't get that there was no on stage or off stage for him. I got the on stage part this time though.

Over the next few years, as life worked on me, I got married and divorced, my parents died, I saw Blue in Harvard Square in front of Brine's Sporting Goods and Warburton's being the "street cat" that he is, as I drank a cup of coffee and opened my mail. Slowly, "Miss Wunderlich" began to make sense. I remembered those teachers who had made a difference in my life. My eighth grade English teacher Mr. Cooper, Mr. Harlow, the supervisor of the oceanography program that I was consumed by in boarding school, Professor Stoneburner who nurtured my love of language in college, Gary Miranda, the poet I was taking a weekly workshop with then. And I have to add Robert Bly, Gioia Timpanelli, and Martín Prechtel who, along with Blue, are my current teachers.

Several years ago, I went to "Blue's Tuesday Night Storytelling" to give myself something in a time when life was nipping at my heels. It was the right move—I've been going ever since to hear the stories we all have to tell from the established tellers, the up and coming, and those who are just tellin' the story of their lives. For Blue's is a place where there is always praise for what you do in this life, praise for who you are, and who you are struggling to become. Where there is always praise for this life.

Robert B. Smyth began Yellow Moon Press in 1978 out of a one bedroom apartment in Cambridgeport, to help perpetuate "The Oral Tradition" and the spoken word. Twenty five years later, it has 54 active titles of storytelling, poetry, and music. They include titles that have been chosen as ALA Notable Children's Recordings, and received Parents Choice Gold, Silver, and Honor Awards, Anne Izard Storytelling Choice Awards, and Storytelling World Awards.

Ahhhh !

A Song for a Neighbor

Werner Sollors

Palms, connected at the pulse,
Fluttering through the air,
Weaving in Harvard Square
A dream of butterflies.

"O-thel-lo!," a magic voice,
Shouting, singing, high, low,
"How did that story go?"
Of freedom, jail, and hope on wings?

"Brother Baraka, don't come late!"
A blue beret, a dot of bright
Colors, glowing in the night,
And dancing in the day.

After the lecture, I await His say,
Adding a magic wand of gold
To others' monologues, long and cold:
"The Mind! The Hope! Yeah! Yeah!!!"

Flapping, gliding, thought anew,
Palms, connected at the wrists,
Sparkling eyes, a song, and twists
Of story-body, Brother Blue.

Werner Sollors teaches Afro-American Studies and English at Harvard University,
and is the author of *Neither Black Nor White Yet Both: Thematic Explorations of Interracial
Literature* and of *Beyond Ethnicity: Consent and Descent in American Culture*, and other
works.

AHHHH!

A Song for Brother Blue

Lenny Solomon

Sun is rising, it's early morn;
After 20 years of living it's like you were just born;
Saints and sinners I have heard the call;
I've finally learned the lesson that to hate is all wrong;
From you, my Brother Blue, this song's for you my Brother Blue.

Look at the little fishes swimming down the stream;
Wonder if the bottom holds the answer to a dream;
Swimming kind of carefree in the lazy flow;
Thinking 'bout the fact that we're always on the go;
Like you, my Brother Blue, this song's for you my Brother Blue.

See the sky, it is calling, the trees echo the sound;
Grace is following you everywhere, you will never, never be
   down again,
No, no, not you, my Brother Blue,
This song's for you my Brother Blue.

Mary and her brother came to town;
Dragging their belongings and their faces from the ground;
Asked a stranger where they might find some rest;
He just smiled, said they had passed the test;
For you, my Brother Blue, this song's for you my Brother Blue.

See the sky, it is calling, the trees echo the sound;
Grace is following you everywhere, you will never, never be
   down again,
No, no, not you, my Brother Blue,
This song's for you my Brother Blue.

Ahhhh!

So if you're a'hurtin' and you're feeling low;
Wondering 'bout something you think you ought to know;
If the weight is heavy, think that it's the end;
Smile to your neighbor and you might have a friend,
To help you, like my Brother Blue, this song's for you my Brother
Blue.

See the sky, it is calling, the trees echo the sound;
Grace is following you everywhere, you will never, never be
down again,
No, no, not you, my Brother Blue,
This song's for you my Brother Blue.

Singer/songwriter/musician Lenny Solomon has known Blue for over 30 years. Lenny still performs in the Cambridge/Boston area with his band, Solomon.

AHHHH!

For Brother Blue

Brita Stendahl

Once upon a time a blue-eyed woman came from the Northland to Cambridge, Massachusetts. Her eyes widened from what she saw, her ears throbbed from what she heard, and her head smarted from all she had to take in. It was so different from the little university town where she had resided before. Here at Harvard Square, if she just stood still, people from the whole wide world would come stolling down the street. Most of them who walked two and two seemed to carry on a serious dialogue, some were laughing out loud, some were old and bearded, but most of those who thronged around the newspaper stand were young students. And it was a most colorful scene.

In the midst of this shifting and noisy crowd one day stood Hugh Hill, trying to make himself heard by the circle that had formed around him. He was a colorful bird who was different, indeed. A storyteller who did not stand still. His feet danced, his hands fluttered, ripple after ripple flittered throughout his whole body, and his voice repeated again and again: Ahhhh.

The woman was astonished. She soon learned his name and that he studied at the Divinity School, where he often performed. There she made his acquaintance. She told him that she too had grown up having stories told to her, but Hugh's manner of storytelling was so confusing. She said, "You put your body between the story and the listener, and thereby it seems to me, it loses its balance and misses its impact." He said, "Show me what you mean. Coach me."

So this young woman from the Northland told him about the careful design of Hans Christian Andersen's fairytales, about the sturdy structure of the Icelandic sagas, about Selma Lagerlof's judicious strategy of repetition in her stories. In short, the blue-eyed woman sought to demonstrate through her Scandinavian heritage what she considered good storytelling should be.

Ahhhh!

It all seems so foolish of me in retrospect—I have to admit that I was that unwise young woman—trying to coach a force of nature, a huge talent. Luckily, Hugh Hill mastered his talent by following his tradition of storytelling. Thus he became Brother Blue. And as Brother Blue, he has entertained thousands of people in many lands and touched their hearts. His butterfly metaphor flies from the claustrophobic pupa to be free among the flowers. The chains of slavery break, and the world opens to dance and to song.

In the defense of his doctoral dissertation Hugh Hill demonstrated what he knew about storytelling before a doctoral committee that had gathered in a prison cellblock. At that very same time an uprising broke out in another section of the prison, but there was no sign of rioting among the prisoners in Brother Blue's audience.

Krister Stendahl and I are immensely grateful that we have had the privilege to get to know Blue and his wife Ruth. We get postcards from all over the map from places where Blue has been performing.

The image that comes to my mind when thinking of Blue is that of St. George and the dragon with Blue enacting them both. The evil dragon is writhing and twisting to drive its poison into St. George's thigh. St. George raises his lance and strikes, and, forcing the creature down, he severs the head from the coiling body. Why is St. George slaying the dragon? Because of the Princess. She stands there at the side, very still, her hands folded. The Princess is Ruth. At every performance I have attended Ruth has always been there. When Blue depicts the virtues of the Good, it is Ruth he portrays. For her, he has been slaying the dragon. Again, and again, and again. Ahhh.

Brita Stendahl has been teaching Scandinavian Literature in the Harvard Freshman Seminar Program, and in the Radcliffe Seminars Program. She is the author of several books, including *The Force of Tradition* and *Fredrika Bremer 1801-1865*. Brita has written articles in major newspapers and magazines both in Sweden and the US. She is a regular reviewer for the literary magazine *World Literature Today*. She and her husband, Krister Stendahl, have three children, eight grandchildren, and one great-grandchild. They reside in Cambridge, Massachusetts.

Krister Stendahl is Andrew W. Mellon Professor of Divinity Emeritus at Harvard University and Bishop Emeritus of Stockholm, Sweden. He is the author of several books, including *The School of St. Matthew* and a collection of essays called *Meanings*.

Ahhhh!

Brother Blue: Reflections and a Poem

Ed Stivender

It is indeed an honor to participate in the founding of what surely amounts to a new literary genre—the first time I saw Blue.

It was in the winter of 1976, I think. Having retired from teaching the year before, I was working with the Plum Cake Players Children's Theater in Hartford, Connecticut. At a particular Monday night's rehearsal, one of our number, Judith, spoke of a wise teacher she had encountered the week before on the Boston Common, a man named Brother Blue. She suggested that members of our group travel up some Friday night to the church where he regularly performed. From the tone of her voice, I thought it might be a kind of pilgrimage. It was.

Five of us caravaned up the following Friday night, found the church and went in. We were a little early. There were only two people there before us, a thin man I assumed was the sexton and a woman. The sexton welcomed us, and said that the man we had come to see would be there any minute, and we should make ourselves comfortable. A few others straggled in and he greeted them as well.

Then the man took off his overcoat and revealed his blue mufti, and I realized that this was the man himself. He had greeted us as the Baal Shem Tov or Nasrudin would have, tongue in cheek.

And then he began to speak, and we were soon enthralled by his wisdom, springing from the most simple images—butterflies, school-teachers, his brother, his very breath: "ahhh…"

Throughout his presentation, he frequently deferred to his sweetheart, his wife Ruth Hill, sitting in the front pew. Although the women in the room were free to swoon, he made it clear where his allegiance, his true love, was. In my mind this added to his power, his grace. Only years later would I realize, as I watched this genius in a variety of settings, how central Ruth is to that power and that grace. We drove back to Milford

Ahhhh!

somewhat amazed. I knew that I had been in the presence of a Master.

My only response was a bit of a song I composed in reflecting on the truth that he shared:

> Inside of me, inside of you
> There is a music room
> And you can go there,
> Anytime you want to,
> You can blow there
> Any tune you want to.
> That room is open to the sky.
> That room is open to God's eye.

As the years went by I saw him several times, each time bringing his audience into the warm space of his wisdom, each time with Ruth as his anchor, the person who held on to the kite line no matter how high he lofted, no matter what wild wind.

It was my honor to introduce him in 1980 at the Sister's Row tent at the National Storytelling Festival in Jonesborough, Tennessee. It was before the Festival got high tech—there were two fifty-watt bulbs above the stage. But that didn't bother Blue. He brought his own light— within.

Several times he has approached me after new or difficult work and held me in his gaze with a word of encouragement or wisdom. He is a man who can make you feel as if you were the only person on the world (besides Ruth) worthy of his attention.

I don't know how he does it. Truly. How he keeps such a joyous view of the world, such a light touch, such a gentle tread on this troubled earth.

There is no one in the world like him.

Too bad he is not Catholic. The Church needs more saints who are both holy and happily married. And who better to deflate the pomp of the Antichrist than Baal Shem Blue.

Ed Stivender is a Philadelphia native, Shakespearean actor, banjo player, teacher, theologian, Mummer, dreamer, juggler, and raconteur. He has been a featured performer at the National Storytelling Festival, the Cape Clear Island International Storytelling Festival in Ireland, and our own Philadelphia Folk Festival. The National Storytelling Association inducted Ed into its Circle of Excellence in 1996. He is the author or two books of tales: *Raised Catholic, Can You Tell?* and *Still Catholic After All These Fears.* He has also released several audio and video recordings of his performances.

Ahhhh!

To "B" or Not to "B"

Ruth Stotter

Bedecked with Balloons and Butterflies

Bubbly, Bouncy, Beaming

Blessed and Blessing

A reverent of tales.

This Being

Bold, Bright and Brilliant

Shows us a new "Blue" print of story meaning

I believe in this man, and say

"YES, to Be, to Being, and to Brother Blue!"

Ruth Stotter is the author of *About Story*, *More About Story*, and *The Golden Axe*. She is the former director of the Dominican University Storytelling Program in San Rafael, California. Brother Blue performed on her radio program, KUSF-FM, *The Oral Tradition*.

Ahhhh!

A Tribute to Sister Ruth

Eleanora E. Tate

"Give her of the fruit of her hands; and let her own works praise her in the gates."

Proverbs 31:31

I cannot think of Brother Blue—Dr. Hugh Morgan Hill—without also thinking almost immediately of his wife and soulmate, Ruth Edmonds Hill, the calm, smiling, patient, wise woman whose care and love has made Brother Blue who he is. Those who know them well also know that Sister Ruth is a scholar and a storyteller in her own right.

I first saw Brother Blue and Sister Ruth in 1987 in Berea, Kentucky at the Fifth Annual National Festival of Black Storytelling, as it was then called, sponsored by the National Association of Black Storytellers. This was my husband, Zack Hamlett, and my initiation into hearing professional and amateur African American storytellers come together to orally "spread the word."

A children's book author—I therefore call myself a "literary storyteller"—I was mesmerized by the calabash of spoken stories. Zack, who tells his stories through photography, was equally caught. But the man who grabbed our attention most was the barefoot gentleman with ribbons and balloons attached to his blue suit. He rose from his seat and began to deliver a story that by turn became a praise song, a sorrow song, a poem, a prayer, a sermon, a rap.

This was Brother Blue, a featured storyteller at the festival, and a poet, a minister, Ph.D., storyteller, lover of language, lover of life. As his performance went on and on and on, I noticed a lady who sat quietly in her seat near the front, her head cocked to one side, watching and listening intently. When it was apparent that Brother Blue's time had ended—but he hadn't—this lady came to the front and peacefully stood

Ahhhh!

to one side, then calmly escorted him back to his seat amid appreciative, respectful applause. That was, I later discovered, Sister Ruth, Brother Blue's wife.

As we continued to attend festivals, I would look forward to seeing the Hills. I noticed that Ruth Edmonds Hill almost always stands quietly in the background of her famous husband — keeping Brother Blue on time, guiding him to and from appointments, to meals, to rest. In her own way, she inspired me in my own marital journey.

I began corresponding with Sister Ruth in 1991, the year Zack, Beulah White, a cadre of organizers and I were in the final stages of hosting our award-winning Ninth National Festival of Black Storytelling in South Carolina. By that time, I had become national president of the National Association of Black Storytellers.

Sister Ruth wrote to me that she was the audiovisual coordinator at the prestigious Schlesinger Library of Radcliffe College in Cambridge, and coordinator of the Black Women Oral History Project there. This was an exhaustive project that began in 1976, and ended in December 1984 with a traveling photographic exhibition "Women of Courage" and a catalogue that includes all the participants in the oral history project. She previously had been a library director and archivist at Harvard, was an accomplished photographer, and gave oral history workshops and lectures.

Sister Ruth added in her letter, "I had previously written only about Brother Blue, but I would also like an opportunity to make a presentation. Both Brother Blue and I are interested in the possibility of school residencies. We would both prefer to work with high school students, but are willing to go as low as the seventh grade. We recently spent the day at a high school in a nearby town. In the morning I talked about oral history and the contributions of twentieth century black women to American society. Following a lunch break, Brother Blue met with drama and literature students. We would enjoy doing something like that again."

She also sent me their itinerary, complete with telephone numbers, contact names and addresses. According to the itinerary, between October 7—when they left Boston—until November 14, when they arrived in Myrtle Beach, the site of our festival's headquarters hotel— they had traveled to Chicago; Salt Lake City, Utah; Portland, Oregon; Spokane, Washington; Sacramento, California; back to Chicago; on to Toronto; over to New York; down to Washington, D.C.; up to Boston;

Ahhhh!

and finally, to Myrtle Beach. What a schedule! I remember getting exhausted just reading it.

As I have come to know more about her, I've found that Sister Ruth previously had coordinated schedules even more frenetic than that, including living with and sharing stories with coal-mining families in Virginia and other regions, and still kept the same peaceful outlook that she maintains to this day.

As John Cech wrote in his article "Breaking Chains: Brother Blue, Storyteller," published back in 1981, "it is neither a casually lived nor an easy life. Ruth tries to keep a modicum of order in it, handling all of the daily details of correspondence (with can be voluminous), bookings, accommodations, and promises—for copies of tapes or articles, for a story that must be told for a certain person at a certain place and time, for making arrangements for performances at a hospital or a prison that wasn't included in the original itinerary."

Cech also wrote that Brother Blue "runs on very little sleep"; that he "lives on air" and a vegetarian diet. "Ruth produced a high-protein drink for him from somewhere one afternoon because she knew he would not stop for food once he began his workshop. She often asked him if he had to go to the bathroom. She must ask because he might well forget to do that until it is nearly too late, and the car or the performance has to be brought to a screeching halt for nature's call."

So I say to Sister Ruth, who knows Brother Blue better than anyone else, who is his caretaker, lover, nurse, and best friend these many years, my admiration, respect, and tribute to Brother Blue is through you:

"Who can find a virtuous woman? For her price is far above rubies; the heart of her husband doth safely trust in her, so that he shall have no need of spoil."

Proverbs 31:10, 11

Eleanora E. Tate is the author of nine books for children. Her newest book is *The Minstrel's Melody*, an American Girl History Mystery recently named a 2001 Notable Children's Trade Book in the Field of Social Studies. Her book, *The Secret of Gumbo Grove*, is a Parents' Choice Gold Award winner. Her stories and essays have appeared in *American Girl*, *Goldfinch*, *Scholastic Storyworks* and *Book Links* magazines, and in *African American Review's* and *Obsidian III Journal's* Children's Literature editions. She is a former national president of the National Association of Black Storytellers, Inc., and co-recipient of the 1999 Zora Neale Hurston Award. She lives with her husband, photographer Zach Hamlett, III, in Durham, NC.

Ahhhh!

To Dance as Story

Amy Tighe Inkiala

I had apprenticed at the knee, so to speak, of some of the finest story-tellers. There, I learned I had been called for Story. But I didn't know that that call would require me to abandon storytelling for a while. I tried to drown myself in alcohol, which was at times hilarious or great fun, but always had an undercurrent of sadness. I tried to write of others' stories, to support others in their storytelling. I gave away all of my books and stopped going to yard sales, stopped looking for old and odd storybooks for sale. But no matter how much I gave up storytelling, I could never get rid of Brother Blue. He was always showing up at the same lonely movie I went to, always on the same corner walking just where I was walking. Once, he was in the first row of a lecture where I was in the back row, and he stood up in front of everyone there and started testifying and mesmerizing, as only he can, and I had to smile. I went to self help groups and all I heard were stories that he had told, or that others had told in his presence which made me talk less and listen harder—anything just to not tell my own story. But perhaps that is where Story was leading me. To stop, and listen, and learn Story in its deepest form.

One day, I ran into him on the Red Line. Blue is kind of hard to ignore, and if he sees you, you are pretty much captive. I can't remember what was hurting so much that day, but something was and I was feisty and argumentative, my way of grieving…We welcomed each other, and I sat next to him, ready to challenge after any niceties. I said, "So, Brother Blue, tell me, just what is storytelling for you?" And without hesitation he said "It's God talking to God, about God." Some bells are just clearer than others and that day, his saph-fire tone reverberates. Do you hear me? Do you know that sapphire comes from a word meaning dear, cherished by the planet Saturn? Right as we cross the Salt and

Ahhhh!

Pepper Bridge, to descend into the city I have failed in so often, here is this man I have seen for 20 years in every facet of his life and mine—performing Harvard Square concerts, unknowingly keeping me company with his lonely late night radio show, stirring up trouble, being a pest, an enigma, a joke, a deeper shaman than perhaps he'll ever know—saying storytelling is God talking to God about God. And I believe him completely. I know he is right—completely. Park Street Station next, change for the Green Line.

And all the times I have yelled back at God, or pleaded with God and tried to get God to see me. All of the times when it seemed that no one else would, I had to love that self in me who would journey, and did journey, even when I hated the road. And all the times I have thought that stories should be sweet and charming and swell and all the other storytellers had perfect and happy endings, knowing that my stories would only detail this disfigured ancestry of mine. So, swearing at the God who had made it so, and hating the world who would not, it seemed, deign to listen, I tried to quiet the storyteller in me, who just never stopped. But to an odd man who dressed in blue, it was all so simple. It's just God talking to God about God.

That pristine sapphire bell of his has never left me and it never will. Sometimes I thought I would outgrow Brother Blue, outgrow this desire to tell, this call for Story. But you cannot outgrow what you truly are, what you have been truly named to be. When someone like Brother Blue talks to you, tells you who you are and what he sees, you too, become a part of that sacred trinity.

There are times I think I am a just a small part of God. There are times I think my stories have some part of God in them. I always think that when I want to tell, the people who listen must be God, for surely I am not a part of them.

And then there are times when I do not think at all, and just tell. Just listen. Just know. If I never tell my kid or the stars or my cats or the empty space in the car or a roomful of people another story again, it would not matter. Because, if I am careful, very careful and very clear, I will not have to tell a story. I will get to be an invitation to Story, I will get to dance as Story, I will get to be someone else's Brother Blue, (probably without the balloons) and follow in his beloved footsteps.

Ahhhh!

I once was lost, and thanks to Blue's amazing grace, I now am found. There are so many journeys in this life, and I am sure I have more ahead. But now I know who I am and what I am doing, and for me, it's one day on the Red Line with Brother Blue that has made all the difference.

Amy Tighe Inkiala's love of storytelling and writing has helped her in her life. After her brother's death, she used storytelling to heal. She began to study and then graduated from a three year program for Integrated Kabbalistic Healing©, learning to bring a profound spiritual practice to storytelling for healing. Knowing and working with Brother Blue has been one of the most important experiences in her life, and she hopes her work honors him always.

Ahhhh!

Telling Without a Net:
Brother Blue's Way

Tony Toledo

When Brother Blue tells a story he flavors it with inspiration, savors it with "ahhhhh" and simmers it with joy. He is a teller that operates in the here and now. And I mean the HERE and the NOW. When he tells, he improvises, he raps, he swings, he yells, he whispers. Most of all, he puts his all into the telling in that instant. Would that we all might take such a glorious risk. When he tells he risks being the fool; when we are foolish we are vulnerable, and in our vulnerability lies our strength.

Brother Blue is one of the strongest tellers I know. Oh yes, I know there are days when he tells stories that don't quite click. When people politely clean their nails and yawn. He's had 'em and so have I. So has anybody who has been telling stories longer than fifteen minutes. Let me tell you though, when Brother Blue is "on," his telling is absolutely magical. His story wraps around you like a lover's hug, and believe you me, that story feels grand. His heart just opens up, and he shows us his laughter and his tears, his passion and his fears, his love and his forgiveness.

You see, when Brother Blue tells a story he does it without a net. His stories come from a lifetime of experiences, rather than a scripted page. He is willing to open his mouth and see what comes out. He trusts that a story will come. So many of his fellow storytellers (and I include myself in this observation), tell only what they have rehearsed and refined and polished to a shiny glow. And shiny glows alone do not a grand story make. A grand story has a solid heart, a foundation, a connection from teller to ear. There is also something undefinable, magical in a living story. Brother Blue has that in his telling.

Blue has a heart as big as barn. It is no accident that he is the founder

AHHHH!

of The Bookcellar Storytelling Swap. He listens to every teller and finds a silver thread to point out to the rest of us. Whether it's the first time you have ever told, your knees knocking, voice cracking, smile forced and failing, or you are a seasoned pro who flawlessly relates a saga with twenty seven different voices while doing a handstand, Blue listens to the heart of the story and shares with you what he loved about it. His love of that story is absolutely real. That is the key to the success of the Tuesday Story Swap series. Every fiber in his body is listening when someone is telling. His listening and sharing and unconditional love is a beacon of hope and encouragement when I get into a blue funk. Blue's passion and love of storytelling is as real as the sky is blue.

Blue is so into stories and conversation that he forgets to eat. That has never happened to me. It just shows me how present Blue is when you talk to him. Recently at Mike and Bonnie Myers' dinner table, Blue and Ruth and Mike and Bonnie and I were gabbing about life and stories, future and past, looking at the world's problems and bantering ideas like ping pong balls. It took Blue forever to eat his dinner because he was so engrossed in the conversation. Though if he doesn't eat he'll blow away. Ruth makes sure he eats.

As Blue flies and flutters through his stories, Ruth Hill is the beacon that brings him home again. The two of them are a matched set. I cannot imagine one without the other. They are yin and yang. Blue is gregarious, Ruth quiet. Blue hardly knows what a watch is, Ruth signals him two more minutes. Ruth delights in details, for Blue everything is a detail. Ruth video tapes her beloved Storyteller. Blue dedicates his storytelling to his lovely wife. The two of them make me smile.

It's a funny thing, though. Blue has achieved a small piece of immortality because a little bit of him lives in the heart of all the people he has touched. There is a little shelf in my heart that is labeled "Bro. Blue." On that shelf is a blue butterfly. It goes off and comes back. And with every story I tell there is a little bit of Blue in it.

Too often in this world things are thought and never said. I am too embarassed, too shy, to say it out loud. Sometimes courage comes in small doses. So I whisper to you both, "Thanks, Blue. Thanks, Ruth. I love you."

Tony Toledo's storytelling has been nurtured by the gentle praise of Brother Blue, and hinted to a halt by the bell of Ruth. Tony tells stories for elementary students across the state through Young Audiences of Massachusetts, he signs "still hungry" and, though he is 43 years old, he reads at a 56 year old level.

Ahhhh!

Prior to Becoming a State Legislator

Steven A. Tolman

For many years prior to becoming a state legislator, I was a baggage handler for railroad passengers passing through South Station. That's where I met Brother Blue and his wife Ruth. It would always brighten my day when I would greet them as they traveled on their way to another destination. I always felt that I was carrying the bags of a celebrity.

As I got to know Brother Blue better over the years, he was a true inspiration to me in my career. Over that time, the man who I thought of as a celebrity became a true friend.

I recall in 1990 when I ran unsuccessfully for State Representative, my campaign sponsored a Family Day. Brother Blue and Ruth joined us to entertain the children with his storytelling. On a very sultry sunny summer day in the broad shade of a massive oak, Blue delighted many children with his tales.

My wife Sue and I will always remember Blue serenading Sue, who was pregnant with our third child at that time, with these words: "Hey little baby, what you gonna do? Hey, little baby, this is Brother Blue!"

In 1994, after I ran a successful campaign for state representative, Brother Blue cheered me on by telling me, "You can carry my bags anytime, and now you can carry my legislation."

Sue and I always delight in hearing from Brother Blue and Ruth when they send us postcards with nice notes from faraway and exotic locations. From the time that I first met him, my relationship with Brother Blue blossomed like a well-tended flower garden. My family and I will always love Brother Blue and Ruth, and we hold them fondly in our hearts.

As a former Red Cap at South Station, Massachusetts, Senator Steven A. Tolman had the pleasure and honor of assisting Brother Blue and Ruth on their many railroad journeys. Steven is now a second term senator representing the Middlesex and Suffolk district, comprising Allston-Brighton, Cambridge, Waltham, and Watertown. Steven is

Ahhhh!

also the Chairman of the Joint Committee on local affairs and lives in Brighton with his wife and three children.

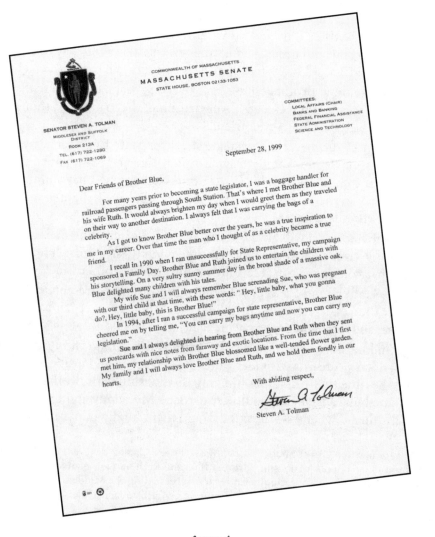

Ahhhh!

Letter Love from Beauty to the Beast

Valerie Tutson

Hey, Brother Blue
How you do?
This is Beauty
Peeking you.

Let me be the Beast to your Beauty, Ruth won't mind, got a story to tell,
now is the time…
Peek a boo
I see you
Ahhh…

Did you know that
I love you?
Well, it's true.
You be Gospel
Shining through
Showing us what God can do

Through you
Through me
Through Beast Beauty and Love Story…

Ahhhh…
Peek a Boo
I see you

True Blue, Brother

Thank you.

Valerie Tutson is a founding member of the Rhode Island Black Storytellers (RIBS)
and a member of the National Association of Black Storytelling (NABS). She believes
that storytelling is a vital part of life, and strives to keep the stories that she hears and
tells alive.

AHHHH!

For Brother Blue and Sister Ruth

Gretchen VanLoozen

Sometimes an experience is so true that it cuts through the daily tapestry of life and opens a window to a more universal world, to a land unseen, hidden by veils.

I used to drive to college in South Florida and many times I remember hearing Brother Blue telling a story on Public Radio. I always wanted to pull over and listen. His spell, as it wove through Shakespeare or any other tale, allowed the veil to flutter and a vision of the other world to peek through.

I learned that Brother Blue and Sister Ruth Hill would be offering a storytelling workshop on my birthday at Blissfest Music Festival. I knew I needed to go and, as my parents would be in town, I wanted my father to go as well.

My father's side of the family was made up of philosophers, teachers, musicians, artists, and doctors. They constantly explored the other side of life's tapestry. I inherited this desire from them, from him.

On July 9, 1998, my father and I walked the wooded path through green-dappled light to the story circle. And there they were, dressed in blue. Sister Ruth the foundation and center, Brother Blue drawing butterflies and weaving images, wielding scissors of words to cut through pretenses while walking the sacred fool's path of truth. Using words to scatter away old truths, confuse and confound old beliefs, then dancing behind humor he painfully exposed the power of privilege. The injustices of classism and racism stood unclothed, stripped by his sharp words. He told the truth to the king, speaking truth to power. And then he told the story behind the story of his brother.

The circle deepened. Moved, each of us now chose the path of courageous vulnerability. Would we take the leap to tell the story only we can tell? Would we take off the mask, step out and show who we are? Yes.

Ahhhh!

I remember, Brother Blue called my father a mensch, and he is.

My father was a Boy Scout long after my brother finished scouting. One day when I worked in a record store, my cool music friends warned me that there was a giant boy scout in my classical music department. With loving embarrassment, I saw it was my father. My dad, a teacher, singer, philosopher, who, as an elementary school principal had large hands of all colors of humanity painted on the halls of the school. He asked native builders of the Everglades Miccasukee tribe to design and build an outdoor environmental education classroom and he set up a community garden for the classes and neighborhood. He raised butterflies and took them to the schools. Blue saw rightly; he is a mensch.

We all told our stories that day, stories of grief, of joy, of birth, of death, reaching a place behind the cloth of performance or self-consciousness, trusting Brother Blue and Sister Ruth to hold a circle sacred enough for us to show our souls.

They taught us true attention. And throughout the entire weekend of Blissfest, they were there, wise blue elders watching, listening, looking carefully for the moments when the cloth would tear and the weave open enough to let them see the truth. To let us all touch the story under the story.

I thank you, Brother Blue and Sister Ruth, for the gifts of deepening and wisdom that you and your lives' work give to all of us. May moments of brilliant truth keep opening for you and through you. Thank you from the heart.

Gretchen Broman VanLoozen is a former Floridian, a singer and a poet since childhood. Struggling to recall ancestral memories of seasons, she lives as a mother, gardener, and healer in beautiful, cold, northern Michigan.

Ahhhh!

Brother Blue

Kay Walsh

So who is this Brother Blue? A man dressed in blue, with jackets, vests, and pockets covered in butterflies. A man who is delighted by children and animals and holds them in adult respect. The respect of having tended to and cared about what is important to these beings. He sings of children, their noises and their grace, and calls on us to find their joy and goodness in ourselves. He speaks of a dog, who loves a man with all his heart, with absolutely no reserve or holding back.

He comes with a wife, Ruth. A woman who lives with, beside, to-gether with this human paradox. Who herself is a wonder to behold, all calm and wisdom full of grace. She holds her own and makes a space for you, Brother Blue, to weave and tell and teach and preach and sing and dance. She guides and reprimands, she controls and is in control of what she does and does not do. Her silence is a story that screams out loud, of courage, patience, intelligence and wild adventures. She is as much a part of every story as Brother Blue's voice. Ruth.

So who is this Brother Blue? I read his book and tears flowed down my cheek, for the great humanity it shows of children living with driven parents. The terrible awe I felt as I read Brother Blue's parent's heroic battle to survive. This drama witnessed and played out, in terrified tandem by him as a child, who watch the near-or no- escape of death or worse for parents, sisters, brothers, or himself.

So who is this Brother Blue? Can he be both the Divinity Ph.D. at Harvard University and the man dressed in blue on the street corner? When he speaks I listen with expectant care, and I know I miss the essence of his message. I ask my son why is he so hard to understand? And my son answers, with a look of disapproval at such a question, "because he speaks in Jazz." And this makes sense to me; he speaks the language of the people's music. A language I have yet to learn.

I went to Arizona for a national storytelling conference and Ruth and

Ahhhh!

Brother Blue were there as honored elders. Aha, a new setting, new people, the Native American will be able to appreciate Brother Blue. I will at last understand this mystical human being. So I watched as the Native Americans went to hear him. I waited. They came out and I ask them what they learned? And they answer, nothing yet. So I waited and they went to his next workshop. And I ask what did they hear. And they answer "him." And so when the next day came I ask the Native Americans what workshops they were going to attend they said, Brother Blue's. And I said, "but yesterday nothing exciting happened." Much with the same look my son gave me "who are you, strange woman from Boston," they answered, "yes, but we are waiting."

In the waiting, not as I knew waiting but as I came to understand waiting, I have learned to listen to Brother Blue with an open heart, and have come to hear what is said on many levels. I look for more, and find it always there.

Kay Walsh is the founder of the Bayside Storytellers, who have been telling healing stories to young and old at inner city settings. She has had two poems published in the *South Boston Literary Gazette* this year, and she is teaching and coaching youth in the Old Colony housing development in South Boston.

Web Dance By Jessa Piaia and Blue at The Cambridge River Festival

Ahhhh!

Truth is a Form of Love

Bob Williams

A math professor from Tufts and I were sitting with a mutual friend who was dying. We were in Portland, Oregon, and in the course of this long night, my friend told me about the joy that attending storytelling sessions in a bookstore in Cambridge was bringing to his life.

Later that summer (1995, I believe) he was in Germany and I was staying in his apartment in Arlington for a week of selling my work in the Boston area. I found a reference to storytelling in the local paper and went.

I was astonished by the variety of stories. As a teacher and member of this culture, I expect more uniformity in things. Some stronger personality usually sets standards that others adopt, but in this delightful case, there was the strongest show of individuality that I remember seeing in any organized endeavor.

I remember Brother Blue singling me out to ask what I thought of one of the stories. I said that I would have crawled there just to hear one phrase from one story, "the janitor of my disease." Blue was pleased, and the stories went on.

Afterwards I talked with Blue and Ruth for an hour or more on the sidewalk. I came back the following Saturday and we talked more. While we were talking a woman came out of a nearby store and was trying to attract Blue's attention. Ruth whispered, "Say hello, Blue, that's the mayor of Cambridge," and he said, "Hello, how are you," before turning quickly back to me and Ruth.

I guess I must have written to them some time thereafter and one of us suggested to the others that Blue and Ruth come to Oregon for some storytelling. They arrived on Amtrak and stayed with me and my wife, Jeanette, for about two weeks. We brought them into Portland nearly every day, 75 miles away, and arranged for storytelling at Portland State University among other places.

Ahhhh!

I wanted them to meet my friend and kind-of guru, Randy Ruland, who lives in Garberville, California, and is quadriplegic. We drove down, taking two days each way to travel, and spent one night and one day there.

The scheduled radio interview was bumped, because Judy Barri, a local environmental activist, had died and the station (KMUD) was given over to a discussion of her life and works. But we did get a chance to meet with Randy and some storytellers he knows, and we did get to see the redwoods together. We walked through a grove to what had been the world's largest tree, now on its side. I arrived in sight of it first and waited for Blue, Ruth, and Jeanette to catch up.

When they came around the bend and spotted it, Blue said, "So, old friend, they got you too."

Ruth and Blue were perfect houseguests. They are vegetarian, and, after dinners, which Ruth prepared for herself and Blue, we would talk a bit before they retired to their little apartment in our downstairs.

As a college kid I had a class called Liberal Arts Seminar, which was two years of perhaps ten students and two professors reading Great Books and meeting twice a week for discussions. All my life since then, I had assumed this would happen for me again. One of my professors, Bill Parsons, now retired, said that he traveled the world looking for the same thing, a repeat of that experience. He had never quite found it.

That class, being with my former professor, Bill Parsons, and his wife, Buffy, and being with Brother Blue and Ruth are all very similar experiences for me. For awhile everything takes a back seat to seeking the Truth.

I told Blue—and I told Bill Parsons—that I want to buy an apartment building, check references, then give rent breaks to tenants who will write a 300-word paper about something they read that week; we would post the papers in the entrance hall, or in an apartment given over to being a library.

Both of these men inspire me in the same way, and I think it must have something to do with the fact that they are so well provided for by a loving partner (Buffy and Ruth) that they have peace from normal distractions.

I also think that the dedication to Truth, which both men have and teach, is a form of Love. It is, in part, a desire to help others avoid the mistakes that believing wrong things might lead to.

Ahhhh!

When my wife and I went to Cambridge a few summers later we went to Harvard Square where, I told Jeanette, we might see Brother Blue walking around. We did, in front of the Coop.

I walked up to him and called his name. He looked at me and said, "Hello, how are you?" as he had to the mayor, as if we had seen each other earlier that day. We waited for Ruth, then walked to her new office at the Radcliffe Library to have dinner together—lots of tofu of various flavors.

After dinner we shared a taxi to the new storytelling site, another bookstore, called "Foozles," still in Porter Square. It was glorious, once again, and for Jeanette to be there this time was wonderful.

Blue spoke in between stories. I wish I had recorded all of it, because what I did write down, I used later in my business.

He said, "Find something beautiful and be a fool for it," and, "You never know which two people can become a critical mass and transform the future."

I am grateful just for that, if nothing else.

Bob and Jeanette Williams are co-founders and co-owners of Book Darts, which feature a quote from Brother Blue on each package. Bob is a retired high school English teacher and a former Federal convict (for refusing to go into the Vietnam era army). He has worked as a philosophy professor, university archivist, boatwright, printer, catalog librarian, youth services agency administrator, paperboy, and firewood cutter, in no particular order.

AHHHH!

Ah, Yes! We Know You Well

Charles V. Willie, Ph.D.

Brother Blue and Ruth have been our friends during the twenty-five years we have lived in New England. We know Brother Blue as a storyteller, but we also know him as a minister, healer, and friend. Regarding Ruth, we do not await religious authorities to take the lead; our family already recognizes Ruth as a saint.

We are impressed that she and Blue go out into the streets on some holidays to cheer the lonely.

On major holidays, our two families usually exchange telephone greetings, a custom that has continued for nearly a decade. We do this because we like and admire each other.

Blue has always been attracted to the stranger. Not long after my appointment to the faculty of Harvard's Graduate School of Education, Blue called on me. He asked permission to attend some of my classes, which of course was granted. Halfway through most of my lectures Blue would be moved to comment on the presentation. His discussions of the messages I was trying to convey were thoughtful and honest. After those brief interludes, the class would continue. To my surprise, the students liked Brother Blue's commentary and I increasingly welcomed and appreciated his interpretive remarks. They were appropriate and full of wisdom. Through weekly interactions such as these, Brother Blue and I became dear friends.

Now Brother Blue and Ruth are friends of all the members of our family. We have dined and "broken bread" together in our home. We talk with each other often about the high times and low times in our lives, and we keep in constant communication despite the extensive travelling schedule of the Hugh Morgan and Ruth Hill household, with postal cards arriving from near and far.

Ahhhh!

358

Charles Vert Willie is the Charles William Eliot Professor of Education Emeritus, Harvard Graduate School of Education. He is a graduate of Morehouse College, where he was a classmate with Martin Luther King, Jr. He earned a Ph.D. degree at the Maxwell School at Syracuse University and served as chair of its Department of Sociology and vice president of the University before coming to Harvard in 1974. Professor Willie is Board Chair of the Judge Baker Convention of the Episcopal Church. He preached the ordination sermon for the service in which the first women in the USA were ordained as priests.

Mike Ahern

Ahhhh!

Getting It All Together

Phil Wilson

As Blue says, "Bringing together all the colors of the human race to live in peace and harmony" is an ideal I have always cherished. Throughout my career, my bands—The Rainbow Band, The Berklee International Dues Band, The Rainbow All Stars—have reflected this ideal, being populated by musicians from all over the world. If we can play beautiful music together, maybe we can learn to live together.

In 1976, I put together a recording of some of my favorite musicians. The album *Getting It All Together* was released on the Outrageous Records label. I had worked with Blue as a chairman of the Afro-American Department of the New England Conservatory.

Boston, to say nothing of the entire country, was in the midst of a great deal of racial turmoil, exacerbated by the public school busing program. Wishing to make a strong statement as to the fundamental injustice behind this ongoing turmoil, I called Blue to ask him if he would take part in the recording session.

My idea was to play "America the Beautiful" behind Blue as he spoke of the historical realities that led us to this moment in history, with the hope that in airing transgressions past and present, we could advance understanding and begin to learn to live together in peace and harmony. "America *Be* Beautiful" was the result of our collaboration, and it has been used in churches and classrooms all over the world to help further the understanding of this ongoing struggle.

Phil Wilson is recognized world wide as a leading jazz trombonist, composer/ arranger, and jazz educator. He was one of Woody Herman's major soloists, a Grammy-nominated arranger for Buddy Rich, as well as a pioneer of jazz education, helping the Berklee College of Music implement its curriculum over the past thirty-seven years.

Ahhhh!

Something Worth Hearing

Raelinda Woad

A god, a goddess, a parallel consciousness being, and a storyteller went into a bar. This particular bar existed only in time, but not in space, so instead of getting a beer, you got the amount of time it took you to drink the beer. Well, after 3 or 4 rounds they'd accumulated quite a few hours of extra 'Now' around their table. Since they couldn't go anywhere until it was used up, they challenged each other to a creation contest. The rules were simple: create something so powerful it could not be overcome.

1976 *Getting It All Together* recording session - L to R: Andy Mcghee, Allen Dawson, Phil Wilson, Mae Arnette, Brother Blue, Ray Santisi, Whit Browne

Ahhhh!

Now, because of its inherent dangers, such a contest was actually illegal, but only in universe standard time. Universal laws did not apply inside a bubble of beer time.

The god began. Suavely sidestepping the fact that he was glued into the Now of beer time, he created his challenge out of language, and past tense language at that. A gibe at the storyteller perhaps?

"Once," he said, "there was a space dragon. His back stretched across the entire Milky Way. His eyes burned with a thousand suns. Each time he yawned, he swallowed a million worlds. The lash of his tail created worm holes in the fabric and flow of space. He could not be overcome."

And over their table floated the dragon, flickering on the edge of existence, dangerously powerful even in its half-real state. It eyed the other contestants and yawned hungrily.

The goddess calmly picked up the tale.

"But alas," she said, "across the sea of space came a storm of hurricane strength. Time itself rose up in huge waves and came crashing down on the dragon. With each crash did he age a thousand years. Soon he was nothing but dust, dust scattered between the stars. And the storm raged on. It could not be overcome."

And over the table a tempest was brewing. Powerful waves of time began pounding against the sides of their little bubble of beer time.

Thousands of years' worth of Later were churning inside a few tiny hours of Now. The god's hair turned to silver.

Without blinking a mind, the parallel consciousness being picked up the thread.

"But then," it said, "did the very walls of reality rip and tear. And through the gap was revealed the Universe of Nothingness, the great vacuum. The stormy waves of time were sucked through and swallowed up into emptiness."

And over the table a patch of nothingness appeared and began to grow.

"Whew," said the god nervously.

"My," said the goddess, edging away from the table.

But they still had several beers' worth of Now to use up before they could leave the table, and the nothingness continued to grow. The parallel consciousness being chortled goodbye and then stopped thinking about itself on that plane of reality and was safely gone.

Ahhhh!

362

The great nothingness billowed out from the table, swallowing every-thing. The god and the goddess joined hands, lifted their chins, and faced their doom, elegant to the end.

But at that moment the storyteller spoke.

"And then a butterfly appeared."

And over the table a butterfly appeared—a little flutter of blue be-tween the three beings and nothingness.

The storyteller continued.

"And the butterfly turned to the nothingness and said, 'tell me your story.'"

And over the table the butterfly began to listen.

But the nothingness laughed and said, "I am nothingness. There is no story."

But over the table the butterfly continued to listen with such complete interest and such complete acceptance and love, that the nothingness couldn't help it, couldn't resist the butterfly's belief that it had something inside it, something worth hearing.

And it unbound like a coccoon and out flew not one but thousands of stories, like a flickering cloud of butterflies with wings of words. The god and goddess clapped their hands as the beautiful stories broke through their little bubble of Now and whirled through the bar. The bartender barely had time to say, "who let a storyteller in here," when they burst out of the bar, a river of wing flashes tumbling across the heavens, carrying stories from star to star. And the more the little butterfly listened, the more there was, such was its power. The power of listening cannot be overcome.

Raelinda Woad has been telling her *True Stories...That Haven't Quite Hap-pened Yet* in coffeehouses and clubs from coast to coast. She has organized several spoken word programs at Cambridge's legendary Club Passim, including Story-LAB, a storytelling concert series. And she spends a lot of time at Brother Blue and Ruth Hill's weekly coffeehouse, listening.

Ahhhh!

Massachusetts House of Representatives

Resolutions

HONORING BROTHER BLUE.

WHEREAS, THE ESTEEMED BROTHER BLUE WILL BE HONORED IN A TRIBUTE BOOK IN MARCH IN THE YEAR 2001, AFTER MANY YEARS OF DEDICATED SERVICE TO THIS COMMUNITY AS A STORYTELLER IN CAMBRIDGE AND ACROSS THE UNITED STATES; AND

WHEREAS, BROTHER BLUE'S WONDERFUL IMAGINATION AND THEATRICAL STORYTELLING HAS ENRICHED THE LIVES AND BROADENED THE WORLD-VIEW OF GENERATIONS OF CHILDREN AND ADULTS; AND

WHEREAS, BROTHER BLUE'S STORIES HAVE FOSTERED A SENSE OF COMMUNITY AND COLLECTIVE SPIRIT BY INSPIRING AUDIENCES OF ALL AGES, RACES, AND ETHNICITY; AND

WHEREAS, BROTHER BLUE HAS RECEIVED MANY ACCOLADES FOR HIS CONTRIBUTIONS TO OUR COMMUNITY, AMONG THEM THE LIFETIME ACHIEVEMENT AWARD IN JUNE, 1999 BY THE NATIONAL STORYTELLING NETWORK FOR SUSTAINED AND EXEMPLARY CONTRIBUTIONS TO STORYTELLING IN AMERICA; AND

WHEREAS, BROTHER BLUE HAS BEEN HONORED WITH A PEACE AND JUSTICE AWARD FROM THE CAMBRIDGE PEACE COMMISSION IN RECOGNITION OF HIS POWER OF STORYTELLING; AND

WHEREAS, BROTHER BLUE HAS TAUGHT STORYTELLING IN CHURCHES, PRISONS, COLLEGES, AND LIBRARIES, PASSING ON HIS LOVE OF STORYTELLING TO NEW AUDIENCES; AND

WHEREAS, BROTHER BLUE HAS BEEN AN INNOVATOR IN THE ART OF STORYTELLING DRAWING FREELY FROM THE TRADITIONS OF THE GRIOT, TROUVERE, BARD AND POET ALIKE, AND CREATING A WORLD OF STORIES THAT HAS STIRRED THE HEARTS AND MINDS OF HIS AUDIENCES; AND

WHEREAS, BROTHER BLUE CONTINUES TO SHARE HIS DEEPLY HEARTFELT MESSAGES BRINGING THE ANCIENT TRADITIONS OF STORYTELLING TO LIFE AND IS GREATLY LOVED AND ADMIRED BY ALL WHO HEAR THESE STORIES; THEREFORE BE IT

RESOLVED, THAT THE MASSACHUSETTS HOUSE OF REPRESENTATIVES CONGRATULATES BROTHER BLUE FOR HIS ACCOMPLISHMENTS AND WISHES HIM CONTINUED SUCCESS WHEREVER THE PATH OF STORYTELLING MAY TAKE HIM NEXT; AND BE IT FURTHER

RESOLVED, THAT A COPY OF THESE RESOLUTIONS BE FORWARDED BY THE CLERK OF THE HOUSE OF REPRESENTATIVES TO BROTHER BLUE.

HOUSE OF REPRESENTATIVES, ADOPTED JULY 12, 2000.

_____
SPEAKER OF THE HOUSE

_____
CLERK OF THE HOUSE

OFFERED BY:
_____
REPRESENTATIVE ALICE K. WOLF

Ahhhh!

Brother Blue

Diane Wolkstein

Look!
A butterfly is flying.
How beautiful!
How marvelous!
How unexpected.
How unfathomable.
How delightful.

Dear Blue,
Dearest Blue,
How grateful I am to you.
For choosing to be you.
For choosing to delight in the world,
And to continuously share your delight.
Wherever I am,
I think,
Ah, Blue is about,
Flitting, flying,
Celebrating Joy and Mystery.

There were times
When I was younger
And set on doing
That I sometimes wondered
How you could take so much time
Stopping to make just one flower happy.

Ahhhh!

And now, I know
To be a butterfly is to choose
To love,
To choose to delight
In the world as it is,
Offering each day more delight.

Brother Blue,
Dearest Blue,
You teach me every day
You guide me by your very being.
What matters?
What really matters?
To be present
With each flower
And to spread the joy.
We know so little
But we do know:
We are alive.

I bless you, Brother Blue
And I bless me
And I bless us all
that we can return your love.
I am so grateful to you—
on the ground or in the air—
You are our conduit
Our reminder
Of the connection between all beings.
Fly, fly, fly!
Fly, dearest Blue!

Whether recounting fairy tales or epics, Diane Wolkstein enters and speaks from the heart of each story she tells. Her lively and illuminating presentations have become as legendary as the annual storytelling performances she gives in New York City's Central Park. A storyteller's storyteller as well as a teacher of storytelling, Diane is the author of 21 award-winning books of world folklore, including *The Magic Orange Tree* and *Inanna*. Her books have been translated into ten languages. Diane Wolkstein, along with Brother Blue, was inducted into the National Storytelling Network's Circle of Excellence in 1996.

Ahhhh!

Praising Blue

Dan Yashinsky

Good people
I have come to praise Blue.

Barefoot, bare-tongued, you came
Before the one who made the world
You asked Worldmaker if you could tell the world its first story
If you could accompany creation with your yarns
If the world may be granted unto your story-keeping
If you could be the one who sang the world to sleep
Who made it laugh
Who remembered its origins
Who spoke comfort at its endings
And Worldmaker gave you your name
Called you Brother Blue
Gave you honourable commission
To serve the world
As Storyteller
As Praise-singer
As the one who could most fluently speak
The language of story
Our oldest Mother Tongue

Since our earliest days
Since the Dreaming
Since the earliest of early days
Since the time before stars had names
We have come to you
We have come to Blue
You have told us your stories of butterflies and black children,

Ahhhh!

Of jazz and wisdom,
of love uprising and beauty beheld,
We have gathered to hear you in our first caves,
Beside rough fires, in royal courts,
In caravanserais, in kitchens,
In jail cells and downtown coffeehouses
We have listened to your voice
In the midst of the Black Death
We have hearkened to you on our pilgrimages
We have heard you in our despair
In our deepest trouble we have turned to you
Your stories repair our broken hearts
Joy comes with your dancing
Jubilation comes with your song
Your harmonica can disperse the death-riders
Mercenaries of the Apocalypse

Hero of voices
You make quiet thunder
You shake a spear of breath and dust
A spear of words with a blade of stars
Your red tongue kindles hope
Your earth-brown face draws rain
Rainbows cascade from your lips
Praise-singer
You even praise the caterpillar
The lowliest one
The crawling one
Unregarded, ground-bound, unheard, unspeakable
Until you come to lend your voice
The lost one is in your story
The forgotten one is in your song
You sing strong praises
You sing caterpillar into chrysalis
You sing torpor into flight
You sing mud into sculpture
You are the Storyteller
Without your stories the night is an enemy
Without your stories the prisoner does not even dream of freedom

Ahhhh!

368

Without your stories the last candle burns out
Without your stories the suicide jumps over the bridge
Without your stories the plague sweeps over the sanctuary

Tell your stories as Orpheus
Broke open the heart of the rock
Sing for us, O great Praise-singer
Sing as Homer sang to the ancient Greeks
Sing as Demodokus the Bard sang to Odysseus
Sing as Mandela's griot showed proper honour
Speak as the elder speaks to the tribe
Speak as my newborn son struggles to cry
Speak as the man in the wheelchair writhes out his words
Speak as if the first word has yet to be spoken
Speak as if the final say will never be said

All welcome you, Storyteller
As the butterfly is welcome for bringing spring
As water is welcome on a dry wanderground
As moonlight is welcome to a night-frightened child
As a minor note is welcome to those in love
As weeping is welcome to those in grief
As sanctuary is welcome in plague-ridden times
As silence is welcome in a house loud with television
You are welcome to our gathering
O Storyteller
O Praise-singer
O Blue who praises more than he is praised
O Student of God's Creative Fiction class
O Storyteller who carries the world in his mouth
O Man who has earned the love of Ruth
O Father of all storytellers

Please welcome Brother Blue

Dan Yashinsky is the founder of the Toronto Festival of Storytelling. He's the author of *The Storyteller At Fault*, and the editor of four collections of Canadian storytelling. He's been a member of the tribe of Blue since 1980.

Ahhhh!

There is a Color

Jane Yolen

There is a color for story,
Beyond the white of paper,
The black of print,
And the color they make together.
There is a color for story,
Beyond the red of lips, the pink tongue,
The white and gold teeth,
And the color they make together.
It is a color you can see
From a Cambridge street:
The deep, rumbling blue of the Charles,
The blue slate of sky
Scribbled over by birds,
The wink of a blue butterfly on a man's hand,
As he brings white and black
And red and pink and white and gold
And all the colors together—
                    into the color of story.

Jane Yolen is an author of children's books, fantasy, and science fiction. She is
also a poet, a teacher of writing and literature, and a reviewer of children's
literature. She has been called the Hans Christian Andersen of America and the
Aesop of the twentieth century. Jane Yolen's books and stories have won the
Caldecott Medal, two Nebula Awards, two Christopher Medals, the World
Fantasy Award, three Mythopoeic Fantasy Awards, the Golden Kite Award, the
Jewish Book Award, and the Association of Jewish Libraries Award, and are told
by storytellers all over the world.

Ahhhh!

Blue's Blessing, Our New Religion

Kerry Zagarella

Over the past ten years I have been fortunate enough to become friends with Blue and Ruth, as all the people who have met them could probably attest to. Friendship is a natural consequence of any encounter with them. Their love is actually tangible. It is a physical sensation that occurs when you are near them or hear them speak. Their love is not left up to faith or the hope trapped inside this mustard-seed world. Blue and Ruth drop their love right in your lap; man, they make it very difficult to be an angry cynic.

I have been blessed to be able to work with Blue and Ruth on a variety of community art festivals and numerous benefits. They are not the folks sitting on the couch wondering what to do or how to do it. They aren't the artists asking about the green room or giving you their agent's phone number. They are the folks waiting for trains in the snow. They are the inseparable and the powerful. They are invincible. Well, I just love them and I want to share a particular experience that I cherish.

About seven years ago, at the First Baptist Church in Somerville, there was a monthly open mike run by Ray Weisen. Many folks were there waiting for their 5 minutes of glory (me included, I am addicted to glory) and Brother Blue was the featured reader that evening. I was eight months pregnant with my first child, Gus. Blue and Ruth were so excited for our new upcoming life, and Blue asked if it would be okay if he did a little piece for the new baby. My husband, Neal, and I immediately answered yes, that we would be honored. I happened to have my tape recorder with me that night and recorded the improvisational piece dedicated to our unborn son. This was our son's baptism; it was a sacred blessing that Blue gave our family that night. Forget your dogma and your organized rituals. Blue gave us true religion that night. I was very surprised to have such a genuine spiritual experience in the basement of a church!

Ahhhh!

Our son Gus, now almost eight years old, knows this story very well and has had the opportunity to speak with Blue about it. Gus imagines what it was like inside of me listening to Blue's message. He tells us that he remembers feeling really nice when he heard Blue's story from inside. On many other occasions both of our children, Gus and Henry, have had the opportunity to listen to Blue, to watch him and to learn.

It is so reassuring as a parent to see my kids hanging out with Blue, listening to his stories, and telling their own to him. I especially like it when we are at an event and Blue is dressed in his wonderful ribbons, balloons, and butterflies and before or after his performance he is able to sit with the kids. They talk and share some ideas, and Blue really listens to their ideas. And the costume, well, my kids, who are normally mesmerized by balloons, focus on talking to what is inside that costume— seeing true gifts!

Watching Ruth and Blue work together demonstrates the freedom and power a partnership can bring. I like that my kids, as well as myself, get to see the team work. I often like to wonder how they live at home. I can't imagine it to be very ordinary at all. I wonder how Ruth folds the beautiful garments that she wears. Does she hang her velvet vest in the windows to absorb sunlight for their next journey? Are the woven tapestries she wears wrapped up snug and placed side by side in a large wooden chest filled with sea glass to preserve their natural color and light? Does Blue let his butterflies free when he gets home? Do they fly around them while they cook dinner? Is their house full of balloons and books? Do they eat? Do they sleep? These are the questions reserved for celestial beings.

I have never developed a thumb green enough to cultivate my mustard seed soul. Faith is difficult when you read the papers. But when the gods send us two kind messengers who live their art and radiate kindness and hope, even a cynical heart is persuaded to believe.

Kerry Zagarella has been involved in the North Shore and Cambridge poetry scene for over 12 years. Her work has been published in the *Stone Soup Quarterly*, *The Borderline Magazine*, *Wail! Magazine*, and *This Magazine*. Her work can be heard on a compliation disc entitled *Beat Night at the Electric Cave*. Kerry has performed at Boston First Night, was a member of Boston's first Poetry Slam Performance Team, and competed nationally in Chicago. Kerry has organized many poetry events for the community, and is dedicated to getting poetry to the people and out of the people.

Ahhhh!

The Jazz Cows

Neal Zagarella

Unfailing generosity is a trait that separates Brother Blue from many other creative artists. After achieving even modest success, many performers seem to dismiss the talents of others. Many times I have seen people show up, do their act, and go home, uninterested in the rest of the bill.

In contrast, Blue and Ruth always seem to find a spot up front, and pay rapt attention to everyone that gets on stage. On one ninety-degree summer day, Blue and Ruth carried lawn chairs on the commuter train to Beverly so they could sit and watch four hours of stories, poetry, and music in the hot sun. Blue was scheduled to perform for only twenty minutes.

On a personal note, I will always remember being at an event where Blue was speaking with the poet Billy Barnum. When Blue saw me, he immediately began telling Billy about a poem that he had heard me perform called "The Jazz Cows." For a writer at my beginning, struggling to find my voice, it would have been a tremendous boost for him to just say hello or remember my name.

Not surprisingly, the poem Blue was speaking of (which follows), could not have been written without his influence. It was his performances that opened up so many avenues for me, and I'm sure, many other artists. The importance of jazz and blues in his stories, the discovery of love and wonder in the everyday, the elevation of simple things to grace and wonder, the absolute joy of the telling—all these qualities are evident in Blue's every performance. Most importantly, Blue exemplifies writing that dives deep inside, while always looking outside, free of convention, embracing experimentation.

Ahhhh!

The Jazz Cows

You might not know by just looking at me,
But I'm not normal.
But that's not my problem,
It's yours.
It's not like I call myself Moondoggie,
Or carry an elephant's bone in my mouth.
I don't carry on conversations with my jello,
Or put on black-lace panties to watch William F. Buckley.
No, I got a regular job downtown,
I love my wife, and our two kids are crazy,
Just like all teenagers.
But what you don't know
Is that my best friends are cows.
Cows?
Yes.
But I don't consider that my problem,
It's yours.
It all started one afternoon when I lost my temper at the house.
The kids were playing some awful record
That sounded like my old Ford
Starting up on a frigid winter morning.
My wife was yackity, yackity with her sister on the phone,
And all the noises were hitting me like a dentist drill.
Parts of my head were turning to smoke and dust.
So I drove the old Ford a few miles out of town,
Where the roads get narrow as straw,
And the hills roll like your grandmaw's lap.
I pulled the car over next to this big candycorn field of cows,
Got out, leaned against the fence
And then I…no, it can't be…but
Yes, a cool, low-low, sweet moan,
A flame burning like Billie Holiday,
A throaty waning oooh like Carmen McCrae,
The smoothest silk-stocking notes since Ella Fitzgerald,
At first I checked and fiddled with my car radio.
Nope.
Then I looked far and wide, across the street,
Up on the hill for people.

Ahhhh!

Nope.
Then I reached into my ears, scooped out some wax,
Shook my head real hard, and
Still the jazz.
The deep backalley growl,
The lonely dog whistle cry,
The underground velvet sighs,
All wending and winding,
Scatting and trading
Sadly and gloriously together.
It was the cows!
The wondrous cows,
The amazing talent-tongued hipster herd ensemble.
The jazz cows.
Now, I see that look in your eye,
Your fingers fidgeting around,
Longing for a remote control to switch me off.
Like I'm one of those first guests on the Tonight Show,
The 108-year-old from West Jerkwater that grew a potato
In the shape of Michael Jackson.
And she can make it moonwalk.
But I don't see that as my problem,
It's yours.
Cause I hear them jazz cows crooning.
Every Sunday afternoon I drive out there to hear them jam.
Oh, my wife's like you.
So I tell her I'm meeting the boys to play poker
Or watch the football game,
But I'm always out there with them cows,
Leaning on the fence, tapping my toes,
And just drifting off like smoke
With the breath of each fine melody.
Now I'm sure you're going to tell everybody,
The curiosity seekers will start salivating,
And the media will jump on this
Like it was another Elizabeth Taylor wedding,
And my face will be on the cover of the National Enquirer
Undoubtedly in some deranged pose
Clipped from my junior high school yearbook.
I'll be the humor line ending every newscast

Ahhhh!

And the caravans will roll,
Cameras, tape recorders, super-sensitive microphones
Sound experts, oenophiles, veterinarians, psychiatrists,
Next to the swelled, sagging udder of a cow
Will be run on the entertainment page
Of newspapers coast to coast.
And for all the wrong reasons
People will come.
People will come and expect to hear nothing,
To disprove the hoax,
To expose the deranged, perverted cow-lover-fraud.
And no one will hear the sweet jazz of the cows,
Just a couple of moos amid the people's mocking laughter,
Laughter echoing back like bully-boy taunts through a schoolyard,
As the caravan rolls away
And on to the next wacko-mediaright-star for a week.
But that's not my problem,
It's yours.
Because after you're gone,
It'll just be me,
Them hip, wild cows,
And long afternoons
Of sweet,
Blue
Jazz

Neal Zagarella has been writing and performing poetry in the Greater Boston area for the past fifteen years. He was one of the founders of *WAIL!* Magazine and ran an open mike poetry series on the North Shore for ten years. A collection of his work can be found in a chap book published by This Poet's Press entitled *Big Rats and Little Babies*.

AHHHH!

A Living Example of What the World Should Be Like

Howard Zinn

I am happy to pay tribute to Brother Blue. He is a rare human being, not just because he is a fantastic storyteller, but because behind his stories is a profound consciousness about the world—about justice, about equality, about how human beings should pass their time on Earth. He himself is a living example of what the world should be like. Every time I encounter him (and his wonderful companion Ruth Hill) on Brattle Street, the atmosphere is immediately transformed. He always seems to be dancing along the street rather than merely walking. His smile lights up the street. His walk, his smile, and his unmistakable beret let you know it is him, even when you are far away. I can't imagine Cambridge without him. Everyone knows him, and he seems to know everyone. I am grateful for his presence, and feel blessed to know him. May he and his marvelous spirit go on and on and on.

Howard Zinn is a historian, playwright, and long-time activist in the civil rights and anti-war movements. He is the author of *A People's History of the United States* and other books.

AHHHH!

Biographies of Graphic Contributors

Biographies of other graphic contributors appear with their written pieces. Every effort has been made to credit all artwork. In some cases the creator is not known to us. Please contact us with information on unattributed work.

Michael Ahern is a self-taught artist striving to open up the story. He lives in the Boston area. — page 196 & 358

Deb Sparrow is an artist and resident of Tempe, Arizona. Sparrow's artwork includes painting, photography and monotype. Today she continues to apply the gestural vocabulary of the brush to music, dance and storytelling. Her work comes from having fallen in love with Chinese painting as a child, and her study as an adult with the painter Fan Tchun Pi. — page 304 & 328

Theresa Shimer met and was inspired by Brother Blue while attending the Boston School of the Museum of Fine Arts. She now resides in Orange, California, where she is involved in several projects, including a children's book, *When I Was Old and You Were Young.* — page 204

Jessa Piaia is a Cambridge-based dancer, clown, and character actress who presents Women in History Programs; In the early '80s, she danced on the streets of Cambridge and Boston doing impromptu moves to accompany Brother Blue's stories; In this series of snaps, they appeared at the Cambridge River Festival event in Central Square in 1982. — page 353

Susan Wilson is a professional photographer who has taken photos of performers ranging from Taj Mahal to Bill Harley. She is also the author of three books on Boston history, *Sites & Insights*, *Garden of Memories: A Guide to Historic Forest Hills* and most recently, *Literary Trail of Greater Boston.* She lives and works in Cambridge, MA. — front cover and lower back cover photos

Ahhhh!

Footnotes

From Pages 250 & 251

[1] G. Nagy, *Plato's Rhapsody and Homer's Music: The Poetics of the Panathenaic Festival in Classical Athens* (Cambridge MA and Athens 2002).

[2] For background on this narratological framing, see p. 126 n. 74 of P. Hadot, "Physique et poésie dans le *Timée* de Platon," *Revue de théologie et de philosophie* 115 91983) 113-133.

[3] On the related idea that the written text needs as its own 'reinforcement' (*boêthoos, boêtheia*) the living voice of the author or extensions of the author, see Plato *Phaedrus* 275e, 276c.

[4] On models of composition-in-performance in oral poetics, see A. B. Lord, *The Singer of Tales* (Harvard Studies in Comparative Literature 24; Cambridge MA 1960; second edition 2000, with Introduction, vii-xxix, by S. Mitchell and G. Nagy).

Ahhhh !